Path of the Purified Heart

Path of the Purified Heart

The Spiritual Journey as Transformation

LAURA DUNHAM

*For Don,
brother on the path —
Blessings!)
Laura
February, 2012*

CASCADE *Books* · Eugene, Oregon

PATH OF THE PURIFIED HEART
The Spiritual Journey as Transformation

Cascade Books
An Imprint of Wipf and Stock Publishers
199 W. 8th Ave., Suite 3
Eugene, OR 97401

www.wipfandstock.com

ISBN 13: 978-1-61097-874-3

Cataloging-in-Publication data:

Dunham, Laura.

Path of the purified heart : the spiritual journey as transformation / Laura Dunham.

viii + 196 p. ; 23 cm. Includes bibliographical references.

ISBN 13: 978-1-61097-874-3

1. Spirituality—Christianity. 2. Spiritual formation. I. Title.

BV4501.3 .D851 2012

Manufactured in the U.S.A.

Dedication

For the spiritual companions who shared my journey and whose encouragement sustained me during the preparation of this book,

For my husband, Alden, whose continuing love and support lasted throughout the preparation and writing process, despite the many ways in which it disrupted his life,

For my son, Tom, whose own transformation through my year of purification challenged and complemented my own,

For the Sisters of St. Benedict's Monastery, St. Joseph, MN, whose support of this project through the Studium Scholars program and my oblate candidacy contributed to the shape and content of this book and who continue to inspire me,

And for all the spiritual guides, wise elders and teachers from the past and present who populate these pages, without whose knowledge, experience, and love of God I could not have identified, let alone followed, the path of the purified heart,

Deo Gratias!

Contents

Introduction

As a deer longs for flowing streams, so my soul longs for you,
O God. My soul thirsts for God, for the living God. When shall I
come and behold the face of God?

—Psalm 42[41]:1–2[1]

IN THE SECOND DECADE of the twenty-first century, the changing land-scape of religious traditions and spiritual expressions is everywhere in evidence. Where and how people define and practice spirituality has shifted dramatically. Population growth and religious demographics have moved south and east, from Europe and North America to Latin America and Africa, the Middle East and Asia. The rise of a high-tech global economy has blurred geographic lines along with the traditional identity markers of race, class, and nationality, as well as religion. Combined with instant Internet access to world events and markets and to self-created virtual communities, such dramatic change has created an environment in which the centuries-old power and sway of religious institutions is rapidly eroding. More than dogma and doctrine is desired and demanded by today's religious and spiritual seekers. A personal, transforming experience of the divine and a supportive community have become the heart's desire.

The search for spiritual nourishment drives us, despite the culture we live in. As America's materialistic, success-driven model is exported around the world, people are discovering that this deep hunger cannot be satisfied by wealth or success in the world's terms. However we may try to escape poverty of spirit through acquiring things or using other people, our hearts hunger and our souls thirst for what only God can satisfy.

In a world that increasingly values the individual over the community, it's no wonder that the young are far less likely to follow the

1. All biblical quotations are from the New Revised Standard Version, unless otherwise noted. When Psalm numbers vary, the first number follows Protestant practice and the bracketed number traditional Catholic and Orthodox practice.

1

family religion—if there is one—than ever before. A recent conversation with a university religious studies major whose prestigious scholarship has allowed him to study in Nepal, India, Mongolia, West Africa and Indonesia, reveals a new interreligious trend. Roman Catholic by birth and practice through high school, my young friend told me that while he remains rooted in this tradition, he does not feel circumscribed by it. He views his affiliation as part of an increasingly complex identity, cultivated through time spent and relationships developed with those of other cultures and religious traditions. "I identify with Catholicism but don't think of myself as Catholic," he says. His life experience, even as a twenty-two-year-old, has been broad and deep, and he isn't willing to settle for anything less in his spiritual search.

Well-known biblical scholar Marcus Borg notes that about half of his university students have grown up outside the church. They consistently describe Christianity as "literalistic, anti-intellectual, self-righteous, judgmental and bigoted." [2] Borg suggests that while such distorted views are found in the media, their ultimate source is a religion based on beliefs rather than on the way of the heart.

As traditional boundaries blur and cross-spiritual trends become more common, the interfaith and multicultural dialogues of the last generation are replaced by the shared spiritual practices of today, often stripped of the contexts that gave them birth and meaning. A neighbor recently described a class on mindfulness she took through the Duke Center for Integrative Medicine. "Was the class focused more on Buddhist or Christian meditation and mindfulness practices?" I asked. "Neither," she responded. "It showed us how to quiet our minds to release stress in our bodies." Modern medicine may be recognizing the mind-body-spirit connections that endure in the spiritual practices of ancient traditions, but no homage is paid to their sources or deep significance.

Even within the great religious and spiritual traditions, not all who explore the pathways to wisdom find what they are seeking. Often these paths remain hidden from all but the most diligent or closed to the un-initiated. Seekers may turn instead to one charismatic guru or another, drifting with popular trends until, disappointed and disillusioned, they abandon their search. Those who do remain within faith communions may know very little about their own religious traditions. While much lost in the mists of the past has been recovered through research and

2. Borg, *Heart of Christianity*, 21.

new discoveries, sorting through all that is labeled "spiritual" today to find pearls of wisdom and enduring truth is more challenging than ever.

As people's religious roots become increasingly shallow or nonexistent, they tend to lose their way. Overwhelmed by choices and personal preferences, many end up like the seeds that can't take root in rocky soil in Jesus' Parable of the Sower (Matt 13, Mark 4, and Luke 8). While the idealistic young, like my erstwhile Catholic friend, may share common values, without being firmly planted in deep soil they are subject to the shifting winds of political opinion and cultural trends. People who consider themselves "spiritual but not religious" may also be so focused on direct experience of the divine that they are unaware of the spiritual knowledge, frameworks, and rich contexts that underpin their experiences, leaving them spiritually connected but uninformed. In the midst of life's challenges, religious roots and a spiritual community ground us and offer the support and guidance we need based on the experience and wisdom of the ages.

While I respect all deeply rooted spiritual pathways to God, it is the Christian path I have followed in my own life, although not without encountering a few interesting byways and unexpected detours. What I present in this book is offered to anyone looking for a rooted spirituality, especially those who are or ever were by birth or by choice part of one of the three great streams of Christianity—Roman Catholic, Eastern Orthodox, and Protestant.

This book is for those hungry for a deep relationship with God and a life transformed by that relationship. They are not satisfied with anything less than an authentic, personal experience of God. They want to know more about Jesus of Nazareth and the meaning of the mysteries surrounding his birth, life, death, and resurrection. They are not willing to settle for a shallow, uninformed faith focused on a narrow belief system or none at all, but rather one that will guide them along a well-defined, clearly marked pathway leading to the heart of God. They also seek companions and a community for mutual support on the spiritual path.

For Christians, the body of Christ is the community of those intentionally being formed in his likeness. The church is meant to be that beloved community reflecting God's reign on earth but it, like other human institutions, falls short of its ideal state. Those whose expectations remain unfulfilled by their experience of "organized religion" may simply give up on church and search outside it for the beloved community that reflects Christ's love and upholds them throughout their lives. Within such a community they hope to fulfill their desires for spiritual nourishment, growth, and friendship. Yet Christians are meant to grow into spiritually mature, wise, loving people prepared to share their gifts and resources for the well-being of all of God's creation through the body of Christ.

The early church referred to Christ's followers as "saints." This title was not limited to those beatified by miracles and exemplary lives but was applied to all the faithful. The standards for Christian believers and communities were high and inspiring, not in terms of wealth or position but rather in intention and commitment. Spiritual formation—even transformation—was the norm within these early faith communions, and those who were to partake of the sacred liturgies and sacraments of the church were expected to undergo a rigorous process to prepare to take their places within their communities as fully formed saints.

Few Christian churches in our own time ask as much of their members. Consequently, each year there are fewer well-formed Christians—those who have been instructed, nourished, and supported in their faith over their lifetimes. Christianity is now expressed in so many different ways that it is sometimes difficult even to discern among them our common heritage and shared core message. That was true in the early centuries of the Christian era as well, as competing versions of the Jesus story vied for authenticity until the New Testament canon was firmly fixed. The discovery of previously unknown early manuscripts in recent times has brought forward several other serious contenders for authenticity, while advancing scholarship within the existing canon has proved illuminating and challenging to orthodoxy.

As the church evolved from the first-century home-based gatherings of believers in communities around the Mediterranean Sea to the state religion in Emperor Constantine's time, the early fourth century, church leaders in concert with heads of state began to assert authority over matters of faith. Scriptures and beliefs labeled heretical were peeled away, often by force. The major upheaval of the eleventh century, the Catholic-Orthodox split over the theological language of the Nicene Creed, was followed in the sixteenth century by the Protestant Reformation, then the Catholic Counter-Reformation. The splintering process that has resulted in all the various entities constituting the

Christian church today has continued, and the "one holy, catholic, apostolic church" envisioned in the Nicene Creed eludes our grasp.

Despite the myriad of forms, creeds, doctrines, and belief systems that constitute modern Christianity, the spiritual pathway of transformation still lies at the heart of our common faith. It is revealed in the birth, life, death, resurrection, and ascension of Jesus and is as available to his followers as it ever was. So it is important to note that the spiritual journey we will take together in this book focuses on discovering and recovering what Christians hold in common rather than on what continues to divide us. After all, it is God who called the church into being as the beloved community, and it is through God's divine will that it will be transformed.

While we do not give up on the church, neither do we give over to it the responsibility for our own personal and spiritual transformation, the work of an entire lifetime in concert with the leading of the Holy Spirit. We are all works in progress, called to co-create with God lives that reflect God's love and mercy, and continually to be transformed into the image of Jesus, the Christ.

All who hunger and thirst for a loving, forgiving, generous God will encounter God on the path. Like the father of the lost son in Luke's Gospel, God runs down the path to meet us, rejoicing that the one who was lost is found and welcoming us home with great thanksgiving and celebration. It is said that the whole gospel may be found in that passage from Luke 15. We will learn on the journey that God awaits each of us in the same way.

While God is revealed to us through the natural world, God's creation, and through Sacred Scripture, God's inspired Word, this is also true of other religions. But only Christianity can claim that God's most significant revelation came in the form of a person, Jesus Christ, in whose image we are invited to become transformed and by whose death and resurrection we are offered forgiveness and new life. Those who have left the Christian faith because of quarrels with God or the church or have found other pathways to the divine may have uprooted themselves in ways harmful to their spiritual development, for unless we become firmly rooted in one tradition that allows us the freedom to explore our own spirituality and become deeply formed by our chosen spiritual path, we may try throughout our lifetimes to piece together a spirituality that doesn't hold through the trials of life.

In my experience, many Christians have lost faith because they have been unable to resolve one of its most basic challenges: why, if God is all powerful and all good, bad things happen to good people. This theodicy question, as it is known, causes many to get stuck in their anger and grief as they try to make sense of human suffering and God's seeming abandonment of even the faithful. If we cannot come to terms with why suffering occurs and in what ways it can be redemptive, we cannot develop into mature adults, emotionally or spiritually. At the heart of the Christian faith is a God who loves us unconditionally and wills what is for our highest good. Suffering, even though we may not understand it, is often instructive and awakens us to better choices we might have made or draws us into a deeper compassion for others. God's ways are mysterious and hidden, but we are accompanied by God's advocate, the Holy Spirit, who comforts and guides us along every step of our spiritual journeys. This personal, loving, faithful, and forgiving God, revealed to us in Christ, separates the Christian tradition from all other religions and remains the heart of our faith.

In recent years, as Christians, particularly in America, have become more the creatures of the dominant culture than countercultural, they have become separated from the processes of spiritual formation offered throughout most of Christian history to both new and mature believers. The catechumens of past centuries—those preparing for church membership—were taught by church leaders over a period of months, not weeks, and were required to leave worship before the Eucharist or Holy Communion was served, as they were not yet prepared to receive it. Until they were familiar with the Old Testament, they were not allowed to hear from the New. John's Gospel, considered the most mystical, was the last to which they were exposed. They memorized catechisms— doctrines and creeds of the traditions—as well as extensive passages of Scripture so they would have those treasures to guide them throughout their lifetimes.

Now, congregations seeking new members may invite visitors to join with only the briefest of introductions to the faith. Some churches are reluctant to wear their denominational labels on the outside for fear people will pass them by on their way to the nondenominational mega-churches. Congregations that do offer new member and confirmation classes for baptized children normally don't require anything further of their members. Once people become members, they are encouraged to worship weekly, take adult education classes, contribute their gifts and resources, and join in fellowship and mission opportunities but are not required to do so. Conservative faith communions generally do expect more, especially tithing, or contributing 10 percent of their income to the church. Across the board much of the traditional transmission of the faith through the family and the church has been lost. As a result, many end up leaving church, looking for more spiritual nourishment than they are typically offered. Yet the Christian tradition offers depth, richness, sustenance, and power beyond what most exposed to it in the contemporary church have experienced.

To find this depth, to become deep Christians, we may need to search on our own or with small like-minded groups for the pathway that leads to the heart of God. From the beginning, that way has been the path of the purified heart. A purified heart is one that yearns for union with God. Crusted over with a lifetime of beliefs, thoughts, and patterns of behavior that separate us from God, our hearts need cleansing and healing. On this path we learn, step by step, to entrust our lives to God. We already have God's unconditional love but need reassurance of that. In order to receive God in the deepest sense, we prepare ourselves to take on the likeness of Christ by casting off all the accumulated debris that gets between us and the subject of our heart's desire. This process is the work of a lifetime, supported by the leading of God's Spirit of Love. Thankfully, we have been blessed throughout the ages with many wise, holy guides who show us the way on this path despite the obstacles that appear and the places where we get stuck. As your host on this spiritual journey, I will connect you with a number of these guides who have illumined my own path.

Before we begin to take this journey together, I want to share with you that I am Christian by birth and by choice. I practice my faith within the Protestant Reformed tradition, in which I am an ordained minister, and within the Western monastic tradition, in which I am a Benedictine oblate, affiliated with a Roman Catholic monastery that follows the sixth-century Rule of St. Benedict. Over the years I have studied and explored these traditions, along with Eastern Orthodoxy (which claims to be the oldest intact expression of the Christian faith), mysticism, and the wisdom tradition. Along the way I have experienced many styles of worship in churches throughout the world. I have taken and led pilgrimages to a number of sacred sites and experienced the holiness of these places.

I've participated in ministries of peace and justice in the Middle East and Europe, as well as within the United States. I've attended services at synagogues and mosques, meditated with Buddhists, studied and taught spiritual healing.

My spiritual explorations have opened me to receive what God may offer through a particular people in a particular time and setting. An ecumenist, I have learned that none of us, despite—or perhaps because of—our belief systems, has the complete truth, a unified vision of the whole. We are like a tapestry, which on the back side looks chaotic—a tangle of colored threads without a discernible pattern—but on the front makes a beautiful work of art. God sees the whole as well as each individual thread. Yet God remains a mystery, at times drawing us closer, at times seeming inaccessible. If we want to know what God is like we have only to look at Jesus, the Christ, or listen to his teachings. At the same time we want not only spiritual knowledge but also to experience directly for ourselves who God is. I have been encouraged along this pathway to God by the guides who have journeyed ahead of us and generously have shared their experiences through the ages, remaining some of our best teachers in the faith.

Despite—or perhaps because of—my excursions down other byways along the religious and spiritual roadways, I am wholly committed to the Christian path, which is deep and wide and open enough to include anyone who wants to explore this way to the heart of God. It has room for skeptics and critics, contemplatives and mystics, and even those who are absolutely sure that their expression of Christianity is a piece of the true cross.

As I pondered how best to present the richness of the Christian faith and tradition, I found two motifs emerging. The first follows the calendar and liturgical years from one September, when I first received the inspiration for this book, to the following September, when the manuscript was completed. It was clear to me from the start that this phase of my own journey must begin, as all approaches to God must, with a deep purification process, so that I would be prepared, through God's grace, for what I would encounter and what would be revealed to me on the journey. This process proved to be far more extensive and long-lasting than I had anticipated and brought both welcome and unwelcome surprises. And yet, as I have learned along the path of the purified heart, all is in divine order, and I am grateful for all that I experienced. What happened during this year of my purification, as I have called it, is revealed in five of the chapters that follow. Interspersed with these chapters are the discovery and description of the path itself as it has been walked by countless followers of Christ through the ages.

The book's second motif follows another ancient and mysterious path, that of the labyrinth, a metaphor for the spiritual journey. We will explore and walk the labyrinth together as we follow its path to the center, where we will find what we have been seeking and rest in the heart of God. Then, refreshed and restored to wholeness, we will return from our journey transformed.

PART ONE

Purification

The Journey to the Center

ONE

Beginning My Year of Purification

Enter through the narrow gate; for the gate is wide and the road
is easy that leads to destruction, and there are many who take it.
For the gate is narrow and the road is hard that leads to life, and
there are few who find it.

—Matthew 7:13–14

THAT SUMMER SEEMED ENDLESS in North Carolina. The intense heat
and humidity came on fiercely in mid-May and wouldn't let up until mid-October. There were weeks when the temperature exceeded 100
degrees nearly every day. By mid-August I wondered with growing concern whether this extreme heat was going to be the "new normal." Would
human, animal, and plant life survive these alarming environmental
conditions? I concluded that the ants constructing habitats beneath the
bricks of our front walk had a better chance than most humans. These
industrious creatures organize themselves into highly complex communities that work together for a common purpose. Surely that's what it will
take for humanity to adapt in a rapidly changing world, I thought.

As a transplanted Midwesterner, I longed to escape back to the
perfect Michigan summers of my youth. A kind of lassitude or torpor
set in with the heat, and I felt myself sliding into *acedia*. One of the
original "eight vices" (later combined with sloth in the "seven deadly
sins"), *acedia* was described by the influential desert monk John Cassian
in the early fifth century as "a harsh, terrible demon" of listlessness,[1]
which takes advantage of our boredom and indifference to lead us astray.
Kathleen Norris' recent book, *Acedia and Me*, documents her own battle
with this demon and brings it once again into the foreground of passions
to be overcome on our spiritual journeys.

---

1. John Cassian, "On the Eight Vices," in *The Philokalia*, vol. 1, 88.

By mid-August I was seriously ready for summer to be over. To turn my attention from the weather, I began thinking about the new academic year that would soon begin. January may be the beginning of the calendar year, but for someone who always loved school and taught first in high school and then in university, September, with its promise of activity focused on new learning and teaching, was when the year began for me.

My academic career ended some time ago, but later, when I entered the ministry, I still looked forward to September. Church classes, small groups, and community events would begin again, and people seemed eager to re-engage matters of the mind, heart, and spirit in the fall.

If the calendar and academic years aren't enough to consider, the church observes yet a third year, beginning with Advent, the anticipation of and preparation for the birth of Christ. The four weeks of Advent arrive in late November or early December. The church's year then progresses through each liturgical season following Advent: Christmas, then Epiphany, celebrating the visit of the Magi to the Christ child, followed by a couple of months of Ordinary Time until Ash Wednesday, the beginning of Lent. The forty days of Lent plus Sundays leads through Holy Week to Easter, a time of cosmic darkness and light around the events surrounding Jesus' death and resurrection.

Although Protestants don't as a rule celebrate Christ's Ascension, it comes forty days after Easter and ten days before Pentecost, a major festival celebrating Jesus' sending the Holy Spirit to the apostles in Jerusalem. Once Pentecost is over, the longest period in the liturgical calendar settles in for the summer and early fall—Ordinary Time, which can seem endless, given how close together the celebrations of the major events in the life of Christ occur. Unbroken until All Saints' Day in early November, Ordinary Time creeps in its petty pace from day to day, and often is experienced as a welcome down time by exhausted church pastors and music directors. Eventually, the church year is brought to a close by Christ the King (or Reign of Christ) Sunday in late November, just a week before it all starts over again with Advent.

I enjoy the changing liturgical colors throughout the church year, from the purples or blues of Advent and Lent to the white or gold of the high holy days. I especially like the flaming red of Pentecost, used only one Sunday of the year in my tradition, although it also appears on days that commemorate martyrs of the faith in Catholicism. Mostly, the green of Ordinary Time is worn in clergy vestments and stoles and seen in pulpit hangings in worship spaces to remind people what time of year it is. During the summer, green evokes the full flowering of the natural world and also represents the heart and healing.

Most of life is lived during Ordinary Time. Each day presents fresh opportunities for transformation through the ordinary moments of life, for releasing what we've clung to that no longer serves us well, facing challenges, and continuing to open our hearts to God's love and Jesus' call to follow him.

That summer, during the long period of Ordinary Time, I waited for fall to bring renewed energy, the regathering of communities, and relief from the relentless heat. It seemed a good time to consider a new writing project. Now retired from the ministry, with no ongoing commitments to teach classes, lead groups, preach weekly, or attend to congregational life, I was free to pursue a long-standing interest. Writing had been essential to each of my three careers as an English professor, a financial planner and newspaper columnist, and a pastor. Now it offered a vehicle through which to express and share the spiritual lessons and insights I had gained through the years. It was time to let the next project emerge.

What had drawn my interest for some time was the narrow way, the less known and traveled path within Christianity. Researching and writing about this subject would shed light on Jesus' teachings to his inner circle of disciples and reveal the deeper meanings of his life, death, and resurrection. I thought I might develop some course material that could be used in a variety of settings—churches, spirituality workshops, and retreat centers. So, fighting off the demon of *acedia* in the midst of the scorching August heat, I began to research and uncover material for this planned course. I quickly found my intellectual curiosity kicking in as I scoured my own library, then ordered books that would reveal more about this fascinating subject.

September did not bring a break in the weather but did offer a welcome change: a retreat with two dear spiritual companions, Meg and Mary, to Mary's lake house a couple of hours from home. The three of us have offered each other spiritual direction and support for several years through our biweekly phone calls and semiannual retreats. The lake house was the perfect place for us to spend a couple of days in quiet meditation, prayer, and conversation.

We began our retreat the morning of the fall equinox with the spiritual practice of *lectio divina*, the divine reading of Scripture so central to the Benedictine monastic tradition. *Lectio* is a process of reading Scripture or other sacred material with an ear to hearing how God is speaking to us through the text. It's reflective and potentially transformative, leading naturally into meditation, prayer, and contemplation of God. That morning I remember selecting the scriptural passage we would reflect on together. It sprang out at me from the page, suggesting that it was chosen for us. The passage was from Matthew 15:10–20, where Jesus teaches the Pharisees and his disciples that it is not what is put into the mouth that defiles but what comes out. The ritual purification of the legalistic Pharisees stands in sharp contrast to the purification of the heart that seeks union with God.

We spent a good bit of time reflecting on this passage because it was speaking to each of us in a different way. As often happens, we shared insights for each other as well as for ourselves. I spoke with Meg and Mary about the course I had begun to work on that would help people understand the deeper meanings in scriptures such as this. They liked the idea but felt a course wasn't enough. It must be a book, they insisted. I heard God speaking through them that morning and knew they were right. And so this project was conceived. It would be a book not so much on the hidden path as the forgotten way to the heart of God that lies deep within our Christian tradition. That path seemed to open before me and beckon me forward through the passage of Scripture we explored together that hot September day.

Thus began my own year-long journey on the path of the purified heart, which from that day I pursued on two tracks. The first was the research and reflection that would lead to the writing of the book. This process was familiar to me as a former academic. I had already produced several books, though none quite as demanding as this one turned out to be. The second track was my own personal process, which would accompany the preparation of the book, a vital part of my spiritual journey that would take me deeper than I had ever gone before into the spiritual practices of the Christian tradition. I would explore, expand, and experience the practices intended to purify my own heart and draw me closer to the heart of God.

From that day forward I held this project as a sacred charge. I committed to a set of disciplines not only to keep me centered on God but also to strip away all that would distract me from this Spirit-led work. I set my feet on the path of the purified heart, not just to read and write about, but to embody and express in every dimension of my life. That was clear from the outset. I felt guided to take this radical step and to expect far more of myself than ever before. The icon writers of old underwent rituals of purification before beginning their sacred tasks so that the paints they worked with would be alchemically transformed into the luminous images through which the faithful could catch a glimpse of heaven. Like them, I approached my own preparation as an act of devotion.

Now, a year later, while my heart remains far from pure, I can truly say that my life was and continues to be transformed in both subtle and significant ways through my commitment to this essential stage of the spiritual journey leading to union with God. Just how will become evident as we begin to walk the path I invite you to take with me. It starts at the entrance to the labyrinth, the sacred symbol of the spiritual journey.

TWO

The Labyrinth as the Spiritual Journey

> Ask, and it will be given you; search, and you will find; knock, and the door will be opened for you. For everyone who asks receives, and everyone who searches finds and for everyone who knocks, the door will be opened.
>
> —Matthew 7:7–8

WHILE THE LABYRINTH IS an ancient symbol, it has become much more widely known in the past twenty years, largely owing to the work of the Reverend Lauren Artress, an Episcopal priest. Her 1995 book, *Walking a Sacred Path: Rediscovering the Labyrinth as a Spiritual Tool*, sparked a revival of interest in using the labyrinth as a spiritual practice. Since then other good studies have appeared and thousands of labyrinths have been identified and created around the world. Artress now leads Veriditas, which trains builders of labyrinths. For those new to the labyrinth, *Walking a Sacred Path* is still the place to start, as was confirmed when I reread the book not long ago.

My own encounters with labyrinths began around 1997. Since then I have walked dozens of them in many locations, including the mother of them all, the eleven-circuit labyrinth still intact on the floor of one of the most sacred sites on earth, Chartres Cathedral in France. More will be said later about this magnificent labyrinth and thirteenth-century cathedral. These experiences inspired me to choose the labyrinth as a central motif of this book, along with the year of the purification of the heart.

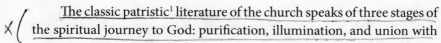

The classic patristic[1] literature of the church speaks of three stages of the spiritual journey to God: purification, illumination, and union with

---

1. "Patristic" refers to the work of the "church fathers," usually monks who were also priests. It is now common to refer to the early teachers and leaders of the faith as "holy elders" or "wise elders," a more inclusive practice I have adopted here.

God. The Eastern Orthodox call this third stage *theosis*, or "deification," believing that union with God is possible in this lifetime, not only in the life to come. While pursuing my own purification process with intensity this past year, I can attest that for most of us the first stage, purification, probably comprises at least 90 percent of the entire journey. We may occasionally reach and even sustain for a time the heights and depths of illumination and divine union through the action of the Holy Spirit, and any of us may experience such an act of grace. But few—mostly contemplatives and mystics—live fully in this state while on earth. Jesus taught that the kingdom of God is within us. Discovering and experiencing that truth figure significantly in the spiritual journey.

The transfiguration of Christ, found in the Synoptic Gospels (Matthew, Mark, and Luke), describes one of those mystical mountain-top moments of illumination for Peter, James, and John, who witnessed Jesus' deification, his union with God. Most Eastern Orthodox icons of the transfiguration depict the three disciples shrinking from the blinding light revealing the presence of God, which is characteristic of such moments. Glimpses of these spiritual heights are all most of us are likely to get in this life, unless we pursue God with our whole selves. Having to descend from the mountaintop to the flat land motivates us to continue trudging along the purification path until we open ourselves more fully to the God who is also seeking us. The Gospels tell us it wasn't long after witnessing the transfiguration that Peter denied Jesus, and all the disciples deserted him and fled. Still, it is possible through the grace of God and our consistent intention and effort on this path to find ourselves eventually transformed in ways we couldn't have imagined when we began. Perseverance in the face of challenges from within and without is essential on the path of the purified heart. As we persist in our pursuit of the One who seeks us, too, we will arrive at our destination and rest in the heart of God.

Few have Damascus Road experiences, like Paul, which dramatically change the course of their lives in an instant. Even he had to take time to realign his entire belief system and worldview in accordance with his experience of the risen Christ, before launching his ministry to the Gentiles. The rest of us continue walking the path through Ordinary Time, looking forward to those sacred moments when we gain new insights or discover the surprises God has waiting for us at every turn of the road—or every circuit of the labyrinth.

Labyrinths have been found in many ancient cultures, usually on the surviving walls of sacred sites. Unlike mazes, which have more than one path and tend to trap the journeyer in their confusing midst, labyrinths have only a single path, and it appears the same going in and coming out. It isn't, though, because we are transformed by the journey itself.

In medieval Christian times, these three stages—walking to the center of the labyrinth, pausing there, and returning—represented the stages of the spiritual journey: purification, illumination, and union with God. Meeting God on the inward path, we discover that our destination is finding our own deepest self within the heart of God. Reaching the center, we rest in God, like the weaned child in Psalm 131 who rests in its mother's arms, the struggle within the child's soul between dependence on the mother and its own autonomy now over. We rest peacefully at the still point, surrendering to Divine Love, before turning again, now forgiven, healed, and transformed through our heart-to-heart union with God, into a bearer of Christ's image who will support others on the life-giving path of the purified heart. The outbound journey becomes symbolic of the new integrated life we carry back into our lives and the life of the world. Returning to the place where we started, we see with new eyes and experience changed hearts.

The labyrinth remains a rich and powerful symbol at each stage of the spiritual journey, and the growing awareness of this among intentional seekers of spiritual transformation accounts for the rapid expansion in the availability of these mystical pathways. By visiting www.labyrinthsociety.org, you can locate those closest to you or in places you'd like to visit around the world.

In the medieval period, devout Christians were encouraged to make pilgrimages to the Holy Land. The so-called "Holy Wars," the Crusades, were intended among other reasons to clear the Islamic presence out of Jerusalem. The Holy City still is sacred to all three religious traditions attributed to the descendants of the Old Testament patriarch Abraham: Judaism, Christianity, and Islam. While for a brief period the crusaders gained control over Jerusalem, pilgrimages were altogether too long, dangerous, and expensive for most of the faithful. In time, alternative sites were designated within Europe, where pilgrims could safely travel and which would serve to give them the experience of pilgrimage. Those memorable travelers in Chaucer's *The Canterbury Tales* were all pilgrims on their way to Canterbury Cathedral, one of the most prominent pilgrimage sites. Another was the cathedral of Santiago de Compostela in western Spain, where the remains of the apostle St. James are said to rest. The Camino de Compostela is still one of the most famous, challenging pilgrimage routes in the world, as depicted in the 2011 film *The Way,* featuring Martin Sheen as a grieving father who walks the Camino as a testament to his son. A third significant site was Chartres Cathedral, where the entire pilgrimage was understood to be represented in the labyrinth itself.

Pilgrimages were not meant to be as easy as signing up for a bus tour of European cathedrals. They began then, as now, with God's call to draw nearer and to release all that separates us from accepting and expressing God's love. For many, they were acts of penance for past sins. For others they offered the hope of healing body, heart, and spirit. The relics of the saints housed in monasteries and cathedrals throughout Europe were thought to hold restorative powers for those who touched them or even came into their presence. Any encounter with the sacred reveals to us parts of ourselves in need of healing, and pilgrimages held out the promise of a life transformed through the power of the divine presence one would meet on the journey as well as at the destination. Forgiven, healed, and transformed, the pilgrim could return home with thanksgiving and a new sense of wholeness, renewed in his or her baptismal vows and reformed in the image of Christ.

As time went by, labyrinths were substituted for the physical journeys, which were difficult for most believers to make, and in our own time their revival and growing popularity gives testimony to the human desire to take the spiritual action of setting one's feet on a path to seek the heart of God. As one steps into the labyrinth, what is known and can be seen is the center, but the way to get there remains a mystery. Deceptive and confusing, the design of the labyrinth, especially the intricate eleven-circuit as opposed to the simpler seven-circuit kind, cleverly disguises how one arrives at the center. To enter a labyrinth means to step out in faith and trust that God will guide you along the path and bring you safely home. Each of the circuits contains twists and turns that resemble our paths through life. The unexpected rises up to meet us. A surprise, perhaps unwelcome but possibly containing an undiscovered gift, awaits us around each corner.

Ultimately, as the pilgrim and serious seeker of God comes to learn and even to accept, all of what we receive is good: the pain and the joys of life and everything in between. We spiritual beings in physical form are given a span of time, however long it may be, to learn how to love as God loves us and to love what God loves. That's really what the journey is about. We make it much more complicated by attempting to have things our way rather than God's way. When we learn, as we approach the illumination stage of the journey, to align our hearts with God's, the journey back out of the labyrinth becomes an expression of our new consciousness of and deeper relationship with God. We may suffer lapses from time to time, but our glimpses of the holy make the path more visible and a joy to walk, accompanied by Christ and the community of saints.

In our own time the labyrinth has taken on a whole new meaning as revealed by Jungian thought. For Jung it represented a kind of mandala, a symbolic, intricately designed pattern of wholeness. Viewed from above, the labyrinth also resembles the right and left hemispheres of the brain, the masculine and the feminine selves, brought into balance by walking it meditatively.

The richness and depth of the labyrinth symbolism is why I chose it to serve in this book as a motif for the spiritual journey as transformation. There were other obvious images which might have served. In ancient monastic literature, for example, the ladder was a popular symbol of the spiritual journey, or at least of a direct pathway to God. Just as in Genesis 28 the ladder Jacob saw in his dream, with angels descending and ascending, illumined for him the way to God, other famous ladders appear in early monastic literature. The works of John Cassian, John Climacus (whose name literally means "John of the Ladder,"), St. Benedict's ladder of humility in chapter 7 of the Rule of Benedict, and St. John of the Cross' ladder are a few of the better known. John Climacus' *The Ladder of Divine Ascent* is a classic that provided many spiritual teachers with a ready-made metaphor for the spiritual journey, and a famous ladder icon found in most Orthodox churches shows the human struggle to reach the top. A recent book by Jim Forest, *The Ladder of the Beatitudes,* even suggests that the blessings at the heart of Jesus' Sermon on the Mount in Matthew's Gospel are constructed as a ladder of divine ascent. The book illustrates how significant ladder symbolism representing stages of spiritual development has been in Christian thought.

As I considered the ladder as opposed to the labyrinth as a central image for this book, it seemed to me that the ladder was a bit too linear, too much a straight line to the top with evenly spaced steps, and that's not how we experience our spiritual journeys. As we've said, most of life is lived on the plains in Ordinary Time, not on the mountaintops. A predominantly male image, the ladder assumes ascension and progress if one is diligent, while the labyrinth is a more balanced masculine-feminine/left brain-right brain image, illustrating that need within each of us to harmonize and integrate these dual dimensions of the self into a unitive whole. In addition, the circuits leading inward offer places to slow down or stop, and it is not uncommon when groups walk the labyrinth together for the ones who see the destination more clearly or are in a hurry to get there to pass by the ones who wish to savor the experience or who aren't ready to move on. The kind of deep reflection and meditative walking the labyrinth deserves takes time to experience and process. To walk too quickly is to miss many of the nuances and hidden messages we might have received had we been in less of a hurry. Remaining open and attentive on the path and taking plenty of time to pause to reflect on the deeper significance of what we are experiencing is a far better approach than moving forward briskly, trying to take control of the pace just as we try to control everything else in our lives.

The labyrinth, because of its many twists and turns, resembles more the "scenic route" of the journey than the fastest or most direct route. The navigation system in your car, if you have one, invites you to choose the quickest, shortest, or most scenic way to your destination and to program in stops along the way. Life presents us with the same choices and offers lessons consistent with what we have chosen. When we walk the labyrinth, we must learn to leave *chronos,* or chronological time, and enter *kairos* time, the more liminal, timeless dimension where our deepest encounters with God await us. Slipping between these experiences of time is not uncommon on the labyrinth.

While the ladder image has its own virtues and carries the weight of tradition, the vertical ladder is a path intended to be scaled only upward. Looking down is perilous and falling back a constant danger that can harm or require us to begin the steep ascent all over again. The classic icon of *The Ladder of Divine Ascent* shows souls on the ladder, some climbing, some falling, others suffering on the ground. While motivating for some, the ladder alone seems incomplete as a metaphor for the entire journey of the soul, especially for those with a fear of heights, which is essentially a fear of falling, of losing control. In contrast, the horizontal path of the labyrinth moves both inward and outward, characteristic of the movement we all make between our inner and outer spiritual journeys: the periods of internal activities—intense reflection, contemplation, and receiving—and the periods of external activities—loving service and self-giving. The entry and exit points of the labyrinth may be seen as encompassing all of our physical existence, spanning birth to death, or as representative of the whole Christian journey from baptism and new life in Christ to life eternal in the kingdom of God. As Jesus taught us, God is not only "up there" in a remote realm we call heaven, or "out there" to be encountered in all of the vast cosmic creation, but "in here" within our own hearts.

A third symbol of the progression of the soul is found in the spiral, which combines aspects of both the circular, horizontal form of the labyrinth and the vertical form of the ladder. The spiral opens up as it moves higher, widening out as our perspectives grow and expand. In *The Naked Now: Learning to See as the Mystics See,* Franciscan priest Richard Rohr notes nine levels of psychological and spiritual development, which he images as a spiraling journey moving wider and higher.[2] These also correspond to stages of the spiritual journey. However, the form and mystery of the labyrinth feels less abstract and more tangible for our purposes.

Walking the labyrinth on a flat surface reveals more clearly the stuck places within ourselves, which slow us down and must be unblocked and released on our way through the purification stage of our journey. It also portrays God at the center of our lives rather than hidden somewhere in the clouds beyond the end of the ladder and shows us that the way out is not down. Instead, refreshed, healed, and transformed, we step back into Ordinary Time, where life awaits us. We may encounter the same jobs and relationships on the return journey, but how we perceive and handle them will change as we are changed. Our hearts open and expand like the mystical rose at the heart of the labyrinth.

The ancients' concept of the human heart was considerably different from ours. The early wise elders used the Greek word *nous* almost interchangeably for the mind, heart, and spirit. The heart was considered the very center of our being, encompassing the rational mind, the seat of our passions, our spiritual connection with God, even our soul, which lives on after death. As the heart governed our connections with God and God's creation, the mind and senses were considered subservient to the

---

2. Rohr, *Naked Now*, 163–66.

heart, which in its purest form had the greater wisdom. This concept was abandoned by the dominant culture in the Age of Enlightenment when science and reason displaced the earlier worldview. The twentieth century's explosion of scientific knowledge shifted how human beings view themselves, and the twenty-first-century high-tech age has brought its own infusion of psychological, neurological, and physical understandings of how we complex humans are wired and operate. However, to God and the illumined of our faith through the centuries, it was always the heart that connected us with our most essential selves, and it was the heart that was to be guarded against the onslaught of passions and images that would tempt us to stray from our path. It is in this holistic sense that I refer to the heart in this book.

Reformed theology teaches that the mind as well as the heart must guide us. While I agree, my experience tells me that the mind alone has been too dominant in the church for too long, and that the heart as the ancients understood it was much wiser, more compassionate, loving, and whole. Love is what guides us along the spiritual path and welcomes us home. The statue of Jesus of the Sacred Heart that graces the table in my meditation room reminds me of the God I seek: "Come to me," Jesus seems to say, "all you that are weary and are carrying heavy burdens, and I will give you rest. Take my yoke upon you, and learn from me; for I am gentle and humble in heart, and you will find rest for your souls. For my yoke is easy, and my burden is light" (Matt 11:28–30). It is this Jesus and his mother, Mary, the soul of self-giving and compassion, who this world desperately need now. It is their love, the love of God that flows through them, drawing us in and uniting us, we desire. The mind, always seeking clarity, certainty, and truth, is never secure without the deeper, spiritual knowledge and wisdom of the heart. The heart's wisdom needs to lead the mind throughout our quest for spiritual transformation.

Whether we find the concept of transformation appealing or scary, it begins at God's invitation and is sustained by the work of the Holy Spirit. Once we are aware of the invitation and then accept it, as we do through a confession of faith at baptism or confirmation, we are continually invited to go deeper and draw closer to the mystery that is God. As we walk on we may find ourselves less prepared than we'd like to be for the growth and change that taking our spiritual journey seriously requires. We see that we may have to make choices that won't always suit those around us, which are countercultural, requiring us to give over control of our lives to God. Part of the journey inward to the center of the labyrinth involves a process of renunciation, turning away from the old life to seek the new in Christ, and especially of *kenosis*, releasing and self-emptying in order to overcome the fearful ego that refuses to give up control, in order to be filled with God. Not all will want to take a journey that propels us out of our comfort zones, but that doesn't mean God will no longer continue to invite us to enter the peaceful still space within where we may rest. Many who have already ventured down the path will want a deeper experience of God, to know and love God more fully and express through intentions and actions the likeness, the consciousness of Christ that is developing. As we take on the mind and heart of Christ, as Paul encourages in Romans 12, we are truly transformed. Then we are able to discern God's loving will for us and fully engage in living it out in every dimension of our lives.

Some may think that being baptized or confirmed into the Christian faith is enough to ensure this kind of transformation or that passing a litmus test of belief that claims accepting Jesus as personal savior guarantees admission to heaven. Depending on your particular expression of the Christian faith, this may be where you are starting. But the journey of the human spirit to the heart of God is deeper, richer, and more hidden than that. As God beckons us to come closer, we discover more within ourselves requiring conversion, inviting us to encounter our own inner darkness, our shadow selves that often block the light of God. The farther we continue on the path, the more we realize that transformation into the likeness of Christ is a process of continual conversion throughout our lifetimes, a process that is never complete.

Unfortunately, many Christians are stuck in the early stages of their spiritual journeys because they haven't understood or been shown the deeper dimensions of their faith. This is by no means limited to any one branch of Christianity. To become deeply Christian in our times, we have to be self-directed learners, seeking out what feels missing in our relationships with God. We need mentors and guides to help us develop our heart connections with the God who loves and accepts us as we are while encouraging us to become more fully who we are meant to be. To become fully human, we follow the example of Jesus, who emptied himself in order to bear the image of God for humanity. Spiritual directors, companions, and communities guide and support us along the path. Wise elders from the past who have grappled with all that lies ahead on the Christian journey are a rich resource, and we will call on many of them in the following pages.

Recognizing and accepting God's loving invitation is just the starting point of our journey to wholeness—knowing and experiencing that love and wanting more, beginning to hunger and thirst for God is what will carry us along, even when the path is hard to follow or out of sight. Without that deep desire we would be passively acted upon rather than actively engaged in a lifelong journey of drawing ever closer to God. So our destination must be clear at the outset, even though we can't see as yet how we are going to get there. We may get lost or stuck along the way, but if we know that our journey will lead us to the heart of God and we experience loving presence and encouragement to keep going, we'll get there. Jesus assured us that if we persistently seek God's realm we will find it if we continue to knock we may be confident that the door will be opened to us. As we step out in faith, following the path laid out for us, we'll be guided safely to our destination.

THREE

Fall
Ordinary Time

Listen carefully, my child, to my instructions, and attend to them
with the ear of your heart. This is advice from one who loves you;
welcome it and faithfully put it into practice . . . This message of
mine is for you, then, if you are ready to give up your own will,
once and for all, and armed with the strong and noble weapons
of obedience to do battle for Jesus, the Christ.

—Prologue to *The Rule of Benedict*

B Y LATE SEPTEMBER MY task lay before me: to write a book about
the path within the Christian tradition through the ages, which
variously had been called the Way, the Royal Way, the Narrow Way, the
Path of the Cross, and the Holiness Path. Over the centuries the path,
overgrown and obscured by shifting political winds, religious wars, and
theological disputes, had at times disappeared, only to reappear again
through the efforts of those devoted to following it.

In our own time, the path has been submerged by churches' struggles to survive in the face of declining membership and resources. I understood that by uncovering and rediscovering this path, pilgrims and
seekers who hungered and thirsted for God could follow it themselves,
drawing on the wisdom of the ages as experienced and taught by those
who had spent their lives on the path. In so doing people could find their
way through the maze that constitutes contemporary Christianity and
recover or discover the depth, richness, and fullness of life it offers. The
labyrinth would represent not a maze but a time-tested way leading to
union with God. While each seeker experiences his or her own spiritual
journey differently, the path has always drawn to it those who desire to
encounter and express the love of God, to become followers of Christ,
to be transformed into his likeness and to express through their lives

God's love for the world. The book was to help them find their way to and along this sacred path.

As the magnitude of this task sunk in, I realized I needed to do much more to prepare myself to write than the normal reading and research that any complex project required. I knew I must undergo a period of deep personal spiritual preparation, a self-cleansing and re-newing of my intention and commitment to offer my whole self to God, to move ever closer to Christ in my thoughts, words, and actions. I had to ensure that not only my mind but especially my heart would be open to God's leading in this process and to shift other priorities in my life in order to focus my full attention on this one. Most of all, I would need to surrender and trust that whatever the outcome, it would be all right.

Anxiety, like a low-grade fever, gripped me, as I realized that every-thing in my life would now change. Would the quality of my thought and writing be adequate? Would I personally be up to the challenge? If I gave it my best, I had to trust that it would be good enough. I just needed to step out in faith and be willing to be guided along this path myself, for I was to experience it in a new way, as a serious seeker of God, a pilgrim on the path of transformation.

It was now almost October, and commitments already made for the next few months rose up to claim my time and energy. It was clear that as part of the cleansing process I would have to step back from most of these in order to concentrate on the new book project. For the past couple of years I'd been more focused on the outer spiritual journey than on inner work. We tend to go through periods when one or the other dimension of the journey dominates. After an intense period of inner work, we are ready to bring what we've learned and how we've grown into our loving service. And the reverse is true. People focused on social action and mission can end up burned out if they don't retreat and spend enough time in prayer and meditation with God. Two organizations that helped me learn that are the Center for Action and Contemplation in Albuquerque, NM, founded by Father Richard Rohr, who's been an im-portant teacher for me, and the Church of the Saviour in Washington, DC, which offers various ministries attached to house churches that stress both inner and outer work. Traveling to Bosnia in 1995, during the tragic war that country experienced, with an ecumenical group from the Church of the Saviour, was profoundly transforming for me, as was their Servant Leadership School, which I later brought to a community in which I served in ministry.

So it was time to turn inward again to prepare for my sacred task. That meant relinquishing several connections important to me. About a month before the September retreat that resulted in my committing to this work, I had begun to sing in the choir of the congregation I attended. Music has always been a large part of my life, but I hadn't had time to sing in a choir for many years. Now that I was retired from the ministry, I found I could as easily sit in the choir loft as the pew on Sunday morning. Sacred music, especially as played on full-voiced organs, raises the vibration within a sacred space and feels as though it lifts us closer to God. Choral singing and meditative chant do the same. I decided to stick with the choir through the Christmas season and then re-evaluate whether or not it was supporting what was now my first priority.

A much larger commitment would be drawing to a close in a few weeks, by mid-October. For the preceding year and a half I'd been involved with a new nonprofit I'd helped create, Power of One. It was birthed when a friend in Washington, DC invited me to meet with him and another woman one afternoon, when I happened to be in town. The conversation that day blossomed into a global project that would gather people on the National Mall to declare the power of each individual and all of us together to co-create a peaceful, sustainable planet. Nothing like aiming high! The project was meant to attract a core group committed to sustainability and peace from the U.S., Europe, and Asia. Despite many fits and starts, the event was drawing close, and I could already see that I would have to step back from any further involvement in order to concentrate on the book project. I couldn't work intensively with both.

My monthly spiritual writing group would actually support the new project and give me a ready-made group of readers for the thoughts and ideas beginning to flow, so that would definitely remain on my calendar.

The biweekly calls with Meg and Mary, the spiritual companions who had helped give birth to the project at Mary's lake house, would definitely continue and be an essential part of the support system I needed to get me through the year I expected the project to take.

I had already pulled back from any teaching commitments, and the only spiritual healing work I was doing was with small groups and mostly involved distance healing. That would also continue.

Another regular commitment would have to go. For some time I had been making five to ten trips a year from my current home in Chapel Hill, North Carolina to my hometown, Detroit, trying to support the city through the devastating economic downturn that had hit it hard. I served on the board of a neighborhood development organization dedicated to building a healthy community. After a conversation with the executive director, I decided I would stay on the board for a while longer, although I'd have to relinquish chairing a key committee and participate by phone and email instead of in person. My fiftieth high school reunion, which I'd helped organize, had taken place a few weeks earlier, so that responsibility—and the fun that accompanied being with old friends—was over, too.

As I cleared the decks to concentrate on the book project, I realized I would need more spiritual support. In turning to the deep inner work that would be necessary, I would need to rearrange my office and prayer-healing-meditation room so that the atmosphere would radiate sacred space. In the meditation room, I removed clutter and placed around it objects and pictures representing my journey. The Jesus of the Sacred Heart statue that came out of a Catholic church in upstate New York years ago was front and center on the altar made by a friend in New Mexico. Over Jesus' head was a round stained glass piece that had hung over the entry to our little chapel built by the same friend. This work of art, entitled "The Perfect Chalice of a Garden," had emerged from a dream I'd had years before, and a gifted stained glass artist was able to create what I had envisioned. The piece depicts a sun's rays pouring into a golden chalice, with a background of the mountains, ponderosa pines, high desert, and blue pond that could be seen through the window of our chapel. Overhead an eagle flew in a clear blue sky. This glass is one of my treasures and appeared on the cover of a previous book. As the light in the room changes throughout the day so do the colors of the glass, illuminating different parts of the scene, and the whole effect with the chalice sitting just above Jesus' head is stunning. I covered the altar with a cloth gifted to me in Scotland. The blue ceramic Communion and baptismal sets received in honor of my ordination to the ministry completed the table.

Pictures of Mother Mary and Mary Magdalene, those women beloved of Jesus, hang around the room, along with framed photos of fellow pilgrims with whom I have traveled to do healing work in Bosnia,

Egypt, Scotland, England, and Panama. On the table next to the chair in which I pray and meditate sits a Bible, devotional books, and a set of healing oils in a heart-shaped red box given to me by my sister.

Setting up a sacred space in which we feel connected with the holy is a pleasurable task each of us on this path may undertake. I am blessed to have a whole room to devote to this space, but a corner of a room is sufficient. Whatever evokes the presence of Christ for you will do. Over the years I have accumulated sacred objects that help embody my faith and the love I feel for the guides on my path. Although Protestants in general and Presbyterians in particular aren't known for supplementing their prayers with sacred objects, I find that they comfort and ground me and support centering on God.

My office needed rearranging, too. I set inspiring pictures around my desk. A bookcase in my line of vision while I'm sitting at my laptop holds other special objects to remind me to keep on task: small statues of Mary Magdalene and St. Francis, a black Madonna from France, an angel sculpted by my friend Mary's mother, the Rama cross from the monastery where we stayed in Bosnia, and a pietà and ceramic praying hands that had belonged to my mother. Directly in view as I look up, the well-known icon of Christ *Pantocrator*, Sustainer of the World, meets my eyes, blesses me, and reminds me to follow him. Later on I'll share the story of encountering the original *Pantocrator* icon in a Sinai desert monastery. That stunning image of Christ opened a window for me into the heart of God, as icons are intended to do.

A silver and turquoise Episcopal rosary given to me by a former spiritual director lay on my desk next to a candle from Michigan held in a Celtic jar from the holy island of Iona, Scotland. A small soapstone heart with the inscription "Peace," given to me by Mary, lay alongside. I often pick it up and rub it when I'm thinking. A vintage statue of a beautiful angel reading a book provides inspiration. Perhaps it's my book she's reading!

I cleared out the bookcase in my office and began to fill it up with all the books I already owned and would acquire as research for this book. These reminded me of the wisdom that other teachers and guides had brought forth so that we might become enlightened, and I was grateful to each of them who shared spiritual knowledge and experience to light our paths. White lined tablets filled with notes would also accumulate on my desk, as I recorded thoughts and images.

Over my left shoulder hangs a photo of the interior of Chartres Cathedral with its breathtaking inlaid stone labyrinth exposed, and behind me is a rosewood labyrinth board, an eleven-circuit replica of the one at Chartres. When I can't walk a real labyrinth, I can always use this one, tracing with my finger during meditation the path that carries us forward to its mysterious center.

Arranging the space and designating it as sacred signified my intention to do what I was committed to do. I couldn't look at all of those objects and what they represented without feeling both supported and compelled to keep moving, even when I was tired or distracted.

I knew it would be important to have the support of my husband and adult son in this work as well. Both of them have health challenges, and when any of us is having a bad day, we all are affected. We had set up our household as a "mutual care society." Tom, my son, lives in a cottage right behind us and shares in errand-running and dog care. Although my husband, Alden, deals with Parkinson's disease and painful arthritis, he manages to play a bit of tennis nearly every day and to function independently most of the time. My health is good, so as long as they are well I can concentrate on my work.

In October both of them were doing well, and with the event on the National Mall behind me, I booked a four-day retreat in the mountains of western North Carolina, where a program being led by a former seminary classmate offered a perfect opportunity to experience the peak of fall colors and the crisp autumn weather with spiritual companions. The Montreat Conference Center, belonging to the Presbyterian Church (USA), had beckoned to me many times before, as recently as six months earlier, when Meg, Mary, another friend, and I had enjoyed a private retreat during Holy Week. This time the program was run by Columbia Theological Seminary, from which I received my Master of Divinity degree some years before, followed by a Certificate in Spiritual Formation. The program's subject was the Liturgy of the Hours, the communal prayer of the Benedictine monastic tradition for the past 1500 years. Praying and chanting the Psalms, interspersed with Scripture and other sacred readings, constituted the Divine Office or Liturgy of the Hours of the Benedictines and framed their daily lives. Originally, the office consisted of seven daily prayer services, following the sixth-century Rule of St. Benedict. It still does in the stricter observance Cistercian (Trappist) order, spun off in the Middle Ages. Most Benedictine monasteries now observe four services a day: morning, noon, and evening prayer, plus Eucharist, or Mass.

I had been delighted to learn that a class focusing on the Liturgy of the Hours from the Catholic tradition was being offered by a Presbyterian seminary and being taught by a Presbyterian pastor. I had long felt that our denomination was short on spiritual formation, while Catholicism and Orthodoxy had deeper spiritual roots. In the course of preparing this book I would rediscover these roots in my own Reformed tradition, but at this point I was looking forward to the experience of being with spiritual people in a beautiful setting, learning about something that intrigued me. For years I had frequented Benedictine and Trappist monasteries in New Mexico, Colorado, South Carolina, Alabama, Kentucky, and Georgia near where I was living at the time. I loved the sense of God's presence I found in each of these holy places, the praying-singing community, the deep silence and solitude, the natural surroundings that connected us with God's creation, and the exceptionally gracious hospitality offered. Each monastery had its own character and personality, and I treasured them all

When in 1997 I first read Kathleen Norris's exceptional portrayal of Benedictine monastic life in *The Cloister Walk*, I became aware that this hospitality, which accepts each stranger as Christ, extended beyond an occasional visit to a monastery. This opportunity is open not only to Catholics but also to anyone who wishes to follow the Rule of Benedict to the best of his or her ability apart from monastic life. Like other of the religious orders within the Catholic tradition, the Benedictines opened a path to women and men of religious conviction who wished to join with them to live out their faith according to the Rule and to support the work and life of the monastery. This is the path of the oblate. Oblates affiliate with a particular monastery and spend usually a year or more in formation—study, prayer, and discernment—in preparation for their final commitment as oblates. This commitment may be renewed annually or eventually for a lifetime. I had found this concept appealing back in 1997 but didn't feel it was the right time to pursue it.

Now the Liturgy of the Hours class at Montreat was offering an immersion into the liturgy and music of the Benedictine tradition, and it seemed that the time might be right after all. The program's leader, a seminary classmate, was a gifted musician. We read a couple of intriguing books in preparation for the class, including Brother David Steindl-

Rast's *The Music of Silence: A Sacred Journey Through the Hours of the Day.* Brother David is a Benedictine monk whose life is steeped in the Liturgy of the Hours, and as I read his description of the *kairos* time each hour represents, symbolized by its own angel, I felt myself being drawn in more deeply. I hadn't known of my colleague's longstanding interest in the Divine Office, or *Opus Dei,* the work of God, as the Liturgy is also known, and was pleasantly surprised to find that he had composed a substantial body of music for every hour, which I hope he will publish someday. As we gathered to pray the Liturgy, he and his wife would lead us in song and prayer, which are really one and the same in these ancient liturgies based mostly on the Psalms. St. Benedict insisted that the entire Psalter of 150 psalms be chanted in a week's time or two weeks at most, although now it generally takes a cycle three to four weeks long to cover them all. This way the monastics absorb the Scripture in a visceral way, which can be called up to infuse private and public prayer in any situation. Although Benedict even in the sixth century desired that his monks be literate so they could read the Scripture themselves in the meditative form of *lectio divina,* memorizing Scripture was also expected. The Psalms afforded the whole array of human experience and stages of one's spiritual journey to ruminate on day by day, year by year. The Liturgy of the Hours was a key part of monastic spiritual formation, and I began to appreciate its rhythms and nuances as it came into focus for me during these few days.

I also enjoyed the community that formed at Montreat, especially in the small groups in which we processed our experiences and shared insights and struggles on our journeys. Several of us began to think aloud about becoming Benedictine oblates. My classmate shared that he and several others had formed a small virtual community called "Presbyterian Benedictines" consisting of those in our denomination drawn to follow the Benedictine Rule. Although it was not an active group, the knowledge that it existed began to trigger in me the desire to explore the oblate path further. I had scarcely returned from Montreat when I did so.

When I went to the Presbyterian Benedictines website, I recognized several people I knew. Later I was to discover that a significant number of colleagues in ministry are oblates because this path combines a structure, a specific community with which to affiliate, and a long-standing tradition still alive and rich. I began to explore on the Internet more about the Benedictines and their monasteries in the U.S. I also pulled out my copy of *The Cloister Walk* and began to reread it. Then I couldn't put it down. Something that had started within me years before when I had made retreats to half a dozen monasteries was now forming in a more tangible way in my consciousness and spirit. The strong pull I was feeling was an unmistakable sign that God was leading me to the next step on my path, to become a Benedictine oblate. I would lose nothing—not my ordination, not my spiritual practices, not my own church community. Instead, because of the open hospitality of the Benedictines, I would gain a new community, a set of spiritual practices to augment and strengthen my own, and a Rule of Life that asked more of me than I presently was giving. These were all remarkably consistent with my desire for self-purification and offered a built-in support system for this process.

Within three weeks of returning from Montreat I had selected the monastery I would affiliate with, St. John's Abbey in Collegeville, Minnesota, the one Kathleen Norris had described most vividly in *The Cloister Walk.* I communicated with the Oblate Director and arranged to receive the materials for my initial oblate candidate commitment ceremony. I selected a minister friend who had just moved to our area to officiate, and in mid-November, I became a candidate affiliated with St. John's Abbey. Although St. John's is a long way from my home in North Carolina, it seemed a good fit for me, with its university, school of theology, Ecumenical Institute, Liturgical Press, Episcopal House of Prayer, and many other resources. I could complete the work required for the year of candidacy at home and planned to visit the monastery a couple of times during the year.

My spiritual practices now shifted to include morning and evening prayer services as outlined in one of several Benedictine resources I had acquired. My Scripture reading broadened to include daily passages from both testaments, at least one of which I reflected on using *lectio divina*, the sacred reading practice leading into meditation, prayer, and contemplation. I added devotional readings from the spiritual classics, and found myself spending at least an hour and a half in the morning and half an hour or more in the evening in prayer and meditation. On evenings when I had to go out, even to choir practice, I found that I preferred to stay home and quietly process the day. The less activity that intervened, the better I liked it. My contemplative side began to take back from my active side what it needed for spiritual nourishment. The deep inner work that would be necessary for this year of purification had begun. As Advent approached, I began to make plans to visit my new monastic community for the upcoming Advent Retreat in mid-December.

Meanwhile, I was spending several hours a day in research and reading. all of it fascinating to me. One source led to another, and I couldn't get enough of engaging with religious and spiritual texts of many kinds. The wide variety of them is reflected in the bibliography, but the more I read the more I realized how much more I wanted to know. I had bookshelves in my house lined with all the books I'd been reading on spirituality for the past twenty years, a number of which I reread with new perceptions, but I especially wanted to learn more about the monastic traditions and Eastern Orthodoxy, which were not featured in my seminary education. Days were spent in reading, punctuated by the Liturgy of the Hours, prayer, and meditating on Scripture, not unlike the rhythm of life in the monastery, minus one crucial component—community.

I had begun updating almost daily the journal in which I'd been recording reflections on my life for many years because it helped me keep track of this period, which began to blur in my mind, so deeply absorbed was I in the work. It also helped me revive a spiritual practice I had neglected for some time, the daily examen, based on the exercises of St. Ignatius of Loyola, the sixteenth-century founder of the Jesuit order. The daily examen is a helpful discipline for reflecting on where you are meeting God throughout each day and in each event of your life. Practiced at least every evening, it helps us hold ourselves accountable to God for our time, thoughts, and actions.

While a thirty-day or nine-month program of Ignatian exercises works best if done with support over a specific period of time to cement the practice, I had studied it before and simply needed to start doing it again. I found it essential to my process of self-purification because it forced me to be totally honest with myself and God. The examen helps us look closely at the dark underbelly of ourselves, the shadow side, where the ego takes us when it's afraid we're going to put it in its place— anywhere that makes it relinquish its firm grip on controlling our lives. It forces us to confront the passions and behaviors that separate us from God and to gently, with God's help, release them. The examen also supports our process of giving over our lives to God, surrendering in trust that God desires what is for our highest good, and trying to listen and discern what that is. As long as we align with that highest good, we are able to stay on the path that leads through Christ to God.

It's not easy to look at our shadow sides, that darkness within that keeps emerging just when we think we've conquered our self-justification, pride, and need to control every situation we are in. But it's absolutely necessary for serious seekers on the path of transformation. We may fool ourselves—we've all had plenty of experience with that—but we can't kid or hide from God, and the examen directs the spotlight onto our relationships with God.

Working with the examen also underlined for me the importance of spiritual companionship on the journey. Spiritual direction is well known in the Catholic and Episcopal faith communions, although few actually take advantage of it. It is less known and used by Protestants and nondenominational Christians. Spiritual direction may be confused with pastoral counseling, usually provided by a congregation's minister or priest or someone trained in that field. Counseling deals mostly with human relationship issues, the particular challenges we are facing, such as grief, forgiveness, and the like. It's similar to therapy, although from a faith perspective. Facing our issues and getting help dealing with them is much a part of the common culture these days, and that's a good thing, but spiritual direction is something else.

A trained spiritual director helps us "listen with the ear of the heart," as St. Benedict teaches, to God's invitations and initiatives in our lives. As we grow in our capacity to hear and discern God's call and sense God's presence, we more intentionally place God firmly in the center of our lives, just as the center of the labyrinth invites and draws us to that place of illumination where God awaits us. Always it is God who does the inviting, and we are expected to RSVP. God is still waiting for some of us to say yes to the multitude of invitations that have gone unanswered or been turned down. A good spiritual director is deeply spiritual her- or himself and listens on our behalf to help us discern how God is speaking to our hearts and to guide our responses. She or he will encourage us to deepen our prayer practices and suggest other spiritual disciplines to open up the channel through which we are more likely to hear God. He or she follows our progress, notes the obstacles we are encountering, and gently supports our finding or resuming our places on the path of our own spiritual journeys.

An organization like Spiritual Directors International can help locate someone to work with, but a better suggestion may be to find a director through a recommendation or through a local spiritual center. At the time this book project emerged I was without a spiritual director. Trained as one myself, I preferred to share what I was hearing and discerning with the spiritual companions who had known me for years, who always had helpful things to say. However, I could see that it was time to go back into direction on a deeper level with someone who would understand the process I was involved with and had gone down that path herself. One person came to mind but wasn't available. I would wait several months until the right person emerged, in God's *kairos* time, not chronological time.

Meanwhile, Ordinary Time was drawing to a close. All Saints' Day, when the church celebrates the saints of the faith, including those unsung, follows Halloween, All Hallow's Eve. I've always liked this Sunday when the Christian community remembers those who have set an example for the rest of us and have passed on. In my tradition we generally sing the hymn also often sung at memorial services, "For All the Saints": "For all the saints who from their labors rest,/Who Thee by faith before the world confessed,/Thy Name, O Jesus, be forever blessed./Alleluia! Alleluia!" The verse I resonate with comes later: "O blest communion, fellowship divine!/We feebly struggle, they in glory shine;/Yet all are one in Thee, for all are Thine./Allelluia! Alleluia!"[1]

The Protestant tradition does not acknowledge sainthood in the same way the Catholic and Orthodox traditions do. We do hold up, however, many in the faith whose courage and love served to illumine the path for those of us feebly struggling. The Catholic and Eastern Orthodox have a wide constellation of saints, many from the dim past, who were important to their tradition but remain largely unknown. I can't help but think that we all have the capacity for sainthood as we feebly struggle on our paths, for God graces us with the strength to carry on, comforting and guiding us over the most difficult terrain. The lives of the saints of old may not be historically accurate, but their stories nonetheless inspire those on the path of spiritual transformation.

Although I was reluctant to add another time commitment to my schedule, I was asked in October to offer a weekend class in spiritual energy healing for a small interested group. Since I could do it at my

1. How and Williams, *Presbyterian Hymnal*, 526–27.

home and use materials from my spring class, I agreed. In mid-November I taught this group how to help people release blockages in their own energy fields and restore balance and peace to their bodies, minds, and hearts. This practice is fully compatible with the Christian tradition. Jesus, the healer, taught something similar to his disciples, although it's one of those pathways within our tradition that remains hidden to most and therefore suspect to some. I've encountered a number of Catholic sisters who practice Reiki, a well-known form of spiritual energy healing often used in alternative medicine settings. If our intentions are for the highest good of the people we are working with, offering healing in this way can be helpful as a supplement to conventional processes.

Thanksgiving brought a visit from family who live in New Jersey, a welcome respite from the intensity of the past few months. Around that time I became increasingly concerned about my son's health, as he complained of occasional breathing problems. After a fairly stable fall, it seemed the approaching winter would bring new health challenges for our household.

Meanwhile, the church's liturgical year was now rapidly drawing to a close. Christ the King or Reign of Christ Sunday comes at last in late November, wrapping up thirty-three Sundays of Ordinary Time distributed throughout the liturgical year. This number is of course symbolic both of Jesus' age at his death and of the Trinity—Father, Son, and Holy Ghost, or Creator, Christ, and Holy Spirit, for those who prefer gender-inclusive language. By the time this Sunday comes, I feel ready to move to the next liturgical season: Advent.

In three short months, from the dog days of mid-August to the oblate candidacy which began in mid-November, just at the end of Ordinary Time, my time had become anything but ordinary. My brush with *acedia* retreated in the rear view mirror, as God beckoned and I followed, awaiting the next circuit on the labyrinth.

FOUR

Stepping onto the Path

Blessed are the pure in heart, for they will see God.

—Matthew 5:8

I appeal to you therefore, brothers and sisters, by the mercies of
God, to present your bodies as a living sacrifice, holy and acceptable to God, which is your spiritual worship. Do not be con-
formed to this world, but be transformed by the renewing of your
minds, so that you may discern what is the will of God—what is
good and acceptable and perfect.

—Romans 12:1–2

THE SPIRITUAL JOURNEY TAKES place over a lifetime, as we experience the opportunities and challenges offered us and become increasingly aware of God's presence in each event and through each stage
of our development. If spiritual awakening begins with an insight, an expansion of the heart, a glimpse of the ineffable, it is followed by a lifetime
of continual conversion from the patterns of thoughts and actions that
separate us from God. For most of us, conversion is a gradual process.
We take a step forward here, a step backward there. Our spiritual growth
may be supported within our faith communities through worship and
the sacraments, Bible study, prayer, and service. For intentional seekers
of God on the path of personal and spiritual transformation, especially
those unconnected to a worshiping community, these practices are only
the basic elements of a deeper, more extensive process.

To desire to experience the spiritual journey as transformation
raises the quest to another order of magnitude. Transformation of any
kind brings about a radical change of consciousness, which leads to a
changed life. To be spiritually transformed into the image of Christ is
to undergo a profound shift of mind, heart, and spirit through which
we are restored to full humanity—but not without cost. In an interview

with Cynthia Bourgeault, the Trappist priest Thomas Keating remarked that "the false self does not just drop dead on request; it's very firmly grounded in the subconscious—so much so that even when we buy in to the spiritual journey and its values consciously, this false self just laughs at them and keeps right on going."[1]

Overcoming the less developed, less mature self that clings to whatever satisfies its needs in order to become the fully human true self is the most challenging part of the inner journey toward God. Unless we have a clear sense of what we will gain on this path we are not likely to let go of what we perceive to be a comfortable, secure life or a belief system resistant to change. Perhaps that's why those who know they need to be saved from themselves and their circumstances are more likely to place their hope in Christ. The dramatic growth of Christianity in the Third World and among those seeking security during our own uncertain times would seem to be evidence of that.

The path leading to new life in God through Christ accommodates people at all stages of personal and spiritual development. Persistence in the face of obstacles or uncertainty will be required of all who seek a deep relationship. The consciousness of union with God and God's creation, made manifest through the life, death, and resurrection of Jesus, is centered in a soul-level understanding and experiencing of the interconnectedness of all life and our mutual dependence. This illumined consciousness sees all of creation as one vast, intricate, beautiful, creative expression of God's love held in relationship and unity.

To experience this consciousness, this integration of awareness, perception, and understanding, is to recognize that God's love is the glue holding the universe together and that even the minutest quark, whether a particle of matter or a wave of potential, expresses divine order and will. While not all who hold this consciousness will necessarily be Christian (Jesus was not, after all), neither does every Christian hold it.

The spiritual journey described in this book, then, is specifically intended to prepare us for and lead to the transformation of our hearts, minds, and spirits into the likeness of Christ, so that we may live out that consciousness of unity and love under the reign of God within the beloved community.

The implications of profound transformation touch every dimension of life. When we see through this lens and truly love God with all

1. Bourgeault, "Awakening to the Presence," in *The Inner Journey*, 49.

* And it has to be something now, (heaven) as well as not later.

of our being, we come to love what God loves: the whole creation. We understand that all of God's creatures share a common story and destiny. When we know that we cannot be separated from the love of God, we discover that what God has been creating through eons of time is the beloved community. This community, called the kingdom of God, kingdom of heaven, realm or reign of God, is peaceful and fruitful, as it co-creates with God ever more abundant life.

The beloved community is the redemption of humanity's fall from grace as captured in the Genesis story of Adam and Eve. It is the restoration of right relationships within the human community, with nature, and with God. It exemplifies the new world inhabited by people who not only obey God's commandments but do so willingly and joyfully, devoting themselves with praise and thanksgiving to serving one another as reflections of God's gracious love in Christ. Those who inhabit the beloved community are the ones Jesus spoke of in the Beatitudes contained in the Sermons on the Mount (Matt 5) and on the Plain (Luke 6): the humble, merciful, righteous, generous, peaceable, and pure of heart. Those who desire to live without separation from God seek to discern and follow God's guidance in all things. Individual freedom is preserved within the beloved community, but that freedom is expressed through choices that reflect the highest good for each person and for the whole body of Christ.

The phrase in the Lord's Prayer "on earth as it is in heaven" is fulfilled in the beloved community. The wisdom traditions have emphasized the significance of "as above, so below," an axiom of correspondence between the higher dimensions of non-physical matter and the three-dimensional world of matter that we inhabit on earth. To take on the mind and heart of Christ is to exist in both dimensions simultaneously, attuned to both and experiencing their interconnection, rather than seeing them in a dualistic way as separate.

Science is revealing to us vast networks of living things and systems that support life. Visionaries can see and feel these networks as streams of light and energy joined in *perichorisis,* an interpenetration of one dimension with another in a kind of cosmic dance. This indwelling, interdimensional force illumines our natural relationship with All That Is, another name for God. *Perichorisis* makes concrete sense of the Holy Trinity, which most of us take on faith because the concept of the three-personed God is beyond our comprehension. If we think of Jesus as the perfect son through a 1:1 correspondence between the human and divine dimensions, it becomes conceivable that we, too, may become united with God through our likeness to Christ. As the Orthodox would say, the fullest expression of Christianity is "deification," the unity between the human and the divine reached in the third stage of the spiritual journey. The Holy Spirit, the agency of this correspondence, is God's loving breath of life.

Belonging to the beloved community is our birthright, our inheritance, as expressions of God's love in created form. Through our own thoughts, intentions, and actions, however, we distort our relationships with God and prevent the beloved community from being that full reflection of divine love. God continually invites us to join the dance but does not coerce. The great gift of free will has not been rescinded. So we must choose carefully the kind of relationship with God we want and whose image we want to reflect.

We learn from Sacred Scripture and story that those who have fallen from the closest relationships with God have fully understood what they were choosing. The story of Lucifer, the brightest of angels, gives testimony. Choosing power over love was his downfall, because within God's being these aspects cannot be separated. Jean Pierre de Caussade, the eighteenth-century Jesuit spiritual director, observes in *Abandonment to Divine Providence* that Lucifer was "a brilliant intelligence, the most enlightened of all, but an intelligence discontented with God and his order." De Caussade goes on to say that our acceptance of God's will regulates the heart and places us in union with divine will, while iniquity is an expression of discontent with God.[2] Jesus clearly understood this, as following his baptism he resisted in his forty-day wilderness experience the three temptations of the human mind, heart, and spirit as he prepared himself for his earthly ministry. Unfortunately, most of us, even lifelong Christians, have scarcely a clue what we are refusing by not choosing to embrace fully God's love and will for our lives and for the creation.

To step onto the path of the labyrinth to begin an intentional, intense process of self-purification is to pray, with fear and trembling, "Thy will be done!" This affirmation we have prayed a thousand times in the Lord's Prayer is itself an act through which we surrender our imagined human sovereignty over our own lives to God. Trusting that God

2. De Caussade, *Abandonment to Divine Will*, 192.

loves us and wants only what is for our highest good, we agree to allow ourselves to be sculpted into beautiful expressions of both our human and God's divine natures, reflections of God's love and wisdom. Our inner work is to cooperate as God restores us to the human state before the Fall. Jesus, in his role as Redeemer, provides the pattern and points the way. This inner work must be our focus on the journey into the heart of the labyrinth, where the God we long to know awaits.

While the importance of the outer Christian journey will be emphasized in Part Three of this book, as a response to union with God, inner work takes precedence at this stage and becomes a lifelong task. If we bring to mission and service our own judgments, biases, and limited understanding, these could damage the relationships we are trying to build within the beloved community and the wider world. An example from my own seminary days may suffice.

For several weeks in 1993, a group of classmates and I undertook an urban ministry immersion experience in Atlanta. We were to visit the housing projects, soup kitchens, and homeless shelters of the city's underbelly, encounter its poor and underserved populations, listen to their stories, observe their living conditions, and reflect on how we in our future ministries might share Christ's love with them. However good our intentions, we didn't know how to feel about or behave toward what we saw. One classmate visited an elderly, ill woman in a housing project living in a filthy apartment filled with the detritus of a lifetime. The woman couldn't take care of herself, let alone her apartment, and so our group decided that we would take a day to clean Ms. Lena's apartment, then try to enlist a neighbor, relative, or agency to provide ongoing care for her.

We showed up at the project with our cleaning supplies on a holiday, when all the neighbors were home to watch the spectacle. The stench in the apartment was too much for me, so I worked outside sorting through the accumulation of Ms. Lena's possessions as they were hauled out onto the lawn. They either went into freshly sprayed boxes to discourage the roach population or were consigned to the dumpster. At one point, when everything movable was spread out on the lawn so that the cleaning contingent could do its work, Ms. Lena stuck her head out the window and mused, "I didn't know I had so much stuff." As the afternoon wore on, we heaved carloads of what we considered trash, including an ancient, broken TV set and reams of old newspapers, into the dumpster. Eventually, when the apartment was as clean as our group could make it, the remaining goods were carted back upstairs and put in place. Exhausted and filthy but satisfied with ourselves and our day's work, we headed home. The next day, when the classmate who had initiated our endeavor revisited Ms. Lena, she found to her surprise that all that stuff we had thrown in the dumpster was back in the apartment, roaches and all. Apparently Ms. Lena surmised we were stealing her stuff and enlisted her neighbors to raid the dumpster and bring it all back inside.

Our own preparation for ministry may have been enriched by this experience, as we learned lasting lessons about imposing our own beliefs and standards on others, the difficulty of trying to break the cycle of poverty, and the importance of building trusting relationships before trying to change other people's lives for them. What did Ms. Lena and her neighbors gain in the process? A day's entertainment, a little kindness and attention paid to the children who gathered, as we passed out candy and gum, but in the end probably a confirmation of their own biases about folks who don't understand them trying to help and nothing really changing. Did they experience the love of Christ through us? Did they glimpse the beloved community in which we all might live together in harmony and peace? If so, it was only through God's grace.

Being well intentioned, believing we are following Christ's teaching to feed and care for the least, the last, and the lost, isn't enough. First we need to see ourselves also as standing in great need of grace. Otherwise, we have missed the mark. Social activists are subject to dejection and burn-out because people don't respond as expected and nothing seems to change. As I reflect on this experience years later, I see that what was missing that day was a sense of mutuality, the quality of relationship that levels the playing field and recognizes how we depend on one another. At times, one's need is greater, at times another's is. Our efforts with Ms. Lena lacked any sense that she and her neighbors might have something to offer us. We were doing ministry to, not with. This understanding only comes through developing relationships with a sense of humility. Our experience that day was one of those transforming moments through which God reveals the work we still need to do to truly love our neighbors as ourselves. Loving ourselves is also part of that challenge!

While Christian churches today generally do engage in "equipping the saints for ministry" across national, racial, gender, and cultural divides, mission workers and service teams are still likely to learn more about themselves than the people they hope to serve. The ancient philosophers as well as the desert wise elders taught the importance of knowing the self. And that is why the inner journey, the work we do on ourselves with God's loving guidance and the support of our communities, must be primary.

In the early church those preparing to be baptized, the catechumen, were taught not only the basic creeds and confessions of faith, such as "Jesus is Lord," and an early form of the Apostles' Creed, but also that the circumstances of Jesus' birth and the events of his life, death, and resurrection were the pattern for them to follow on their own spiritual paths before they were sent out to "make disciples of all nations" (Matt 28:19). This catechumenate, or curriculum, was transmitted orally. It would be decades after the formation of the first house churches that the earliest written Gospel accounts appeared, and dozens, even hundreds of accounts, may have been in circulation. Even by the fourth century, when Christianity became institutionalized, copies of the four canonical Gospels, Matthew, Mark, Luke, and John, were scarce. The oral tradition prevailed for centuries, well after Western monastics made it their sacred duty to copy, translate, and preserve the key texts of Scripture. Only in our own lifetimes have most Christians been able or encouraged to read Scripture for themselves.

When the catechumens were instructed, those who had known Jesus or had known others who knew him passed on their memories and experiences, which varied in the telling. It was the stories people remembered, the parables and the healings, along with the pattern of Jesus' life in five movements: rebirth through baptism, transfiguration, crucifixion, resurrection, and ascension. These movements, which eventually became known as the "Lesser Mysteries," presented Jesus' biography as metaphor, even as initiations, which those who were his true followers could also experience when they were ready. The "Greater Mysteries" were only transmitted to those more formed in the faith. A passage in the Letter to the Hebrews makes this clear. The writer chides those being prepared to transmit the faith to others: "For though by this time you ought to be teachers, you need someone to teach you again the basic elements of the oracles of God. You need milk, not solid food . . . But solid food is for the mature, for those whose faculties have been trained by practice to distinguish good from evil" (Heb 5:12, 14). The author goes on to say that it is time for "leaving behind the basic teaching about Christ, and not laying again the foundation: repentance from dead works and faith toward God, instruction about baptisms, laying on of hands, resurrection of the dead, and eternal judgment" (Heb 6:1b–2). Here we are given a glimpse of early Christian basic training, but it is the church elders to whom the letter is addressed, and they need to go deeper and learn more.

The highly liturgical Roman Catholic and Eastern Orthodox churches have always transmitted the Lesser Mysteries through liturgy— forms of public worship including ritual, prayer, and the sacraments— that people could experience with their hearts and souls, even if they didn't understand the Latin or Greek words being spoken. Memorization of catechisms and prayers was expected of those confirmed in the faith. Since the Second Vatican Council in the early 1960s, when worship in native languages was mandated, the Catholic Church has revived an extensive curriculum known as the Rite of Christian Initiation for Adults. This instruction and similar programs in other more liturgical Protestant denominations, like the Episcopal and Lutheran, are generally focused on church doctrine, liturgy, creeds, and practices. Other Protestant and nondenominational faith communions use a variety of curricula for children and adults. Material specifically focused on spiritual formation rather than faith development, or what is called Christian education, is less common and varies widely across the whole church.

Not long ago I spoke with a seminary classmate, now a professor of Christian education for ministers and other church leaders responsible for the formation of Christians in their congregations. I asked her what she understood as the difference between Christian education and spiritual formation. She responded that the one focuses more on human development theories and applications, while the other deals with spiritual practices, like prayer and Bible study. The one-semester class in the Master of Divinity program required of those seeking ordination to the ministry was about equally divided into these two parts. Why was there no course specifically on spiritual formation in the curriculum, I questioned? An already packed program of study and budget restraints was her response. I reminded her that when we were in seminary taking a required class on the practice of ministry, only part of one class had been devoted to the theology and practice of stewardship. Ministers in my tradition are required to be proficient in Greek and Hebrew, biblical studies, theology, preaching, and pastoral care but are not specifically trained to support spiritual formation. Even though I was fifty when I finished my Master of Divinity degree, I was still a beginner on the spiritual path, as were most of my classmates going out to serve congregations. Ministry, I learned, consists mainly of on-the-job training.

I recently asked two Orthodox priests, one from the Greek tradition, the other from the Russian, how they handled spiritual formation within their congregations. Both responded that there was no such text as "Orthodoxy 101" but that experiencing the Divine Liturgy and the sacraments was the main means of transmitting the tradition. Greek school for children and adults, Bible study, and other classes usually led by the priest were also offered. I observed this tradition in worship one Sunday at the local Greek Orthodox Church. Icons representing saints and scenes from Scripture are prominently placed at the entrance to and within the sanctuary and are kissed and revered by worshipers as portals to divine energies. Much of the service, throughout which the congregation stands, is conducted in Greek, including the choral responses. The sacrament of Holy Communion is offered to all the baptized, even toddlers, and served by the priest on a common spoon from a chalice containing the consecrated bread and wine.

The liturgical forms, prayers, and practices, including the sacraments that the different faith communions recognize, are essential to any Christian's spiritual formation, as they are designed around God's saving action throughout human history, culminating in the life, death, and resurrection of Christ, and they invite our grateful responses to God's grace. In less liturgical traditions like my own, the sermon, through which the preacher encounters God's word on behalf of the congregation, carries more weight than homilies in the Roman Catholic and Orthodox traditions, and the sacrament of Holy Communion is often given only once a month rather than at least weekly. Communal and pastoral prayers composed by pastors or lay leaders are offered in place of liturgical prayer in the other faith communions. Worship is clearly essential to anyone's spiritual formation, but so is instruction in what the liturgy and order of the Service for the Lord's Day mean and how we are to respond.

The model of Jesus' life as metaphor used in the early church parallels the spiritual path I have been describing, with its three stages of purification (baptism), illumination (transfiguration), and union with God (crucifixion, resurrection, and ascension). It begins with a turning:

away from the old life and toward the new. This act of turning, *metanoia*, is enacted in baptism rites by renunciations of all that in our previous lives has separated us from God, followed by the commitment to begin a new life in Christ, the new creation. It is this turning we must commit to as we begin to walk the path of the labyrinth.

Baptism, the first public act undertaken by Jesus before he began his ministry, is considered a sacrament in most forms of Christianity. (A sacrament is a sacred sign or symbol of a spiritual act or reality.) When Jesus presented himself to John the Baptist to be baptized, John protested that he was not worthy to baptize the one he knew to be greater than he. Nevertheless, he performed the sacrament by immersing Jesus in water. The Gospels tell us that God completed the baptism by acknowledging Jesus as the beloved son with words and the presence of the Holy Spirit in the form of a dove.

The sacrament of baptism in most of our faith communions contains the same two elements: water and the Holy Spirit. Pentecostals and other charismatic Christians place the emphasis on the empowering work of the Holy Spirit as at Pentecost in Acts, but the other communions generally invoke the Trinity while immersing or sprinkling the candidate with water. Just as his immersion into the waters of the Jordan represented for Jesus a kind of death, an end to his former life, and a rebirth, the rising to a new life of public ministry and self-sacrifice, so does it for those of us on the path of the purified heart. For Jesus, the symbolic death and rising of baptism also presaged his crucifixion and resurrection. Baptism was a public act for Jesus, and in Christian churches it is generally performed in the presence of the congregation that commits to supporting the newly baptized in their journeys of faith.

While theological differences remain within the wider church on the methods by which this baptismal rite is administered, most faith communions at least recognize each other's baptisms and do not require another of converts and transfers, as long as they were baptized with water in the name of the Trinity. Before the water and words of institution are administered, however, the candidate for baptism or those who represent a child are asked a set of questions. I encourage you to obtain a copy of those used in your own faith communion, especially if you were baptized as a child, so you know what promises were made on your behalf. Key to these questions is the act of *metanoia* mentioned earlier.

In the *Book of Common Worship* used in the Reformed tradition, these questions read:

> Trusting in the gracious mercy of God, do you turn from the ways of sin and renounce evil and its power in the world?
>
> Do you turn to Jesus Christ and accept him as your Lord and Savior, trusting in his grace and love?
>
> Will you be Christ's faithful disciple, obeying his Word and showing his love?

Alternately:

> Do you renounce all evil, and powers in the world which defy God's righteousness and love?
>
> Do you renounce the ways of sin that separate you from the love of God?
>
> Do you turn to Jesus Christ and accept him as your Lord and Savior?
>
> Will you be Christ's faithful disciple, obeying his Word and showing his love, to your life's end?[3]

These renunciations or turnings must be made before we are ready to accept Christ and become his faithful disciples. Virtually all baptisms performed within the Christian church require them in one form or another. Acts of repentance, penitence, confession, cleansing and purification are built into our common faith, not only at baptism but also whenever we stray from the path and often before taking the Eucharist, or Holy Communion, representing the body and blood of Christ. This Communion in its many forms is the only other sacrament all Christians share.

So our journey inward on the narrow path which leads to life begins with renunciations and releasing patterns of thought and behavior not consistent with God's desire to remake us in Christ's image. In effect, we turn away from the old life before we take on the new life in Christ. The baptismal rites are basic and general, but on this path we will be required to move more specifically and deeply into the practice of *metanoia* at crucial stages of the journey.

3. *Book of Common Worship*, 407–8.

One of the wise teachers in our own time who knows the narrow path well is Mary Margaret Funk, OSB.[4] Sister Meg, as she is known, is a Benedictine monastic[5] who has written a series of well-informed and helpful books, the *"Matters"* series: *Thoughts Matter, Humility Matters, Tools Matter, Lectio Matters,* and *Discernment Matters.* Sister Meg clearly has learned through her study and practice the path of the purified heart. For her, as for me, the source was the desert elders, the abbas and ammas of the first centuries of Christianity, before the schisms and splintering of beliefs and forms took place.

The early communities that formed in the desert wastelands of Egypt, Syria, and Palestine developed guides and teachings that light our way on the path. My own study of the desert elders began with the four volumes of *The Philokalia,* a collection of writings from the fourth to fifteenth centuries translated from the original languages into Greek in the eighteenth and nineteenth centuries and only in the mid-twentieth century into English. These writings and others that have been preserved, though not all translated, represent to Orthodox Christians an intact tradition traceable to the third century, nearly 1800 years ago. Right up to our own time, the Greek Orthodox monks of Mt. Athos, Greece, and the Coptic Orthodox monks of Egypt are instructed in and practice their tradition in much the same way, and there is a great deal to learn from the long line of monastics who have forsaken the world most of us live in to seek God.

Similarly, the Roman Catholic monastic tradition stems from the same early desert elders through the time of John Cassian, the late fourth- and early fifth-century monk credited as being the founder of Western monasticism. After Cassian, the streams of Eastern (predominantly Orthodox) and Western (predominantly Catholic) monasticism begin to diverge. The Catholic Church also has attempted to preserve the apostolic church of Peter in an unbroken line, but not without great internal and external dissension up to our own time. The apostolic succession of priests, for example, who stand in Peter's line, is a contentious and debatable issue for many Christians, particularly in light of recent scholarship and the cultural acceptance of women in church leadership.

---

4. Order of Saint Benedict.

5. "Monastics" is a unisex word referring to both male and female vowed monks and nuns attached to monasteries. The gender-specific terms "nuns" and "convents" are phasing out of usage.

While many Catholic monks are also ordained priests and serve, along with vowed sisters, in dioceses and parishes throughout the world, it is not the apostolic tradition I focus on in this book but rather the one preserved in monastic orders such as the Benedictine and their reformed counterpart, the Cistercian (Trappist) order. This tradition, with which I am affiliated as a Benedictine oblate, has continued unbroken for 1500 years. Other monastic orders, such as the Franciscan, Dominican, and Jesuit, came in later centuries and have made their own significant contributions to the Christian faith. Much of the early path of Christianity was preserved through the desert tradition and monastic life and, outside of monasteries and academic settings, is not well known. It may also be found in the early Celtic monastic communities in Ireland, Scotland, and England.

The desert elders knew the meaning of renunciation. They often took to extremes the forms of self-denial they practiced, which we don't need to do, but self-denial in purposeful moderation and self-control will definitely be part of our path. In *Humility Matters,* Sister Meg Funk identifies four general renunciations that all on the narrow way must make: 1) our former way of life; 2) the thoughts and desires of that life; 3) our own made-up thoughts of God; and 4) our made-up thoughts about ourselves. She goes on to say that each renunciation leads more deeply into an experience of purity of heart. For her, "purity of heart manifests as humility, which is the fruit of the virtuous life."[6]

Continual purification is a process we undergo on this path. It will, through God's grace, lead to a humble heart. Humility as self-emptying, *kenosis* in Greek, is an intentional act of surrender in which we release the desires and patterns of behavior that distort our essential purity and block the love of Christ from fully living within us. We undergo this process willingly, even gladly, to make room for the indwelling Christ. If we are constantly filled with our own ego needs, as most of us are, we leave no space for Christ. We live instead heavily foregrounded, self-absorbed lives taken up with the struggle to feed the never-ending desires that plague us during our waking hours and invade our dreams.

This concept of *kenosis* as self-emptying surrender, of open-handed, open-hearted release and trust in God, is beautifully expressed in the early Christian hymn found in the second chapter of Paul's letter to the Philippians:

6. Funk, *Humility Matters,* 10–11.

> Let the same mind be in you that was in Christ Jesus, who, though
> he was in the form of God, did not regard equality with God as
> something to be exploited, but emptied himself, taking the form
> of a slave, being born in human likeness. And being found in
> human form, he humbled himself and became obedient to the
> point of death—even death on a cross. (Phil 2:5–8)

Visualizing what life might be like for us on the path of the purified
heart helps to keep us moving forward, for as in any process leading to
transformation we may allow fear or discouragement to distract us or
cause us to abandon the path. Once on the spiraling labyrinth, however,
it is difficult to do anything but keep going, no matter how long it takes.

Paul at his most pastoral was continually encouraging the nascent
Christian communities he felt responsible for, urging them not to give
up in the face of hardship and dissension. He also tried to teach them
that they were members of one whole church, not just the local ones
they attended. The memorable chapter 12 in First Corinthians on unity
in diversity, the body of Christ composed of many members, all with
varieties of gifts needed for the whole body to function as God intends,
is as vital a teaching for us today as in the first century. I've heard pastors compare dealing with their congregations and governing bodies
to "herding cats." Collections of individuals who can't be headed in the
same direction existed within the church from its inception.

That's one reason why many devout Christians who wanted to follow the path of spiritual transformation headed out of cities and towns
into places without the usual distractions, where they could be alone
with God, listening for God's voice and praying for guidance. If you
don't have days like that, you may find this path even more challenging.
You don't need to be an introvert to follow the path of the purified heart,
but you do have to learn to be comfortable with silence. When we go on
retreats, we seek God in solitude, perhaps within community, but also
without external and internal distractions.

Early and later forms of monasticism grew out of this deep desire
for God alone, and these forms of monastic life, even if we don't and can't
live in monasteries, hold many lessons for us. Within these small, then
larger communities deep Christians were formed and transformed, men
and women who wanted nothing more than to humbly and obediently
love God with their whole being and take on the consciousness—the
mind and heart—of Christ. They needed spiritual leaders and guides in

the faith who would help them on their paths. As noted earlier, the oral traditions of faith transmission prevailed even in monastic life until the Middle Ages, so only those who knew the Jesus stories and had studied with master spiritual teachers were equipped to teach the others. But knowledge alone was not enough. Unless these master teachers were well-formed Christians themselves, reflecting God's love and grace in their own lives, they were not equipped to lead others on the path.

What characteristics were found in the deeply Christian transmitters of the faith? What were they like? What will we be like when we are fully transformed into the likeness of Christ? Scripture provides many lists of virtues or fruits of the Spirit that give us clues. In addition to humility, these include patience, compassion, charity, joy, uprightness, self-control, trustworthiness, forgiveness, peacefulness, wisdom, a loving heart, gratitude, perseverance, and many more. Such a list can be a bit intimidating! However, if we examine the Greek words for each of these we find much overlap. Boil these down, and we find that someone formed in Christ's image is both loving and wise. There is no illuminating wisdom without love, and no pure love without wisdom. The opposites of love and wisdom are fear and ignorance, [deceit] the two plagues that have dominated human history. All that has been considered sinful may be collapsed into one or both of these categories.

To reflect God's love and light is to be illumined by the light that shines in the darkness that the darkness cannot overcome (John 1:5). That includes our own inner darkness, the shadow self, which God is waiting to transform into light. On the path of the purified heart, we open our whole beings to the wisdom of the heart, God's all-embracing love for us, and become wiser and more loving ourselves.

FIVE

Winter
Advent to Ordinary Time

Almighty God, unto whom all hearts be open, all desires known, and from whom no secrets are hid; cleanse the thoughts of our hearts by the inspiration of thy Holy Spirit, that we may perfectly love thee, and worthily magnify thy holy Name; through Christ our Lord. Amen.

—The Collect for Holy Communion,
The Book of Common Prayer of the Church of England

THE LITURGICAL YEAR ENDED in late November, and the new one began on a note of foreboding. My son's mysterious symptoms were not easily diagnosed. Tom underwent a series of painful tests, including a bronchoscopy during which water was poured into his lungs through a tube. To him it felt like water boarding, and this incident triggered panic attacks that continued for some months. Finally the tests uncovered a chronic disease that attacks the body's vulnerable organs. The bad news was that it had invaded Tom's lungs and spleen; the good news was that the condition often cleared up on its own—unless it attacked the heart or the brain, in which case it would probably be fatal. This was one time we were thankful for the Internet, which helped us research this disease and possible treatments. We also thanked God for the doctor at the University of North Carolina Medical Center, who reassured us that this bout with the disease would probably go away without treatment. If the symptoms persisted or recurred, we were to be in touch.

Tom had had a good fall up until November. Now the weeks of Advent leading up to the Christmas season were filled with anxiety, as we awaited further word on his condition. Strangely, that anxious waiting allowed us to experience Advent in a way that matched the nature of this season. Like the ancient people of God we found ourselves waiting expectantly, hoping that the promises of God would be fulfilled, that out of darkness would come a great light and release the world from its bondage to the powers that destroy and diminish human life. As the days shortened, the longer stretches of darkness invited us to turn inward, away from the cultural Christmas into a time of preparation for the new life to come through the birth of the Christ.

Just as baptism, our reception into the body of Christ, requires from us the renunciation of our former way of life and a turning toward the Christ light, the other three renunciations Sister Meg Funk listed in her books, turning from the thoughts and desires of the old life and from made-up thoughts about God and about ourselves, will be required of us along the path of the purified heart. Unlike baptism, a once and done event, these four turnings are constant points of conversion for us, like the circuits of the labyrinth that lead forward as we are firm in our commitment to Christ, then turn back again as we fall away, then are re-encountered so that we may continue on the path in our journey toward the center.

As Advent began I knew it wasn't enough for me to clear away other commitments that might interfere with the work I had been given, create a sacred working environment, step up my spiritual practices and seek spiritual direction. I needed to examine in the light of Christ whatever still remained within me that separated me from God, whether it was old baggage from the past, incomplete grief and forgiveness work, a heart not fully open to giving and receiving God's love, or patterns of thought and behavior inconsistent with my sense of who God is and who I desired to become on this path. It was time to do some serious inner work. As winter set in, the withdrawal of light invited me to reflect on my own inner darkness and to venture more deeply within to excavate what remained hidden so that it could be brought into the light and transmuted by God's love.

The practice of the examen recorded in my journal became essential, as were contemplative prayer and the Benedictine Liturgy of the Hours, which focused on praying the Psalms. The Psalms cover the whole range of human emotions and allow us to express to God our own feelings without fear of losing God's love. My time at the Montreat Liturgy of the Hours conference had drawn me back into the practice of chanting the Psalms, as monastics have done for centuries, using many forms. A recent revival of Gregorian chant, that beautiful, haunting, pure combination of tones, stimulates the holy presence within us and expresses our longing and love for God. Cynthia Bourgeault's books now populated my shelves, including her *Chanting the Psalms,* which not only teaches this ancient practice but also is accompanied by a CD on which she and others chant many of the forms.

In my twice-daily prayer periods, aided by this ancient form of prayer, I faced myself as honestly as I could, confessing all my failures and shortcomings to God. Some days the tears of compunction, of sorrow and regret that the wise elders tell us are a sign of grace, flowed freely. As this prayer process opened my heart, I began to feel the effects of purging the heart in the loving presence of God. It is only when we trust that the one who loves us unconditionally accepts us just as we are that we are able to strip off the armor of self-protection and self-justification we put up to avoid criticism and judgment.

When we can freely confess and own up to the poor choices we've made, the resources we've wasted, and the trail of hurts we've left in our wake, we find ourselves cleansed, renewed, and, through the grace of God, forgiven. These traditional acts of confession and pardon, offered through the church's rites of repentance and reconciliation, are there to help create in us the contrite hearts that prepare us to perfectly love God, as the Anglican collect makes clear. We can do this only when we have acknowledged and asked God to take away what has prevented us from getting close enough to see God. "Blessed are the pure in heart," is the sixth Beatitude, "for they will see God" (Matt 5:8). That is both truth and a promise. We know that God sees us, but what keeps us on the path is our desire to see God at the end of our journey, directly, face to face. This becomes our single purpose and all else must support and strengthen that purpose.

My own experience of *kenosis* or self-emptying and release during this intense season of Advent revealed this process to be an intentional act of surrender that the immature self of my ego fought all the way. It would pop up when I was deep in prayer to try to reclaim control or resurface when I'd ignore it, letting my more developed self know that it was still around, that my inner work was far from over. At the same time God was drawing me closer—for the whole process was initiated at God's invitation—assuring me that it was okay to continue and to trust that God would not let me fall. This reassurance would prove to be what got me through the time of trial awaiting me in January. But here, deep in Advent, the waiting and watching for the Christ Light to be born into the world was paralleled by my own struggle to overcome the darkness by reaching for the light. Surrender is not a passive process, I learned, but an active one in which we cooperate with God and learn to trust. The image that kept coming to me during this period was that of the weaned child of Psalm 131. No longer a baby nourished solely by breast milk, the child rests on the mother's breast, trusting in her continued love and care. It is like the journey of the soul from infancy to maturity in God.

It is important at this stage of the spiritual journey to take direction not only from the traditional sources—prayer and reflections on Scripture and sacred writings—but also from a spiritual guide with the wisdom and experience to help us see what we may be missing and process what comes up. My spiritual companions, Meg and Mary, sustained me throughout this intense period, and I am most grateful for their love and support. On occasion, when I needed a more direct, immediate response to the prayers of my heart, I would find myself in conversations with a still, small voice within me, whose guidance I received gratefully. Unlike those within the monastic traditions over the centuries, most of us don't have spiritual elders to lay our thoughts before. Christ becomes that for us. We may pray to him until resolution or release comes.

Knowledge of the self is essential at any stage of the spiritual journey, and especially during purification. The enneagram, an ancient Sufi spiritual growth system based on nine personality types, is one very helpful spiritual tool for self-knowledge. As may be apparent to those who have studied the enneagram, I am a One. The One has a need to be perfect and is prone to criticism of self and others. No type is better than another, and each presents its own set of challenges. Richard Rohr[1], the Franciscan friar from whom I first learned about the enneagram, says that if we are not humiliated when we discover the characteristics of our personality type we've missed the point. But there is hope. Even though we can't change our essential type, we may move along the spectrum (or shall we say the labyrinth?) from the unredeemed side of our personality to the redeemed place to which God has been drawing us. And that is, in a nutshell, our inner work and our path, to be the fullest expression we can be of the person God created us to be. For Ones, like Father Richard and me, self-acceptance (love of self) and acceptance of others

---

1. Richard Rohr, OFM, is a master spiritual teacher whose book *Discovering the Enneagram: An Ancient Tool for a New Spiritual Journey,* published in 1992, remains one of the best on the subject.

(loving neighbor as self) become possible only because God has first loved us. Loving as God loves is our greatest challenge and gives our lives direction.

Despite Tom's health crisis and my own intense clearing process, I went ahead with plans to attend the Advent retreat I had signed up for at St. John's Abbey. This visit in mid-December would be my first to the monastery with which I had affiliated as an oblate candidate. Never before having visited Minnesota in the winter, how was I to know that the weekend of the retreat the roof of the Minneapolis Metrodome would collapse under the weight of seventeen inches of new snow? Fortunately, eighty-some miles away in Collegeville, only a foot of snow fell, and it was beautiful to behold for someone who hadn't seen this much snow in years. The abbey guesthouse overlooked the frozen lake, and the vista of tall fir trees against the expanse of snow brought a welcome serenity to my spirit.

During the few weeks since I had undertaken the oblate candidacy I had begun to respond to the nine sets of questions sent by the abbey's oblate director. These were meant to be completed over the coming months as preparation for the final oblate commitment to living a life in accordance with the Rule of Benedict to the best of my ability, in affiliation with the abbey. Each set of questions focused on one dimension of Benedictine spirituality, something I was eager to study not only as part of my new relationship with the abbey but also as background for my own inner work and writing.

As is typical of a former academic, I had already acquired a small library of books on the Rule of Benedict, Benedictine spirituality and life, and the role of the oblate. I discovered that a woman I had met nearly ten years earlier, after a pilgrimage to the holy island of Iona, Scotland, and had known as a scholar of Celtic spirituality, was also a highly regarded commentator on Benedictine and Cistercian life. In fact, I had spent several days with Esther de Waal at her home in Wales, where she had shown me gracious hospitality I now recognized could have come straight from Benedict's sixth-century rule. She had carted me around the Welsh border country to see holy wells, sacred sites, and remains of ancient churches, and, I now remembered, had tried to interest me in the region's Benedictine history as well, to little avail. It turned out that her husband had been the dean of Canterbury Cathedral, one of the most prominent of posts in the Anglican Church of England. I discovered in my library a signed copy of one of her commentaries, *The Way of Simplicity: The Cistercian Tradition*. Since then I have read several more of her books on Benedictine spirituality and found them informed and insightful.

Also hidden among my spirituality collection was the first of several volumes I would come to own by Joan Chittister, OSB, one of the wisest and most prolific of writers on the Benedictine tradition. (I must have picked up *Wisdom Distilled from the Daily: Living the Rule of St. Benedict Today* shortly after first reading Kathleen Norris'S *The Cloister Walk* in 1997.) I was glad to be reminded that both of these exceptional women, Esther de Waal and Sister Joan, had contributed long-forgotten wisdom to my own meager store of knowledge about monastic life years earlier. Finding these books suggested to me that seeds were now sprouting that God had planted in me for a time when I would be ready to hear and respond to what these teachings offered. Even now, I keep beside me for daily reading Sister Joan's commentary, *The Rule of Benedict: A Spirituality for the 21st Century*, the work of a master teacher herself transformed by the monastic life and a gifted communicator of the depth and richness of that experience.

So in late November, when it was time to begin responding to the sets of oblate questions, I felt armed with helpful resources. St. John's Abbey had already sent me a copy of *The Oblate Handbook*, which contained a copy of the Rule, the daily office for morning, noon, and evening prayers, and other useful information. However, the first set of oblate candidate questions dealt with a subject little encountered in my own Reformed tradition: holiness. (We speak instead of "justification" and "sanctification" to describe the work of the Holy Spirit within us, enabling us to conform, insofar as we are willing and able, to the likeness of the Christ. We teach that salvation is a gift of the Spirit freely given to the baptized through the grace of God and the sacrifice of Jesus. Through our grateful response to God's love for us, we seek and reciprocate that love, allowing it to grow and dwell within us, as we are formed into Christ's faithful disciples. In my tradition, we are more likely to speak of this process as spiritual formation than holiness, which seems an inaccessible path for ordinary Christians. Because I was intrigued with this subject and wanted to address it in the substantive way I felt it deserved, I spent considerable time fleshing out my responses. This would also be my way of introducing myself to the oblate director, so I sent off to him my eight single-spaced pages of answers nearly three weeks before my anticipated arrival, when I hoped to meet with him in person and see if in his estimation I'd hit the mark.

What I learned to my chagrin on my first day at St. John's was that what I had sent far exceeded the expected response. "This is too much," were almost the first words out of his mouth when the director met me, a copy of my paper in hand. When I heard how much responsibility he carries at the Abbey, I understood that my oblate candidacy was my process and work, not his. I didn't have to express everything I knew on the subject, just let him know I was reflecting on and praying about it.

Monastics may be formed by *ora et labora*, prayer and work in Benedict's language, but the amount of work in a large, complex institution like St. John's Abbey must at times seem overwhelming. The church as an institution seems to expect its clergy, including the vowed religious, to work or at least be on call 24/7. "Days off" are often taken up by weddings, funerals, and emergencies. Because clergy and those under vows are expected and expect themselves to serve God with their whole being, they may fail to set limits on activity to allow time for recreation and renewal. As a result, burnout is common. As a Type One personality on the enneagram, I was subject to this condition myself and knew I needed to observe the same kind of self-care I urged on others.

Our life lessons often come in surprising ways, and this experience of overdoing my assignment caused me to confront my own intellectual and spiritual pride. My academic habits of research and thorough coverage of a subject, combined with my seminary training in the art of reflection and my own love of language, were well suited for teaching and writing but not for my new role as an oblate. I would need to observe and listen "with the ear of the heart," as St. Benedict begins his Rule. The heart, the source of true wisdom, must govern the mind. As a guest of the monastery, I would need to learn its culture, rules, and expectations, just as the novice monks did when they entered the community for the first time.

I thoroughly enjoyed my three days at the abbey. The guesthouse was lovely and comfortable, the food delicious and plentiful, including the famous homemade johnny bread, and the other retreat participants an interesting group. The monastery's facilities were amazing, with an immense, awe-inspiring chapel designed by the famous German architect Marcel Breuer, alongside the campus of St. John's University. Although it was too snowy to walk around much, I loved the combined religious and academic environment, which suited me well. The retreat itself was led by the abbott, something I found surprising, as I hadn't expected him to be so accessible or so personable. A former chemistry professor, elected by his community to serve for life as their spiritual and administrative leader, Abbott John Klassen has an engaging personality and teaching style that the small group of retreat participants appreciated. The retreat focus was Jesus' parables as proclaiming the reign of God. In the group were lay Catholics, Presbyterians, and Lutherans, as well as an Episcopal priest and even a lone evangelical Christian, who apparently came often to the monastery. Benedictine hospitality was clearly in evidence, and the discussion during and between the presentations was lively.

Abbott John's written notes summarized his approach to the parables:

> While we have heard most of these stories or accounts many times, there are ways to approach them that reveal fresh and provocative meanings. Above all, Jesus was calling people to a new vision of God, a new covenant, to a new ethical vision. In the parables we are invited to make a choice and to come to a decision. We are urged to pay attention and face issues we might prefer to ignore. The parables tell us that it is in the midst of the everyday . . . that our happiness and salvation are worked out. The story of our salvation lies inside the story of our everyday life.[2]

The method of *lectio divina* was one of these approaches, as was a form of *lectio* I had not encountered before, called *viseo divina*. It is a way of seeing the word as well as hearing it. St. John's is famous for not only its johnny bread but for *The Saint John's Bible*, published by its Liturgical Press. This set of books published separately and together in various sizes represent the illumined masterpieces created by the monastics of the Middle Ages. The multicolor illustrations and calligraphy are striking and invite the viewer into a deeper encounter visually than with the text alone. Our group experienced *viseo divina* using a beautiful illustration from Jesus' Parable of the Sower and the Seed. We were all amazed at how much was revealed to us through the visual images. *Viseo* is a process I have added to my own spiritual practices, particularly with icons, so significant within the Orthodox tradition as windows through

2. Klassen, notes from Advent retreat, 2010.

our own reality to the multidimensional realm in which God dwells. *Viseo* is also a perfect way to view the book of nature, God's creation, as it reveals God's love, creativity, and power to us.

Another highlight of this first experience at St. John's Abbey was praying and singing with the monks. We sat in the choir of the huge chapel, all concrete, glass, and brick—cold materials warmed by the voices of the monks and other worshipers as they blended and lifted the vibration within the sacred space to that place where God is met. The only flaw in the experience for me was not being able to receive the body and blood of Christ from the hand of the communicant priest. Only Catholics in good standing may partake in the Eucharist in any Catholic church. The same practice is observed in Orthodox congregations. In the more open Protestant denominations, like my own, all confirmed Christians are welcome at the Lord's Table.

For an ordained minister who has for many years officiated at Holy Communion herself, offering the bread and cup to all, I felt sadness at being excluded from this precious sacrament. I am well aware of the theological and doctrinal differences that separate our faith communions on the matter of the Eucharist and also am aware that some non-Catholics partake anyway. However, I did not want to put the officiating priest in the position of unwittingly or knowingly serving Communion to someone outside his own faith communion. Instead, I prayed, "Jesus, heal your church. Heal us, for we are the cause of this division."

Refreshed from my time at St. John's, I prepared to return home to Chapel Hill. Miraculously, an angel had cleared the foot of snow off my rental car, and I drove early Monday morning on treacherous roads in heavy, slow traffic back to the airport. There I sat, while one flight after another to Raleigh-Durham was canceled because of the weather. Finally my prayers were answered. I got the last seat on the last flight out that night and arrived safely home.

With only two weeks to go before Christmas, I turned from my intense purification process to preparing for Christmas with the family and the local congregation. I particularly love Christmas music of all kinds—hymns, carols, sacred music, even popular tunes—and found myself getting into the joy of the season through the music. I knew I'd probably need to take a break from the church choir after Christmas, so it was a treat to sing with that gifted group at this special time of year.

If the previous summer had been extremely hot, this winter was proving to be an aberration as well, and several brief periods of snow and ice made walking and driving precarious. As if Tom hadn't had enough misery for one season, he slipped on a patch of ice in the dark, fell, and cracked his knee. More pain and x-rays later, a hairline fracture took him down for the count. He was in a soft cast for several weeks, until the knee healed enough for him to walk on it. Meanwhile, his anxiety level stayed in high gear throughout the holidays. Fortunately, my husband, Alden, remained well, unlike the previous year when a life-threatening infection hospitalized him on Christmas Day. This year I was grateful that the three of us had a quiet Christmas and New Year's at home.

Celebrating the birth of Christ is so huge in our culture that remembering how hidden and sacred the original event must have been is a challenge for Christians. I especially love the services of Lessons and Carols—just story and song—and the candlelight service on Christmas Eve that ushers in the night when, like the winter solstice, the season turns to one of growing light rather than growing darkness. This year Christmas felt especially holy to me as a time of giving birth—new life— to something within me that had remained hidden and was intended to spread Christ's light into the world through my own story. The joy Mother Mary must have felt when she gave birth to the child of promise and fulfillment inspired me to continue on my own path of purification.

During the week following Christmas I managed a day trip to visit my spiritual companion Mary, who lived in a nearby community. Mary's peaceful home was filled with angels, harp music, and an elaborate Christmas village display that could have been featured on the evening news. Since I had last visited her, she had created a spiritual center on her property, including a beautiful small chapel and a labyrinth! Needless to say, I was eager to walk the labyrinth and experience its energy and that of the site. Mary had told me the story of how the labyrinth came into being. She was looking for someone experienced in labyrinth building when a man showed up at the door looking for work. Although he knew nothing about labyrinths, he insisted he could build anything, so Mary gave him a pattern, directions, and let him begin. She wanted an eleven-circuit labyrinth like the one at Chartres Cathedral.

This design is not simple to build, especially out of brick pavers, the material Mary chose. Forty-two feet in diameter, the Chartres labyrinth actually has twelve concentric circles with twenty-eight loops, seven on the left side and seven on the right that wind toward the center, another seven on the left going toward the outside, and seven more on the outside right that terminate in a short, straight path leading to the center, consisting of a six-petal rosette or flower of life.

To get all of these dimensions right generally takes a master builder with a team, all of whom understand the basics not only of the design but also of the significance of the labyrinth. Mary's builder was suspicious of the spiritual nature of the labyrinth from the beginning. However, as time wore on and the labyrinth took shape, his attitude and demeanor changed. It was as though he was under the influence of the Holy Spirit, Mary claimed, and weeks later, when the job was finished, he was a man convinced that he had participated in sacred work. And so he had.

As I walked this sacred path for the first time, I felt immense gratitude to God for my own spiritual companions on the journey. Standing in the center, held there by God's love, I felt nourished and healed, ready to make the return journey home. On the way out, one of those conversations with the inner guide began, and, though I don't remember the details, it was clear that I would be supported through the remainder of my own journey along the path of the purified heart. Uplifted by this visit, I felt ready to move forward into the new year and all the challenges and hope it promised.

Epiphany, the twelfth and final day of Christmastide, when Protestants and Catholics celebrate the coming of the Magi to the holy child, is actually Christmas Day for the Eastern Orthodox, who observe a different liturgical calendar. In my tradition, Epiphany is associated with the light of Christ that illumines the world, as in this prayer from *The Book of Common Worship*:

> Lord God of the nations, we have seen the star of your glory rising in splendor. The radiance of your incarnate Word pierces the night that covers the earth and signals the dawn of justice and peace. May his brightness illumine our lives and beckon all nations to walk as one in your light. We ask this through Jesus Christ your Word made flesh, who lives and reigns with you and the Holy Spirit, in the splendor of eternal light, God forever and ever. Amen.[3]

After the highs of the Christmas season, I was in for a rude awakening. The following day the illumination of Christmastide gave way to

---

3. *Book of Common Worship*, 191–92.

Winter: Advent to Ordinary Time   67

darkness, as God showed me how far I still had to travel on the path of the purified heart.

For nearly a year our house had been on the market. Though neither my husband nor my son wanted to move, I had pushed for downsizing to a more affordable, manageable housing arrangement. Having the house on the market was a source of stress for all of us. It meant that we had to be ready for a showing at any time and to explore viable options should it sell. The housing market was as depressed in Chapel Hill as elsewhere, and despite significant price reductions we hadn't received an offer. As the new year began, we needed to evaluate where we stood. A former financial planner (my middle career between higher education and ministry), I handled the family finances and was convinced we'd be better off in a more affordable property. In addition, downsizing felt consistent with my own spiritual path. I was becoming less and less attached to things and longed for a simpler, more environmentally and economically sustainable lifestyle.

That morning after Epiphany, Alden and I got into a disagreement over whether to continue to try to sell or take the house off the market and wait for a better time. After all the time and energy I'd invested in a potential sale, I wasn't ready to give up. Anger and frustration welled up inside me in a way I couldn't ever recall experiencing, and something snapped. Having enough sense to cool off before saying anything I'd regret, I withdrew to my meditation room. I tried to calm down and pray. But something had shattered the core of internal peace I held within like a precious jewel. To me it represented my connection with God, the result of all my spiritual work, the calming influence my family needed to function, and it was gone. I spent the day trying to pray and recover my inner peace, but this meltdown had a message for me I needed to hear. The bigger the hit, the bigger the gift, was Meg's sage advice.

By the next day I got clarity. My whole approach to the sale of the house and our finances had been motivated more by fear—fear of the future, fear of scarcity—than by love of God and family. Despite my good intentions for a more secure and sustainable future, my lower self was in control of the process. What I was projecting was exactly the opposite of the message I'd tried to teach others in the church through the *Graceful Living* book I'd written ten years earlier: to overcome our fears of not having enough by trusting that God's grace is sufficient for all our needs. Clearly I hadn't learned this essential lesson myself, so I had a meltdown.

As I began to process the message and the method of delivery, layers of meaning emerged for me. Although I was shaky for days afterwards, I realized that whether we stayed in the house or moved didn't matter. What mattered was that the needs of each of us and of the family unit were being provided for. I needed to turn my attention away from where we were going to live to how we were going to live trusting in the grace of God. It was time to get on down the road of the purified heart.

This mini dark night of the soul, a kind of purgation, lingered as a reminder to continue to trust and keep my feet on the path laid out before me. The experience felt at the time like the death of the ego, but it helped me release old insecurities and recover my inner core of peace. I could only respond with gratitude. Before long we took the house off the market, rearranged some priorities, and all is working out fine, as it does when we trust in and surrender our wills to God.

When we ask God to burn away the dross to leave only the pure gold, we'd better be prepared for whatever comes. The day after my meltdown, another message came through loud and clear. I needed to take better care of myself physically. However connected I felt spiritually, I still needed to live in my physical body and to preserve it well for the decades more I hoped to live. That meant the excess weight I'd carried for ten years had to come off and I'd have to add regular exercise to my daily schedule. Like half the American population in early January, I decided to go on a diet. The one I chose and followed for the year included lots of protein and veggies but eliminated my two favorite food groups: carbs and sugar.

It helped to look upon this shift in eating habits as the spiritual practice of fasting, turning the experience from a dreaded task to an offering of self to God. It also became a very visible sign of the self-emptying process already begun. I have to say that the fast, common within the Christian tradition, initially held little appeal for me. My mother, raised Lutheran before marrying my Presbyterian father, believed in giving something up for Lent, usually my favorite foods. Just as Catholics traditionally did not eat meat on Fridays, remembering the day of Christ's sacrificial death, fasting to discipline all the physical appetites, not just food, as a form of self-denial and self-purification is a basic spiritual practice.

This shift in perspective has worked well for me. Since I made that connection, it's been easier than I thought to drop the weight. In another sense, this weight was symbolic of all the responsibility I carried for the family. Now, relinquishing it for the sake of the project I felt had been given to me by God made perfect sense, along with adopting a healthier attitude toward self-care. When I hit a plateau and had to push through it to keep losing, it wasn't as great an effort as I'd dreaded it would be. Jesus smiles at me from the meditation room across the hall as I write and reminds me, "My yoke is easy and my burden is light." And so it is.

Now I enjoy a daily walk on our long, sloping cul-de-sac, no matter the weather. A couple of sessions with a personal trainer laid out a pattern of exercise to follow, and a fitness center less than five minutes from home awaits me on days when I'm ready for the strength training I need. My feet are moving forward on the path. After all, walking the labyrinth is good exercise!

Following Epiphany, the liturgical year moves into a stretch of Ordinary Time that ends with Lent. As I dealt with the aftermath of my own "epiphany," the moment of illumination that exposed the inner work that still lay before me, I wanted to explore more deeply the wisdom of the holy elders who'd gone before us on this path. While at St. John's in December I had heard about the nearby women's monastery and college, St. Benedict's, and its Studium Scholars program. After investigating the program, open to people who want to spend a few weeks or longer at St. Benedict's Monastery to study or work on projects like mine, I applied to come to the monastery for the first three weeks in Lent, in March. I felt this would give me an extended time without all the duties and distractions at home to finish the research for the book and begin writing. I would have access to the resources of both monasteries' college libraries and could join the sisters in the Liturgy of the Hours as well as meals within the community. This sounded very appealing. My acceptance into the Studium program followed shortly, and I began to make plans to be away from the family for a full three weeks. That, I knew, would be a challenge, so I surrendered it to God and trusted that all would be in divine order.

As much as I had enjoyed singing with the choir through the Christmas season, I decided to take a break and see if I wanted to continue in the spring. One reason was that in mid-January I began to audit a class at nearby Duke Divinity School on the Spirituality of the Eastern church, taught by a priest from the Russian Orthodox tradition, Father Edward. This class would require a whole new library of books on Eastern

Orthodoxy, which I began to collect and read. The basic texts were the four volumes of *The Philokalia*, the preserved writings of the fourth- to fifteenth century spiritual elders and monks. Other texts included the Russian Orthodox classic, *The Way of the Pilgrim:The Pilgrim on His Way*, that introduced the form of ceaseless prayer for which Orthodoxy is known, the Jesus Prayer, to the common people. I also read around in later writings from the monks of Mt. Athos, the isolated Greek island that houses twenty monasteries still following the ancient traditions, including the exclusion of women even from setting foot on the island. I discovered through my own research another group of writings I found fascinating, in which the basic practices of Orthodoxy were shared. Two of these were written by a Greek Orthodox native of Cyprus who teaches sociology at the University of Maine, Kyriacos Markides. Both *Mountain of Silence* and its sequel, *Gifts of the Desert*, recount Markides's own story of reclaiming his Orthodox faith through numerous encounters with a Mt. Athos monk, Father Maximos. The priest teaches him much as the desert elders of old used to teach their small communities to follow the narrow path to God. This path crisscrosses the Western monastic path and is also recoverable from within my own Protestant tradition, as we will soon see.

This intense journey into Orthodoxy, which began in earnest following Epiphany at the beginning of Ordinary Time, proved enriching and brought me the acquaintance of the two local Orthodox priests, who taught me much about how their current traditions are practiced and just how intact Orthodoxy remains after nearly 1800 years.

In February, I attended a conversation at the University of North Carolina between Father James, the Greek Orthodox priest, and a professor, a self-affirmed agnostic who, ironically, heads the university's religious studies department. Interestingly, both men had grown up in evangelical Christian families and attended the same evangelical college at about the same time. Both had diverged from this early path in significant ways, one to find his spiritual home in Eastern Orthodoxy, the other to explore and publish books about historical inaccuracies in early Christian writings. The one way took the path of the heart, the other the path of the mind, and the differences were striking. The literalism both had rejected within their early faith communion had become for the academic a literal approach to sacred texts and for the priest a deeper experience of God. I came away from this experience feeling once again how limited our human endeavors are when God is not acknowledged as the source and sustainer of life.

Later that month, my friend Meg and I had the opportunity to meet Kathleen Norris, the author who had set me on the monastic path years earlier through her book *The Cloister Walk*. Kathleen was the featured speaker at the Kanuga Conference held at an Episcopal retreat center in the North Carolina mountains. I'd read most of her books over the years and found them marvelous combinations of research, human observation, spiritual insights, and poetic prose. She is also a Benedictine oblate, so I was especially eager to meet her and let her know she'd been instrumental in connecting me with St. John's Abbey. She had spent several lengthy periods at the Ecumenical Institute at St. John's researching and writing her books. A few years ago Kathleen lost her husband, an experience she wrote about at length in her recent book, *Acedia and Me*. I did have a few minutes to talk with her and to thank her for her work. We never know when or how something we say or do will have a positive impact on someone's life, and it is always a gift of grace to find that out.

When I returned home, one task remained for me to undertake before Lent. As a minister retired for several years, I hadn't been active in the local governing body, the presbytery, of which I remained a member. My spiritual journey had been taking me further away each year from politics and conflict, whether global, national, or within the church. A growing split in our denomination centered on the issue of the ordination of partnered gays and lesbians to church leadership, in much the same way as the ordination of women fifty years ago was controversial. My view was simple: God calls, and humans respond to the call. However, thirty years of wrangling over this issue within the denomination was coming to a head in the spring. Presbyteries across the nation were voting on proposed amendments to the church constitution allowing local governing bodies more autonomy in making decisions in the best interests of their churches. In effect, voting in favor of these amendments would mean the end of excluding people from ministry based on sexual orientation.

So I resolved to attend the presbytery meeting at which the amendment would be voted on. I prayed it would not prove so contentious as to further divide the church. After considerable debate the vote was taken and the measure passed. It subsequently was confirmed in the national vote and is now part of the church's constitution, although the issue remains contentious, and some congregations and their leaders are making plans to leave the denomination. It's always sad to see that kind of division within the church and especially painful when it's your own church communion. I appreciated even more the Benedictine commitment to stability, to staying in place and working out divisions with respect for one another and through communal discernment of God's will through the movement of the Holy Spirit.

The four renunciations we must make as we enter onto the path of the purified heart had proved more involved and challenging than I had imagined when Advent began three months earlier. Now Lent loomed ahead of me, and I trusted that this next stage of the journey would unfold in whatever way God intended. "*Thy* will be done," became my constant prayer, and I willed myself to mean it.

SIX

The Purified Heart

Who shall ascend the hill of the Lord? And who shall stand in his holy place? Those who have clean hands and pure hearts, who do not lift up their souls to what is false, and do not swear deceitfully. They will receive blessings from the Lord, and vindication from the God of their salvation. Such is the company of those who seek him, who seek the face of the God of Jacob.

—Psalm 24[23]:3–6

T HE JOURNEY FROM RENUNCIATION to transcendence has character-ized the Christian path from the very beginning. Jesus himself is the incarnation of the path of transformation. Following his baptism in the waters of the Jordan, he was whisked off by the Holy Spirit to the desert for a forty-day solitary sojourn, during which he undertook a physical and spiritual purification before beginning his ministry. He fasted, prayed, and renounced the three temptations of material comfort, ego-driven power, and false gods. Perhaps these three might of all things have been most tempting to him if at any point he had thought of himself as an earthly king, the kind of Messiah the Jewish people longed for, who would save them from Roman oppression and restore Israel's glory days. Instead, his time alone with God in the wilderness prepared him to say no to a kingdom of this world and yes to his destiny within the realm of God.

This very human side of Jesus is what we see first, before all the healing, teaching, and challenging of human authority. The Jesus of the desert is stripped of defenses, totally reliant on and trusting completely in the providence of God. He sought only to live in loving relationship with God and share that love with those willing to be transformed by it. Even before taking up his ministry he teaches us through his sojourn in

73

the desert that we need not fear life's challenges if we maintain a deep and abiding relationship with God.

Christian formation leading to spiritual transformation begins here for the newly baptized. We look at the one who modeled for us what union with God looks like. Then we allow God to form us in Christ's image so that we may anchor that love and light within ourselves to illumine the world of our own time. In order to love God more fully, we choose to turn away from the temptations that would keep us apart from God or cause us to deviate from our true path. Then it becomes a matter of course that we resist certain kinds of thoughts and behaviors in favor of those that draw us closer to God. Ideally, we do this within a supportive community, whether a family, small group, church, or monastery, that represents for us the beloved community signifying God's reign on earth.

This pattern of attraction and repulsion as the two major energy sources within the human personality was observed by two influential early monks formed by desert spirituality, Evagrius Ponticus of the late fourth century and John Cassian of the early fifth century. They noted that we become more like what we are attracted to and less like what we find repulsive. The pattern of drawing away from harmful attractions or passions and moving toward those that are life-giving formed the basis of early monastic life in the wilderness areas of Egypt, Syria, and Palestine. Like Jesus, the desert monastics wanted to be alone with God to follow what they understood as the three-stage spiritual journey presented here: purification, or purgation; illumination; and deification, or union with God.

The best known of the early monks was Anthony of Egypt, often called the Father of Monasticism, who in the late third century relinquished his estate and possessions to live as an anchorite, or hermit, in the desert west of Alexandria. As early as the second century, anchorites had fled the urban centers for the desert in order to commune with God. After Anthony, many others followed. Even though the hermitic life was considered the ideal, it proved too isolated and dangerous both physically and spiritually for all but the hardiest of souls. Small cells began to form, eventually each with a spiritual leader who taught newcomers the spiritual path and the practices that would keep them on it, while holding them accountable for their progress in the faith. The austere conditions of life in the desert were not for the faint-hearted. Extreme asceticism was commonly practiced, including fasting to the point of starvation, self-mortification, exposure to the elements, and the like. The spiritual teachings or sayings of the desert fathers (abbas) and mothers (ammas, although few were women), preserved in texts still studied today, have provided wisdom and guidance for centuries.

Both Western and Eastern monasticism developed from these early common roots. The eastern form continued the pattern of the small cells under the direction of a spiritual leader, which still exists as a monastic model today, although the cenobitic form characterizes most monasticism since the early Middle Ages. Cenobites live in community under the authority of an abbot or prioress, who stands in the place of Christ.

By the mid-fourth century, the first Eastern monasteries appeared, one of which I have visited. St. Catherine's Monastery is located in the Sinai desert of Egypt, where Moses is said to have communed with God and received the stone tablets containing the commandments. The burning bush in Exodus 3, from which God spoke to Moses, is still growing on the monastery grounds, according to the monk who showed it to our group! This beautiful monastery, which hosts pilgrims in gracious comfort, is filled with some of the most precious icons and sacred images of Orthodox spirituality. It is here I saw the stunningly luminous original fifth- or sixth-century Christ *Pantocrator,* Jesus the Sustainer of the World, hanging in plain sight on one of the monastery's stucco walls. To visit St. Catherine's is to travel back in time and experience God through the eyes of the ancients who came to the desert to seek God alone. The bones of St. Catherine's monks over the centuries are stored in cells within the monastery, where the community and its visitors may ponder the brevity of life and honor those who remained steadfast in their faith.

The center of Orthodox monasticism throughout most of its history has been the small, inaccessible island of Mt. Athos, Greece, where twenty monasteries, each with its own heritage and style, offer spiritual sanctuary, community, and training to men with a monastic vocation. The teachings and practices haven't changed much over the centuries, although the conditions are less austere. Recently, Mt. Athos has begun to allow the wider world a glimpse of its extraordinary monastic heritage. On Easter night in 2011, I was astonished to find a special segment on *60 Minutes* filmed on Mt. Athos, in which the black-robed, long-bearded monks went about their daily work and prayer, shadowed by correspondent Bob Simon and the film crew. It took CBS News over two years to get permission to make the feature, and it had been thirty years since the last media interview had been granted. One of the monks remarked, "You have to understand that the words we're saying in today's liturgy are the same words that Christ was saying, are the same words that the saints from the first century were saying," and the second, third, and fourth centuries in an unbroken lineage.[1] The only change welcome on Mt. Athos seems to be inner transformation, not the outer expressions of the contemporary world.

A recent film on Orthodox monasticism, *Living Prayer: Christianity*, features Mt. Athos and St. Catherine's monasteries and Russian churches. In viewing an early release, I found this beautiful film evocative of the depth and mysticism of this richly embodied expression of human devotion to God. It is too little known in the West, although that is probably why it continues to exist in its well-preserved state, and for that we can be grateful.

By the fourth century of the Christian era, cenobitic monastic communities were developing in the West as well. While a number of early rules for monastic life emerged from these first experiments in monastic life, none was as grace-filled as that of St. Benedict of Nursia, Italy. This sixth-century rule became the standard followed in the West, and even today the Rule of Benedict still guides much of Western monasticism. In addition to the Benedictine order, which emerged from the Rule, twelfth-century reforms centered on a stricter observance of the *Opus Dei,* the work of God in liturgy and prayer, led to the more contemplative Cistercian (Trappist) order.

The early Celtic tradition was essentially a blend of desert and Benedictine monasticism, as Geoffrey Moorhouse points out in *Sun Dancing: A Medieval Vision.* For those hardy monks who inhabited the remote and nearly uninhabitable island of Skellig Michael off the coast of western Ireland from the late sixth to the early thirteenth centuries, the ocean was their desert.

Few Christians today know much about monasticism. People are better informed about what is known as the apostolic church, which emerged in the cities and towns, the church of Peter and Paul, and its Roman Catholic, Protestant, and nondenominational descendants.

1. CBS News, "A Visit to Mt. Athos," April 24, 2011.

Bruno Barnhart, OSB, Cam,[2] notes that these two streams of Christian monasticism emerged almost from the start. One seems to be represented in the Gospel of John by the Beloved Disciple, whom Jesus instructs to remain until he comes again, and the other by Peter, who is to follow Jesus. Eastern Christianity, says Father Bruno, remains at the place of origin theologically, spiritually, and geographically, while Western Christianity "moves forward, away from its beginnings . . . and original center."[3] Eastern spirituality seems more mystical, drawing upon a deeper knowing, while the Western form is about forward movement, expressed as the Christian journey. One can see this in the Western spread of Christianity across Europe and the Americas. Father Bruno suggests that many former Christians are attracted to Asian traditions because they resemble the forgotten interior spirituality of the early church in the desert.[4] That insight confirms my own observations about spiritual seekers who, unaware of the deep spirituality within Christianity, look elsewhere and readily adopt practices outside their own traditions, often without reference to their contexts.

The desert elders formed what became the Eastern tradition, and it wasn't until after the time of John Cassian, a pivotal figure for both Eastern and Western monasticism, that the split that eventually created Roman Catholicism and Eastern Orthodoxy took place. By the sixth century, when St. Benedict wrote his famous rule, drawing upon several previous rules but contributing his own unique perspectives, monasticism became and stayed predominantly cenobitic. Other orders followed in later centuries, like the mendicant Franciscans and Dominicans, the contemplative Carmelites, and the scholarly Jesuits. The roots of early monasticism may still be observed and experienced within the relatively intact Benedictine communities worldwide and the Orthodox monasteries of Mt. Athos and communities of the Egyptian Coptics.

By following these early streams of Christianity to the point of divergence we can begin to see not only the differences that emerged and led to the multiple forms of Christianity practiced today, but also our common beginnings. Perhaps these can lead us back to a more authentic

2. Order of St. Benedict Camaldolese. Like the Carthusians, the Camaldolese Benedictines live in community but more as anchorites than cenobites.

3. Barnhardt, "Christian Self-Understanding in Light of the East," in *Purity of Heart and Contemplation*, 292.

4. Ibid., 292–93.

expression of life in Christ, not based on politics, culture, geography, not even on theology, creeds, and doctrines, but rather on the pattern and path Christ followed in his own life, which led to his union with God. As we have seen, it began with the path of the purified heart.

Purification of the heart, then, is the work God works in us so that we may become more Christlike. Not many of us are called to a monastic vocation, but we may nevertheless feel drawn to a life characterized by a devotion to God above all else. It is difficult for those of us who live relatively "normal" lives within the dominant culture to follow this path of the purified heart that longs to see God, as it is not one necessarily honored in contemporary life or by our families and friends. Even within the apostolic church this path is often difficult to find. This is one reason why people are seeking out monasteries and independent communities for the spiritual wisdom they haven't found within their own faith settings and experiences.

While the numbers of vowed religious women and men in both monastic and apostolic communities are declining as their populations age and are not replaced by younger postulants, the numbers of those searching for spiritual guidance and a more satisfying way of life are dramatically on the rise. Within the Benedictine tradition, more than 25,000 oblates affiliated with monasteries around the world now outnumber the vowed monastics. The two monasteries I know best have 700–800 oblates and candidates apiece on their books, not all of whom are active, but who are held in relationship, presenting challenges to the communities' capacity to respond. And these are not all Catholics, by any means. Even non-Catholic clergy are seeking spiritual wisdom outside of their own denominations and finding it within Benedictine hospitality. There are also Anglican, Episcopal, even Lutheran and Methodist monasteries that follow the Rule of Benedict. Other monastic orders, like the Franciscans, also have affiliate programs that attract many Christian seekers.

People who hunger and thirst for God always have sought out those who were farther along in their spiritual journeys than they to teach and guide them or to be their companions. That hasn't changed. The early monastic communities focused on purity of heart throughout the spiritual journey. Even now it is considered the whole Christian journey, learning to give and receive love, and to empty the self so that it can be filled with God.

Cassian, whose writings on purity of heart strongly influenced Benedict, remains one of the dominant voices within Western monasticism. He equated purity of heart with Christian and monastic perfection. His mentor, Evagrius (who eventually fell out of favor with church authorities), called *apatheia*, (detachment from the passions or *logismoi*,) what Cassian called purity of heart. Purity, or *katharos* in Greek, (meant clean, free of contamination,) which implies something more than detachment, a return to a pure state. Throughout this book I refer to a "purified heart," one that is restored to the purity of its original divine state when we unite with God and are able, through God's grace, to recognize our Creator with clarity of vision undistorted by human passions or attachments.

The detachment of the purified heart differs from the concept of detachment within the Buddhist tradition, (in which the self eventually merges with the divine and loses its individuality in transcendence.) Rather, Christian detachment releases that which separates us from God in order to become more attached, (the movement we noted earlier from repulsion to attraction.) Basically, it is the substitution of life-giving desires and attachments for life-destroying tendencies.

By definition, the passions have more emotional than rational content, although thoughts may awaken them. Attractions to the *logismoi*—the eight passions or vices—were to be repelled by specific spiritual practices and replaced with their opposite virtues. The lists of vices and virtues shift somewhat, depending on which of the wise elders is writing, but vices generally included gluttony, lust, avarice, anger, dejection, listlessness, vainglory, and pride. Sister Meg Funk, writing 1,500 years after Cassian, calls them the "eight afflictive thoughts," which she names as food, sex, things, anger, dejection, *acedia*, vainglory, and pride.[5] The traditional "seven deadly sins" were named by the anonymous fourteenth-century mystic, author of *The Cloud of Unknowing*, as pride, wrath, envy, covetousness, sloth, gluttony, and lechery.[6] These were often paired with what eventually became known in the Catholic Church as the four cardinal virtues (prudence, justice, temperance, and courage) and the three theological virtues (faith, hope, and love). Another list of the "heavenly seven" includes humility, patience, abstinence, temperance, perseverance, kindness, and charity. The New Testament epistles are filled with

5. Funk, *Humility Matters*, 9.

6. *Cloud*, 34–35.

virtues lists, as their authors encouraged spiritual transformation among the believers.

The distinctions among all of these passions or vices are not always clear; for example, dejection and *acedia,* also called listlessness or sloth, were later combined, and vainglory and pride appear to be nuances or degrees of the same vice. Charity and love come from the same Latin root, *caritas.* Nonetheless, it's not hard for us to recognize our own most challenging "afflictive thoughts," and I daresay we've probably been afflicted with all of them at one time or another in our lives.

Movement away from the affliction or passion toward the virtue is the Holy Spirit's work of transformation within us. But this does not happen against our will. While we don't have to earn grace because God's love for us is unconditional, we do have to cooperate, to desire to change. This point is crucial. For those on the path of purification of the heart, the desire to be with God must be greater than the desire for whatever our ego-dominant selves believe will satisfy our endless wants and needs. Otherwise, we will have little incentive to do the hard work required to overcome the base passions.

For the early monastics, then, purification meant liberation from the passions and their consequent actions and their replacement with the virtues. The desert elders taught their disciples how to disable the activity of the human will and the lowest levels of human nature that resulted in what the church throughout most of its history has called "sin": that which displaces or separates from God. While sin is an acceptable term for what is literally translated from the Greek word *amartia* as "missing the mark," its derivatives "sinful" and "sinner" often feel harsh and judgmental in our supersensitive culture. Even so, in the Lord's Prayer as recited in English-speaking congregations, we variously ask God to "forgive us our trespasses as we forgive those who trespass against us," "forgive us our debts as we forgive our debtors," or "forgive us our sins as we forgive those who sin against us." While there are nuances of meaning in each of these translations, all acknowledge that we have harmed others intentionally or unintentionally and that we must first forgive the real or imagined grievances we have against others before asking God to forgive us ours. Whether we call a sin a trespass, transgression, or debt (and I believe debt is the most accurate translation of *opheilete* in the Lord's Prayer found in Matthew 6:12), acknowledging our own wrongdoing signifies that we are allowing God to heal us and the consequences of our actions.

Although there is not a one-to-one correspondence between any vice and any virtue, or a common understanding of what each meant in its own context, we can more easily see in the table below the attraction and repulsion movement we undergo in the purification process.

Vices	Virtues
Gluttony	Temperance, moderation
Lust	Chastity, abstinence
Avarice, greed	Charity, generosity, simplicity
Anger	Love, compassion, forgiveness, peace
Dejection	Hope, surrender, faith, trust
Listlessness, sloth (*acedia*)	Patience, perseverance, zeal
Vainglory	Compassion, humility
Pride	Repentance, humility

If these lists seem oversimplified—and they are, given the complexities of life in contemporary society—they still exemplify the human spectrum of both undesirable and desirable traits and movement along the path of the purified heart. The passions are what we carry in with us on the labyrinth, as we walk inward toward the heart of God, and the virtues what we bring back into our lives and the life of the world as we walk back out, transformed by the journey.

For years I have kept a mental "Oh, how fallen" list, named for Lucifer, the bright angel who fell from heavenly glory, as portrayed in John Milton's magnificent narrative poem, *Paradise Lost*. The fallen on my list have included quite a few politicians, religious leaders, and government officials—people who held power and public trust and disgraced themselves, their families, and those who believed in and depended on them. They had farther to fall than the average person, although their sins may have been no worse. Pride, lust, and greed are vices we see all around us, magnified by the media and actually encouraged by our economic materialism and individualism. At times it's hard to believe that people with so much to lose could make such poor choices. As their lives unravel before our eyes through media exposure, their public humiliation provides lessons for the rest of us not only in how not to behave but also the consequences of thoughtless actions. What all appear to have in common is the capacity to compartmentalize and justify to themselves their behavior. Often, they are lonely and isolated in their positions, with insufficient oversight and accountability. Or they hold themselves to impossibly high standards they can't sustain, and act out in self-destructive ways.

It's easy to judge the ones on my fallen list, but how easy has it been for us to resist our own temptations? What keeps us on the straight and narrow and what draws us away? The desert elders had been honed by years of instruction in and experience with fighting off their own demons and so could speak with authority on how to recognize and subdue them, even if just for a little while. Those who reach the third stage of our journey, union with God, are far enough along on this path to have assimilated the virtues that guard them against the vices, but no one living in a physical body with a human mind is ever exempt from temptation. God offers us countless opportunities in life to learn humility, compassion, and all the other virtues, and none of us can do it on our own. The "Oh, how fallen" list is full of people who have tried and failed. Through their suffering, some have become wise and humble people with much to teach others. We can be grateful to these for what we have learned from them and try to avoid their mistakes.

Even with wise elders to guide us, we will veer off the path from time to time. If these guides are not currently present in our lives, they are still available to us through their writings and the examples of their lives. It is essential for serious seekers to live within or be supported by a community of people who desire to become more Christlike. In our own times, unless we are drawn to a monastic vocation, such communities may be found within churches, families, and like-minded self-organizing groups. Those farther along on the path are obliged to assist those behind them, although some of the wise are younger than their elders, as St. Benedict makes clear in his rule, and the innocence of children contains its own wisdom. Recently, I heard Richard Rohr say that our culture is heavily populated with elderly but has few elders in the sense that we have been using this term. These elders are spiritually wise, mature people who have undergone their own trials and emerged with stories to tell and love to share with those still struggling to get through the perils of life on the journey. Aging doesn't guarantee wisdom.

To avoid the temptations to which humans are most vulnerable and keep tracking toward God, fear has often been used as a primary motivator, the stick rather than the carrot. Fear of retribution and eternal damnation for our sins is a frequent theme and graphic image within the Christian faith even today among the most literal of us. Just as fear and ignorance have been throughout human history the strongest obstacles to the realization of the reign of God on earth, the fear of God's wrath was built into Judean-Christian theology from the outset, when God cast Adam and Eve out of the Garden of Eden. For beginners on the spiritual path, the fear of a wrathful, judgmental, even capricious God might have kept them motivated, but the fear of the illumined was to fail to overcome their passions and so act in ways that would draw them away from God's loving presence. A healthy reverence and awe for God's power and mystery is an acceptable form of fear, but to directly experience God's love and the unspeakable joy and peace it brings to the soul is what in the end will keep one's feet on the path. The desire to see, to know, to experience God proves more powerful than any abstract virtue or primitive fear.

This desire, if not present in the beginning, will become stronger as we persevere on our journeys. It is also far more important than any given spiritual practice or technique. Nonetheless, three common elements form the core of all expressions of Christianity: Scripture, prayer, and corporate worship, with its sacraments of baptism and Holy Communion. Dozens of other spiritual practices, like fasting, repentance, and walking the labyrinth, may contribute to individual Christian formation, but these three are essential for all. Scripture is our common story, prayer our communion with God, and worship and the sacraments how the body of Christ is built up and nourished.

These three elements, as we have begun to see, take various forms within the three main streams of our faith. In the relatively unbroken traditions of the Benedictines and the Eastern Orthodox, we find clues to the shared understandings that were misplaced by the constant power shifts and theological debates throughout the sweep of history. We also discover the unique contributions monasticism made to prayer, the study of Scripture, and worship, all of which are experienced within the worshiping community and as daily practices of the devout.

Eastern spirituality has viewed the struggle for purity of heart as taking place in both the body and the soul, centered within the heart.

The early desert elders, as we have seen, saw this struggle as a function of the will overcoming humanity's animal nature. The more we fixate on stimulating and satisfying our senses at the lower levels, the more we place distance between ourselves and God and the rest of God's creation. This path eventually leads to spiritual death. Understanding the passions and how to overcome them are where the conversation starts in Eastern spirituality.[7] Ascetic practices, which punished the body to save the soul, were not uncommon in the desert and seem at odds with the incarnational understanding that the human was made in God's image.

A more moderate understanding of turning away from what would harm to what would support our journey toward God came later. The interaction of mind, body, and spirit turned to God, supported by God's work in us, enables us to subdue the passions and replace them with the desired virtues. Spiritual formation began with Christ and never moved far from his image. The Christian journey became what Benedict would later call *conversatio morum,* a way of life consisting of continual conversion to the things of God rather than the things on which humanity placed more importance. Repentance, that act of renunciation and turning outlined earlier, became one of the highest virtues. As all who have practiced their faith over any length of time know, it is a continual process, God's fire of purification within us watered by our tears of compunction or sorrow for our transgressions.

The desert elders had noted that if one's afflicted thoughts could be cut off before they lodged in the imagination, where they were likely to take shape, become inflamed with desire and acted upon, sin could be destroyed at its roots. One method advocated in the Eastern tradition was that of guarding the heart, consciously turning away from the temptation at the moment of awareness and substituting a more virtuous thought or behavior. This is a practice anyone on the path of the purified heart may readily adopt. When the heart is left unguarded, our thoughts may drift toward whatever we find tempting and soon become a fantasy, taking on more details and turning into a feature-length film. Marketers and advertisers know this well and count on it. When a full-blown fantasy takes hold, we're already in the red zone. It can take all of our willpower and much prayer to repel such a powerful desire.

7. I am indebted to Father Edward Rommen, an Orthodox priest and adjunct instructor at Duke Divinity School, Durham, NC, for his framework of spiritual development within the Eastern tradition.

Unless we have built-in censors to guard our hearts, we can easily skip on down the path of self-indulgence that leads us astray. But we do have such censors, our own internal spiritual guides, those God-given voices of conscience that stop us in our tracks and turn us back to the path. The more we practice guarding the heart, the more we become aware of how subtle as well as blatant some of our temptations are.

Those being spiritually formed in the Christian life were under close supervision and guidance until they developed the inner censors that repelled the vices and the inner attractors that drew them to God. The loving presence and supervision of wise spiritual elders were great blessings to these communities. The elders taught their charges to lay all their errant thoughts before them as often as they occurred so that they wouldn't take hold and hook into the imagination. In that way they acted as guards of the heart for the community. This practice of disclosure is a form of confession as well as a precursor to the daily examen, the internal review that brings into our awareness what went on throughout each day and allows us to reflect on its meaning. We ask God for forgiveness for our errant ways and strength to help us guard our hearts against dangers from without and within.

Confession is not just an act of repentance but also an act of accountability. The ancients believed that God knew all our thoughts and observed all that we did. Psalm 139 [138], known as "The Hound of Heaven," begins, "O Lord, you have searched me and known me. You know when I sit down and when I rise up; you discern my thoughts from afar." Throughout this complex, beautiful Psalm it is clear that God's loving presence penetrates every defense we can erect against it and permeates every dimension of our existence. Only when we believe ourselves to be out of God's reach, instead of united with God through Christ and the Holy Spirit, do we get ourselves into trouble. If there is nowhere to hide from God, then we can't hide from ourselves, either. The only recourse is to confess, to lay everything before God, ask forgiveness and resolve not to let our ego's desires and impulses get the best of us.

We need to know ourselves well enough to know what afflictive thoughts are like magnets pulling us into their orbits in order to back off and head in the opposite direction. We'll never know ourselves as well as God knows us, because we're very good at fooling ourselves. But the more awareness and desire for God we bring to the process of overcoming our harmful attractions, the more help we will receive. We need to learn and set our limits, the parameters beyond which we will not go, and there is little in our culture to guide us, except the kind of powerfully negative examples of the publically fallen mentioned before. When celebrities seek out Dr. Phil in order to understand themselves and for moral guidance, we wonder where the spiritual guides in this culture are hiding. The early monastics were blessed indeed to have spiritual elders to help them draw the lines and stay within them.

Maximos the Confessor, a seventh-century monk martyred for his faith, saw contemplation, the constant remembrance of God, along with a life devoted to service, as effective means of overcoming the passions and guarding the heart. This constant remembrance became a signature practice within the Eastern Orthodox tradition, ceaseless prayer that invoked the name of Jesus for protection against the demons that attack from without and within. Based on Paul's admonition to the Christian community in First Thessalonians 5:17 to "pray without ceasing," what became known as the Jesus Prayer, some form of "Lord Jesus Christ, Son of the Living God, have mercy on me, a sinner," expressed not only one's devotion to and utter reliance on Christ as savior, but guarded the heart against serious error. The Jesus Prayer acted as armor against the temptations.

The prayer, repeated hundreds, then thousands of time a day until it became internalized and self-sustaining even during sleep, was and still is a common monastic practice, like a song without end that plays over and over in your head. Eventually, praying the prayer becomes so habitual that it is difficult to stop. Eastern monastics were taught how to drop the prayer from their minds into their hearts, and when that happened it was firmly embedded within. Eventually the Jesus Prayer became known as the prayer of the heart.

The wisdom of the Jesus Prayer or any form of ceaseless prayer is that it may lead to a purified heart free of the passions on its way to union with God. Long after this practice became a staple of eastern monastic life, the nineteenth-century classic of Russian Orthodox spirituality, *The Way of the Pilgrim: The Pilgrim Continues His Way,* made the Jesus Prayer accessible to the ordinary Christian, like a secret prayer that lies hidden within the human heart. The Orthodox may use knotted prayer ropes, similar to Catholic rosaries, to keep the Jesus prayer before them. In the Reformed and Catholic and other liturgical traditions, the prayer of confession, *kyrie eleison,* "Christ, have mercy upon us," is a form of the Jesus Prayer. I find myself unconsciously uttering the words, "Lord, have mercy," in situations that call for it. Clearly, the Jesus Prayer has embedded itself within our common tradition.

Praying without ceasing turns the mind away from afflictive thoughts until the practice truly becomes a prayer of the heart. In recent times, brain research and cognitive behavior therapy have taught us much about our own neurological wiring, both within the primitive brain and the more highly evolved portions. In treatments of substance abusers, for example, it has been observed that changing behaviors can lead to changed patterns of thought, rather than the other way around. The way to overcome an addiction begins with admitting you have one, then taking steps to stop it. Later you can figure out why you were doing it in the first place and how you can avoid repeating your mistakes, but stopping the behavior comes first.

The Jesus Prayer—the prayer of the heart—constitutes a significant contribution of Orthodoxy to Christian spirituality. It expresses the practice of focusing the mind and heart on God so as to stay connected at all times and avoid the pitfalls of temptation and sin. While this practice may not appeal to everyone, it is simple and accessible, and it works.

Most prayer expresses our understanding of who God is. This kind of prayer is known as the cataphatic way, or *via positiva*, in which we speak of the names and attributes of God. The kind of prayer that begins, "Merciful, gracious, all-powerful God," typical of liturgical prayer spoken in worship or privately—is cataphatic. It tends to express our limited human understanding of God or the qualities of God we particularly wish to call upon at any one time. It may acknowledge and celebrate God's grace, power, and mercy in our lives and may be either liturgical or personal prayer.

The cataphatic way, (described by Dionysius the Areopagite (or Pseudo-Dionysius) in the late fifth or early sixth century,) suggests that God may be known or at least the existence of God may be known through the creation, human understanding, Scripture, and the person of Christ—the means through which God has revealed Godself to us. Dionysius also noted at the other end of the spectrum from the cataphatic way is the apophatic way, *via negativa*, which acknowledges that God is ultimately unknowable and that any attempt to describe God reveals our limited understanding rather than the divine nature. Forms of prayer move along this spectrum. As we grow in our relationships with God in Christ, we experience both cataphatic and apophatic prayer.

The "Our Father" or Lord's Prayer is a form of cataphatic prayer common to all Christians, as it is taken from the Gospels of Matthew and Luke, although recited in different forms, depending on our tradition. It is the one prayer most raised in the church know "by heart," and that's where it lodges. Other prayers used in the weekly worship liturgies are often memorized by worshipers. For Catholics, Orthodox, and Episcopalians, especially, liturgical prayers may be the only forms prayed. In evangelical churches, however, those are rarely used, and personal and corporate prayer composed for the occasion or spontaneous and Spirit-led seem more valued. The Reformed tradition uses both liturgical and occasional prayers.

In addition to the Jesus Prayer, the Orthodox emphasis on engaging the senses in prayer and worship is another significant contribution to our common Christian heritage. Eastern spirituality focuses on the visual images of icons, as already noted, to direct our attention to God through Christ and the saints of the tradition, in order to keep us on our path of purification. Vision is for most of us the most developed of the five senses. If our vision is focused continually on God and exemplary Christians, we are less likely to turn our attention to the things that excite the passions.

The Orthodox look upon icons as windows to God leading to illumination and divine union. Eventually we become living icons ourselves, having taken on the minds and hearts of Christ, transformed in his image. Praying with icons or any kind of image that evokes the holy may also be considered a form of cataphatic prayer. That may lead us into meditation and contemplation, which draw us into the silence where we seek and rest in God. This becomes apophatic prayer, known in Orthodoxy as pure prayer, as it involves no words, just presence. We will say more about the apophatic in the sections on illumination and union, as we encounter the Christian mysteries in deeper ways.

In the same way that praying with images keeps us focused on God, the stimulation of the other senses in prayer and worship is also central to Orthodoxy. Touch is engaged through handling and kissing the icons; taste through the elements of the Eucharist, representing the body and blood of Christ; hearing through spoken prayer, Scripture readings, and music; and smell through the burning of candles and the swinging of incense. In addition, the Divine Liturgy calls for embodiment of faith in gestures: standing, prostration, kneeling, and making the sign of the cross, as is also the case in the Roman Catholic tradition and that of the Protestant liturgical churches. This embodiment and intense engagement of the senses in prayer and worship not only strengthens the worshiper's experience of God but is a form of experiential education.

If you attend a Greek or Russian Orthodox Sunday service, you may not understand a word of what is said, but you will surely grasp the liturgical meaning and movement, the drama and mystery of what is unfolding before you. The iconostasis with its vivid iconographic images acts as a kind of screen separating the inner mysteries of the faith, where the priest and celebrants prepare the Eucharistic meal, from the outer or lesser mysteries that reenact the principal drama of our faith: that Christ has died, Christ is risen, and Christ will come again. As we celebrate this mystery with all the senses engaged, it evokes, inspires, and integrates the whole self into the worship of God. In a sacred space created to focus all attention on the experience of God within a tradition that understands how to fill every pore of our bodies with the glory of God, it is easy to feel close to God and the beloved community.

My own Reformed tradition, in contrast, relies very little on any of the senses other than the auditory: hearing the Word proclaimed and responding appropriately with prayer or hymns. Holy Communion is rarely served every Sunday in our congregations; more common is a monthly celebration of the sacrament. The contrast is sharp and invites reflection. There are historical reasons for the differences, of course, as well as theological ones. The rise of literacy since the Reformation is one, so that reliance on carrying the liturgy through means of the senses wasn't as essential as in ages past. Another is the desire of the Reformers to strip away the trappings of the church down to its essence. But perhaps it is time to live out our common faith in more fully embodied, fully engaged ways, recognizing different learning styles and ways of communicating and experiencing our core Christian understandings.

Both of these important contributions of the Orthodox to Christian spirituality, ceaseless prayer and praying and worshiping with images, emerged from the desire of the early ascetic cells and monastic communities to direct human attention to the things of God. We can learn much from this rich heritage. Rather than adopting or criticizing the ascetical practices of many of the more extreme desert monks, we can take from their example the positive elements that led them farther along the path of the purified heart.

The Western monastic tradition has considerably more breadth than the Eastern, but within the relatively unbroken Benedictine tradition we can observe the same devotion to the path of the purified heart as the way to union with God found in the Orthodox tradition. As mentioned earlier, a pivotal figure for both was the cosmopolitan monk John Cassian (360–435), likely born in the Roman territory now part of Eastern Europe, who studied with both Evagrius in Egypt and John Chrysostom in Constantinople, and lived in Bethlehem, Rome, and France, where he founded two monasteries. His writing, influenced by Orthodox spirituality, helped form monasticism in the West and was cited more than one hundred times in the sixth-century Rule of Benedict.

For Cassian, purity of heart was the essence and goal of the spiritual journey, and Matthew 5:8, ("Blessed are the pure in heart for they will see God,") was its key text, as it had been for Evagrius. Although several kinds of purity were known in the ancient world, such as the ritual purification of both body and sacred space found in the Leviticus holiness code and the spiritual purity of baptism and chastity already part of early Christianity, for Cassian purity of heart was the process by which those devoted to God prepare for eternal life.[8] Holiness or sanctification, terms used more widely in the church than purity of heart, were synonyms. Like the Eastern spiritual elders, Cassian viewed the spiritual journey as progressive, moving from renunciation to transcendence in the ways already described. One fruit or gift of this movement was that the pure of heart could contemplate the transfigured Jesus, while those on the path saw only Jesus among people. Cassian understood that spiritual knowledge and union with God came on the next two stages of the journey, illumination and deification, and that prayer, especially contemplative or pure prayer, was crucial at all three stages.

By Benedict's time (480–547) a century later, Cassian's major writings, *The Institutes* and *Conferences*, were well known in both eastern and Western monasticism. Latin had become the monastic as well as the classical language in the West, and the late fourth-century translation of the Bible from Hebrew and Greek, its original languages, largely owing

---

8. See Columba Stewart, OSB, Introduction to Luckman and Kulzer, eds., *Purity of Heart in Early Ascetic and Monastic Literature*, 1–15, and Stewart, *Cassian the Monk*, 42–47.

to St. Jerome, was readily available and frequently copied in monastic libraries. The Latin Vulgate, as it became known, was the universal Bible translation in the west until the English King James version came along more than a millennium later.

Other monastic rules had also been written, such as the fourth-century Rule of Basil and sixth-century Rule of the Master, which Benedict drew upon, but none would stand the test of time in the way that the Rule of Benedict has done. Benedict felt free to adapt material from previous rules into his own, but one of the outstanding characteristics of his rule was his emphasis on moderation. The asceticism of the Eastern tradition that sometimes carried self-denial to extremes was not for Benedict's houses. His monks and nuns were to be fed enough, clothed and housed sufficiently, and treated fairly. When you read the rule today, it seems surprisingly generous for its times. Monks were allowed a pound of bread and two to three glasses of wine daily, at the discretion of the abbot or abbess, and the ill were allowed meat for nourishment. Clothing allocations and bedding were similarly adequate. Consequently, Benedictine monasteries began to flourish, as they have up to the present. In the early days, noble classes dropped off their children destined for the church, and these early offerings or oblates, as they were known, were included in the life of the community until mature enough to take vows.

Poverty was not a specific vow in Benedictine monasticism, as were celibacy and obedience to God and the abbot or abbess. The unusual addition to these typical monastic vows was stability leading to conversion of life. For Benedict, spiritual formation within the community required a commitment to stay within this "School of the Lord's Service," to be transformed into the image of Christ, to learn to love as God loves, and to become the beloved community exemplifying God's reign on earth. Central to Benedictine life was *ora et labora*, prayer and work. Seven times a day, following Psalm 119:164 ("Seven times a day I will praise you"), the community gathered for prayer. The remaining time was allocated for *lectio divina*, the form of sacred reading of Scripture leading to meditation and contemplative prayer perfected within the Benedictine tradition, and whatever work the monks or nuns were assigned.

My own experience of Benedictine spirituality is described elsewhere, but here three of its most influential and highly developed contributions to Christian spirituality are outlined: praying or chanting the

Psalms, *lectio divina,* and contemplative prayer, which naturally arises out of the *lectio* process.

In most mainstream churches today worship includes a selection of Scripture readings taken from what is known as the Common Lectionary. These readings, usually consisting of an Old Testament passage, a psalm, a Gospel reading, and a text from the Epistles, follow the liturgical year and vary over a three-year cycle. The lectionary has the advantage of shared texts across much of the Christian tradition and is readily available so that people may study the texts during the week. Clergy preach from the lectionary texts and find a variety of readily available resources to draw upon for their sermons or homilies.

In Benedictine monasteries, however, worship centers on the Psalms. This practice came from Judaism into Christianity long before Benedict's time. The early desert monastics and their descendants all memorized and chanted the Psalms, and it is clear that Jesus brought this practice into our faith from his own Judaic tradition. The Synoptic Gospels have Jesus crying out on the cross, "My God, my God, why have you forsaken me?," the first line of Psalm 22 [21]. Assuming he knew it in its entirety, it is likely he chanted it until its end, when the psalm turns from despair to trusting in the righteousness and mercy of God and ends on a note of praise. It seems more likely that Jesus did not go to his death doubting God but even at his darkest moment taught his disciples how to accept God's will, trusting that it has a higher purpose than we can see.

When I was growing up, it was common within the church to memorize familiar psalms, like the 23rd [22nd], which begins "The Lord is my shepherd," and the 100th [99th], "Make a joyful noise unto the Lord." Those of us who are older may have learned these from the King James Bible and still recite them in its archaic language and poetic cadences. Having this store of familiar prayers to draw upon from memory through all of life's passages helps us stay grounded and connected in our faith. I remember when as a seminary intern I paid a weekly visit to an elderly woman with dementia who lived in a nursing home. If I read or recited passages of Scripture she knew, she would recite them along with me. This became our form of communication, because otherwise she was locked within her own silence.

In a similar way, the Psalms—all 150 of them—were the common heritage of Benedictines and a significant part of their spiritual formation. These expressions of human desire, suffering, doubt, rage, and, ultimately, praise for the wonders of creation and the mystery of God's infinite love were to be committed to memory. The Psalms were always spoken aloud, because that embodied practice was known in the classical schools to aid in memorization and in directing the mind and heart to God. (Thoughts cannot wander when the lips are occupied with the sounds of psalmody.) Benedict insisted that all the Psalms be recited during the seven services a day over a one-week period, two weeks at the most. Today, when Benedictines are more likely to worship three to four times a day in addition to the Eucharistic Mass, it takes several weeks to work through the cycle. During the twelfth-century Cistercian reforms the earlier practice of praying through the cycle weekly was revived.

Praying and chanting the Psalms in worship during the four to seven or eight offices a day, along with other worship elements, constitute the Divine Office or Liturgy of Hours. Each hour of the day has its own angel, its own charism, according to Brother David Steindl-Rast in his gem of a book, *Music of Silence*. These hours, typically known by their Latin names, Vigils or Matins, Lauds, the little hours of Prime, Terce, Sext, None, then Vespers and Compline, followed by the Great Silence, observed until Vigils the next day, mark the periods of *ora et labora* that circumscribe monastic life. Benedict even determined which psalms went with which hours, so it's little wonder he insisted that the brothers and sisters learn to chant them not only by heart but *with* heart, chewing and ruminating on each word, each line of significance in defining the whole of life under the reign of God.

Psalmody, or (the art of setting Psalms to music and chanting them) therefore became a high form of art in Benedictine monasteries throughout the world. The ancient beauty of Gregorian chant was common by the tenth century, and its haunting, mysterious tones and melodies have been revived in our own time. Gregorian chant was not the only form of psalmody but the most treasured, consisting of over 3,000 known chants. Hymns, antiphons, and versicles (liturgical introductions to a text), and the doxology (or "Glory be") were also chanted in the Liturgy of the Hours. These, along with liturgical prayers, readings from Scripture and traditional texts in addition to silent pauses for reflection, still make up the remainder of the liturgy.

The art of psalmody, in my experience, is taken very seriously in the Benedictine tradition, and its communities are expected to perform it well. (During one of my recent monastic stays, the community was given a brief refresher on pronunciation and following the patterns of the chant, even though most of them had been chanting together for decades.) Most monasteries have developed their own Liturgy of the Hours prayer books, attentive to inclusive language and sensitive to the "cursing psalms," in which expressions of hatred of enemies may be relegated to the small print.

A few other forms of psalmody have been preserved within Christianity from their oral traditions, most from post-Reformation English sources. However, hymns have for the most part replaced psalms as the primary sung music within congregations. The Benedictine heritage is to be treasured and honored for its long-standing contribution to prayer set to music.

Praying the Psalms and other liturgical prayers of our faith in the cataphatic mode are considered by many the most important form of prayer, as they keep people tracking together in their communion with God and are at the heart of the worship experience. The practice of *lectio divina,* also central to Benedictine spirituality, crosses from the cataphatic to apophatic and leads into what may be the deepest form of prayer, contemplation, which will lead us along the labyrinthine path of the purified heart into the center, where we stand, illumined, in the presence of God.

Lectio divina, like praying the Psalms, did not originate with Benedict, but was highly developed within Benedictine monasticism. In our own time, many have rediscovered *lectio* (pronounced *lectsio*) through Michael Casey's *Sacred Reading: The Ancient Art of Lectio Divina.* Casey, an Australian Cistercian monk, has contributed substantially through his work to a wider interest in spiritual practices previously considered the prerogative of vowed religious, including the art of spiritual direction.

I first encountered *lectio* in the mid-1990s, when following seminary I took a substantial certificate program in spiritual formation not limited to my own Reformed heritage. Having struggled through biblical exegesis for two years in Greek and one in Hebrew, requisite for Ministers of the Word and Sacrament within our tradition, which highly values preaching, "the Word fitly spoken," I was delighted to discover a more meditative, reflective practice in keeping with the inner search for God's word and presence in all of life. Casey places the rediscovery of *lectio* within the post-Vatican II environment dating from the late 1960s that encouraged each religious community to search out and recover its own unique charisms or gifts of Spirit to strengthen its inner life and outreach to the world. *Lectio*, Casey asserts, is "a means of descending to the level of the heart and of finding God."[9] (Descending to the level of the heart, presumably from the head, where the church had dwelt through the age of Scholasticism, the Reformation and Counter-Reformation, appealed to me from the outset.)

Benedict's Rule made provision for each monk or nun to spend several hours each day in sacred reading, both within the Liturgy of the Hours and in his or her cell alone. This is astonishing for a sixth-century rule, because it required literacy of all monastics, and in Latin, at that, (a privilege normally reserved only for the wealthy.) And where were the books to come from which they were to read? It was one thing to hear Scripture or Cassian's *Conferences* read during worship or meals, but quite another to assume that manuscripts would be readily available in abundance within monastic libraries. The production of these manuscripts became, over time, another of Benedictine monasticism's major contributions to the world both within and outside of the cloisters. In fact, monasteries are recognized as *the* centers of learning in the early to late Middle Ages, and (the Benedictines in particular have been credited with bringing enlightenment out of the Dark Ages through their commitment to accurately copying and preserving the best of ancient texts.) Over time, these were shared among monasteries, and copying became not only essential to ensure the spiritual formation of every monk but also a highly developed art form. Even today, St. John's Abbey's Liturgical Press pays homage to this tradition with its beautifully illumined editions of the Bible.

So reading—aloud, of course, as with the Psalms—whether in the oratory, refectory, or cell, was a formative practice within every Benedictine community from the outset. Before books were plentiful, memorization of key passages of Scripture and other texts considered foundational for faith development was common. They were ingested, chewed, ruminated upon and swallowed. Then like the cow's cud, to use a metaphor commonly applied to the process, the texts could be regurgitated when needed, reflected upon, and re-swallowed to be coughed up again at a time when the text would prove instructive or comforting.

9. Casey, *Sacred Reading*, vi.

Whole books of the Bible were digested in this manner, and the process defined a community transformed by an intimate familiarity with the divine word.

Memorization of texts that serve us throughout our lives has, to our detriment, become a lost practice. Even when I was a child, it was common to memorize well-known poems as well as passages of Scripture, the multiplication tables, and important dates in history. I remember as a shy ten-year-old being pushed by my father to perform James Whitcomb Riley's "Little Orphan Annie" for visiting relatives. Such memorization may not develop the higher faculties of our brains, but in an age when we rely on Wikipedia to fill in the blanks in our basic knowledge of the world, there is much to be said for being able to call forth the wisdom of the ages from an inner store.

Lectio divina itself was considered a four-part process of reading (*lectio*), meditation (*meditatio*), prayer (*oratio*), and contemplation (*contemplatio*). It begins with a prayer to be open to perceive and receive a word of guidance, clarification, discernment, or judgment through the text and the process. Then it proceeds through the four stages. This is a perfect daily practice for a seeker of God.

As a pastor in a congregation who preached weekly, I discovered *lectio* suited me and the congregation better, for the most part, than the kind of biblical exegesis or critical interpretation of the text I had been taught in seminary. *Lectio* restored heart and soul to a practice mostly centered in the mind. I loved it. Each week I met with half a dozen pastors—Methodist, Episcopalian, Presbyterian, and even the odd Baptist—to eat lunch, share our concerns about our congregations, and reflect on the upcoming lectionary passages on which we would preach. This became my first routine practice of sustained *lectio divina* within a community of peers. As pastors, we focused more on what we felt our congregations needed to hear than God's word for each of us that day, but these tended to blend, since God has ways of speaking to us personally even when we think our members are the target audience. While we didn't do the complete four-part process in those group sessions, we did listen and read attentively with the ear of the heart, as Benedict would say, and meditated on each passage, wringing from it enough meaning to compose a fifteen- to twenty-minute sermon. As the group bonded, we opened ourselves even more to each text as well as each other, going deeper and becoming more creative over the years.

My first experience of Benedictine group *lectio* dates from a retreat I made to a women's monastery in Colorado. Each morning after breakfast a group of sisters and guests gathered in the comfortable living room of the retreat center, and one sister led a *lectio* session. There the practice included reading the text aloud several times with different voices and even different translations, noting at first a word or phrase that stands out, taking time to ponder that, then listening in a second reading for a little more to come forward, reflecting, then hearing the text a third time, after which a more extended meditation and sharing would occur. Prayer, spoken and silent, would close out each session. We were invited to further meditate on the text and what it had revealed to us, write about it in our journals, and pray with it throughout the day. We didn't take the fourth step of contemplation within the group, but were encouraged to go deeper into wordless presence later on.

This group *lectio* process always seemed to bring out exactly what each person needed to hear that day, and the sharing of insights among the group contributed to the voices heard in the text. Since that time, *lectio* has become central to my own spiritual practice. Anyone who takes the process seriously and continues the practice will find that it bears much fruit. It is also readily adaptable to Bible study in community groups and congregations. I personally belong to two such groups, one in a congregation and one created by a small group of us. In these days when it seems that little is offered within churches for those eager to go beyond the basics of the Christian faith, *lectio* is a spiritual practice that can bridge the gap between the beginner and the more developed spiritual seeker.

Father Casey's book will greatly assist anyone starting to work with *lectio divina,* as well as those who have practiced it for years. He notes that at each stage of the process our experience of Christ becomes more and more interior. As meditation on the Word follows the initial reading and hearing of the chosen text, it invites reflection not only on the passage but how it relates to something in our lives. That naturally leads into the third step, prayer, probably the cataphatic kind, in which we talk with God, from the heart, about our reflections, needs and concerns, and express our gratitude for God's love and gracious presence in our lives. At the conclusion of this portion of the prayer, we may desire to drop into deep silence, allowing ourselves to be enveloped by the Mystery as long as we are able to stay in that place, suspended in time. The practice of *lectio* within a community that understands its communal relationship with one another and with God deepens and supports this grace-filled practice.

If you are ready for a more thorough immersion into the deep waters of *lectio* and are prepared to strap on a lifejacket and brave the currents, I recommend a more recent book that made an impact on me, Mary Margaret Funk's *Lectio Matters: Before the Burning Bush*. Sister Meg's approach to *lectio* is both practical and profound. Taking as her text the entire book of Jonah, Sr. Meg recounts how deeply she plunged into this text on many levels. Eventually it led to her being able, finally, to share the story of her own near drowning and rescue by God in the gripping *Into the Depths*, published in 2011, which felt in some ways like an exorcism of old demons and a merciful healing. *Lectio* takes you deep, if you'll let it, and God knows just how deep to take you before you come up for air.

Sister Meg's practice in *Lectio Matters* included elements of the biblical exegesis I'd been taught, placing the text in its historical-critical-textual contexts, as well as calling on training I'd had in graduate school decades ago in the study of literature. Her process moves through the literal voice of the text perceived through logic, the symbolic voice that draws on intuition, the moral voice that appeals to the sense of right and wrong, and the mystical voice received by the spiritual senses. This thoroughgoing extended process of *lectio divina* could keep you hooked into a particular passage or book of the Bible for months in order to mine its depths, extract its precious gems, and apply it to your life. This kind of sustained study becomes *lectio continua,* as you stay with it over a period of time.

Lectio is not limited to Scripture and may be applied to anything in God's creation that opens the windows of our mind, heart, body, and senses to God's work in and around us. Meditating on the natural world, art and literature, events, and our own experience can lead us into a deeper relationship with God in Christ and to moments of intense illumination. We may be grateful to the Benedictine tradition for developing, preserving, and raising to a high art this essential spiritual practice.

A particular contribution the Benedictines and Cistercians made to the fourth step of the *lectio* process, contemplation, will be explored more deeply in Parts Two and Three, because it is more commonly experienced in the later stages of the spiritual journey. Here I want to mention the importance of contemplative prayer to both Eastern and Western spirituality and the work of the three Cistercian (Trappist) monks who brought this practice forward into our own time: William Meninger, Basil Pennington, and Thomas Keating.

These wise elders met early in their monastic lives, and Father William brought his understanding of contemplative prayer from his study of the great fourteenth-century mystical classic, *The Cloud of Unknowing*, to his brothers. Each of the three began to perfect a form of this apophatic style of prayer. Father Thomas called his "centering prayer" and eventually created an organization devoted to its teaching and practice, Contemplative Outreach (www.contemplativeoutreach.org). Resources, events, and teachers/facilitators trained in centering prayer and *lectio divina* may be found on this site. Father Basil passed away in 2005, but the other two still teach and write about this deceptively simple but deep spiritual practice that has helped many find their way to God.

Because the Eastern Orthodox and Benedictine traditions have been around throughout most of Christian history, their contributions to our common heritage have been profound and lasting. Although Eastern and Western monasticism began to go their separate ways as early as the fifth century, following Cassian's time, it wasn't until the great schism of 1054 that cultural, political, and theological differences led to the irrevocable split between these two great streams of Christianity. Five hundred years later, another schism, the Protestant Reformation, splintered the church of Jesus Christ further. Now, five hundred years after the Reformation, the latest turning is the amorphous emerging church movement, yet to be defined but sharing a common recognition of the need for institutional change. According to one source, there are now some 38,000 denominations and faith communions labeled as Christian worldwide, a staggering number suggesting that the body of Christ is so fragmented as to make its unity in diversity visible only to God![10] It seems that the Christian labyrinth, with only one path leading to the center, has become a maze, confusing those who step onto it, turn this way and that and can't find their way either to God or back to where they started. All we can do in such a world is trust that God will once again do a new thing and lead the body of Christ to become whatever it is meant to be.

10. http://christianity.about.com/od/denominations/p/christiantoday.htm.

My own search has been to recover a common path through this maze, to strip away all but its common core, and turn it back into a labyrinth, this path of the purified heart drawn from the eastern and western spiritual traditions. While multiculturalism and inclusiveness are essential for any future vision of the church, nothing must be preferred to following Christ, as Benedict's Rule teaches us.

Here is where we pick up the path which took a major detour five hundred years ago with the Protestant Reformation. Although the roots of the Reformation were planted in the fifthteenth century, the date in 1517 when Martin Luther, then a German Augustinian priest, nailed his famous Ninety-Five Theses to the door of the Wittenberg Castle church is often taken as its first offshoot. At the heart of the split from Roman Catholicism was the Reformers' outrage over pervasive abuse and corruption throughout the institutional church. Ultimately, the papal hierarchy was held accountable for its moral and financial excesses, including the selling of indulgences to pray souls out of purgatory, as though God's forgiveness were a monetary exchange with Rome as its treasury. That practice was only the most visible tip of the iceberg. Luther, also a theology professor, taught that faith in Jesus Christ and Scripture alone, *Sola Scriptura*, were the means of grace. He called for a priesthood of all believers, without the intermediaries of the church hierarchy, and translated the Latin Vulgate into German, making the Bible available and its interpretation open to church laity.

Luther's theology differed from that of other Reformers, such as Ulrich Zwingli and John Calvin, but its essence—God's freely offered grace through faith in Christ as the means of salvation—was a shared understanding. The Reformation was to continue for over a hundred years and to become as embroiled in politics and theological debate as previous schisms. So many mergers and derivatives from the Lutheran, Reformed, and Anabaptist communions have occurred that it would be tedious and confusing to thread our way through them. What is important to our conversation is how spiritual formation within Christian communities and transformation of seekers of God into the likeness of Christ were viewed in the emerging Protestant traditions. (What did Protestant, especially Reformed, spirituality look like? Was it appreciably different from Eastern and Western monastic spirituality? What did and can it contribute to the development of Christian spirituality?)

Truthfully, these questions became mine as I plunged into this material, for my own Reformed tradition is noted more for its theology, educated clergy, sense of order within a civil society, and worldwide mission than its spirituality. I had to return to sources studied in my post-seminary spirituality program and new ones for the answers. What I found surprised me at times. Retrieving my 1991 edition of Howard Rice's *Reformed Spirituality: An Introduction for Believers,* I reread Morton Kelsey's introduction. Kelsey, an Episcopal priest and Jungian psychologist, points out that Reformed spirituality has largely been lost, as it has in the wider church. However, he also said that John Calvin (1509–1564), the French theologian and pastor considered the founder of the Reformed tradition, practiced a method of Bible reading that "is very close to the meditative method of the Benedictines, known as *lectio divina.*"[11] In fact, as Rice says later on in the book, "One could say that the ideal of Reformed Protestantism was that each Christian home become a little monastery in the world," with morning and evening prayer. Without the monastic model, Rice goes on to say, Reformed Christianity has "too easily adjusted to the particular culture of its time."[12] It's interesting to me that the emergent church movement over the past decades has generated new ecumenical monastic communities, like Taize in France, centered around liturgical chant, and the Iona Community in Scotland with a global membership, adapting Celtic spirituality, itself a blend of the ancient Druidical and Culdee religions, with the Benedicine tradition. Taize chant and its uniquely contemplative services, along with the Iona Community's distinctive prayers and music, have made their way into mainstream churches. In Durham, North Carolina, close to my home, a new monastic model called Rutba House is drawing worldwide attention as a mixed style of communal living, as people search for what seems missing in the traditional church.

Even Calvin, it seemed, was drawn to spiritual practices typical of the Benedictine tradition. In addition to *lectio divina* and a form of Liturgy of the Hours, he practiced extended solitary contemplative prayer. He also promoted the spiritual disciplines of righteousness, frugality, generosity, fasting, and holiness, the fruit of life on the path of the purified heart. I was delighted to rediscover with new eyes the consisten-

11. Kelsey, "Introduction," in *Reformed Spirituality*, 15.
12. Rice, *Reformed Spirituality,* 60.

cies in the spiritual practices of the Reformed tradition with Western monasticism.

There are significant differences, of course. The intellect is more highly valued than the heart in this tradition. It insists that Christian life is corporate more than individual, that we are the people of God and of God's Word. The book of nature is also a more prominent feature in the landscape of Reformed spirituality, especially the desire to tame the passions through bringing order out of chaos. Yet I found so many similarities to the gifts of the monastic traditions that I felt the path was being cleared of overgrown brush before my eyes.

Richard Baxter, a nineteenth-century Reformed pastor, called for four spiritual practices that sounded familiar: prayer; study, principally of the Bible using a form of *lectio divina*; spiritual guidance; and practice, ethical living or the outer journey we will explore in more depth as we take the return journey on the labyrinth.

The notoriously somber Puritans practiced contemplative prayer, repeated words like "Jesus" and "love" as used in centering prayer, talked about meditation and mental prayer, and used both *lectio* and *viseo divina*, although they weren't called that. E. Glenn Hinson in "Puritan Spirituality" writes that Puritanism *was* spirituality: "Puritans were to Protestantism what contemplatives and ascetics were to the medieval church." While monks sought sainthood in monasteries, Puritans sought it everywhere: "in homes, schools, town halls, shops, as well as churches, . . . zealous of heart religion manifested in transformation of life and manners."[13]

Theology professor and Presbyterian minister Belden Lane's 2011 book, *Ravished by Beauty: The Surprising Legacy of Reformed Spirituality*, devotes considerable space to describing how the Puritan highly developed sense of longing and passion was redirected into a desire for God, just as in the monastic traditions. For the Puritans, recreating the New Eden out of the wilderness of the New World was the transformation they sought through bringing order and civilized society to the wild New England landscape. The Eastern desert and early Celtic ascetics, on the other hand, made no such attempts, as the barrenness and harshness of the landscape contributed to their desire for God alone. Lane's previous book, *The Solace of Fierce Landscapes*, much of which is set in the high desert of New Mexico, where I used to live and which still

13. Hinson in Senn, ed., *Protestant Spiritual Traditions*, 65.

has a piece of my heart, perfectly captures the difference between these two approaches. The Reformed approach feels cataphatic, centered in manifesting heaven on earth, while desert spirituality is decidedly apophatic, (drawing the seeker like a magnet into the unrelenting silence of the elusive divinity.) Both spiritualities, however, find in wild nature the terrible beauty and mystery of God. As Lane notes in *Ravished by Beauty*, this recognition would argue for an environmental ethic based on "God's own longing for a restored cosmos"[14] that only recently has begun to emerge within the Reformed or any other Christian tradition.

The Reformers did make a significant break from the medieval tradition of discovering multiple levels of meaning in a text during *lectio divina*. They strove instead for the text's plain meaning, informed by the Holy Spirit and accessible to the priesthood of all believers. That approach can lead to a narrow literalism more restrictive of than open to the movement of the Holy Spirit, as in Christian fundamentalism. The Spirit is still moving, however, as evidenced by the number of high-visibility evangelical Christian leaders who, through their own spiritual conversions, have begun to move beyond literalism and take people along with them into a more expanded view of Scripture and God's saving grace. Pastor Rob Bell's controversial *Love Wins* and Brian McLaren's recent work both challenge from inside the church a theology of damnation, summarized as "if you aren't saved you're going to hell."

Calvin, to his credit, insisted on placing Scripture within its context, (not engaging in "prooftexting," the common practice of pulling out a line of text to prove a point without acknowledging the historical or critical contexts from which it came.) Like the monastics before him, Calvin was prone to interpreting the Old Testament in light of the New, making one Bible out of the sacred scripture of both Jews and Christians.

Calvin made no distinction between the Word read and the Word proclaimed, placing great emphasis in worship on preaching, which he called "the audible Eucharist," while Holy Communion was the "visible Eucharist."[15] As already noted, differing theological understandings of Eucharist keep the three streams of Christianity divided at the Lord's Table. However, the sharing of Christ's body and blood occupies a central place in all three, as well it should.

14. Lane, *Ravished by Beauty*, 223.
15. Rice, *Reformed Spirituality*, 105.

The more I read around in Protestant spirituality, the less unique it appears. Marjorie Thompson's popular 1995 study, *Soul Feast: An Invitation to Christian Spirituality*, covers *lectio divina*, contemplative prayer, prayer of the heart, including the Jesus Prayer, worship, the daily examen, fasting as self-emptying, spiritual direction, and ends with the practice of developing and observing a rule of life, which she defines as "a pattern of spiritual disciplines that provide structure and direction for growth in holiness."[16] She mentions, of course, the Rule of Benedict. What is new here is not the practices themselves but their introduction to a largely Protestant, non-monastic audience. A dozen years ago a friend and I co-taught a multi-week class in a Presbyterian church called "Spiritual Sampler," using Thompson's book and other sources as texts. The class was very well attended, as it covered unfamiliar ground for this highly educated group of mature Christians, including clergy, who were eager to learn what they had not been adequately exposed to in their many years of spiritual formation. What has been lost is now being found, not only within the Reformed tradition, but other Protestant spirituality as well.

In *Protestant Spiritual Traditions*, Frank Senn focuses on seven spiritualities: Lutheran, Reformed, Anabaptist, Anglican (Episcopal), Puritan, Pietism, and Methodist. The essays on each of these provide more confirmation that little has emerged in the past five hundred years that is substantially different as far as spiritual practices are concerned from what had been developed by the early Eastern and Western monastics. As martyred Lutheran theologian Dietrich Bonhoffer observed, "the life of faith is nothing if not an unending struggle of the spirit with every available weapon against the flesh."[17] Back to the desert wisdom of the early church!

The theology of these faith communions may differ but the spiritual practices are remarkably similar. For Anglicans (Episcopalians), the authority of Scripture, the creeds of the undivided church from the early centuries, apostolic patterns of ministry, and the two sacraments of baptism and Eucharist are central. Some from this tradition, which does not have a dominant theologian, say that it never left the Catholic Church. Its liturgy resembles Catholic mass in many ways, though it uses the

16. Thompson, *Soul Feast*, 138.

17. Senn, *Protestant Spiritual Traditions*, 15.

Book of Common Prayer. It also has a holiness path within it, which is part of our path of the purified heart.

It is well known that John Wesley, the Anglican who founded what became Methodism, also walked the holiness path, wrote about it and taught it to his followers. Like the path I have described, it was formed out of a deep desire to follow Christ by conforming one's life to his teaching and God's love. In my view, Methodism contributed a strong, much-needed heart dimension to Protestant spirituality. Wesley's notable mystical experience, when his heart was "strangely warmed," will be recounted later. What is clear here is that though nuances and even radical shifts exist from one denomination to another, what they have in common is that their spiritual practices are almost without exception drawn from our common Christian heritage as transmitted through eastern and western monasticism.

Within a period of two hundred years following the Reformation, the Protestant faith had begun to take a multitude of forms, almost personalities, in the sense that most were the products of one major theologian's or founder's views. Yet all were still visibly linked with their origins through their spiritual practices.

One tragic sidebar to the story of the Reformation was the damage that the zealous Reformers wreaked upon some of the most beautiful art and architecture of Europe. Cathedrals and monasteries, chapels and local churches were savaged by those who strove to eradicate what they considered papist idols and imagery. I have been in European cathedrals whose original stone altars were hammered and hacked, bearing still these marks of that destructive rage so foreign to true spiritual transformation. Religious tyrants are found in every age, including our own. Yet our faith is built on a solid foundation and on hope, and we are about to step into the last turn on the inward journey of the purified heart, ready and eager to receive the illumination we have sought.

PART TWO

Illumination

Resting in the Center

SEVEN

Spring
Lent to Pentecost

The righteous flourish like the palm tree,
and grow like a cedar in Lebanon.
They are planted in the house of the Lord;
they flourish in the courts of our God.
In old age they still produce fruit;
They are always green and full of sap
Showing that the Lord is upright.

— Psalm 92:12–15a

SUMMER'S HEAT MAY LINGER well into the fall in North Carolina, but spring comes early. By the first week in March the redbuds and flowering cherries are in bloom and the daffodils past their prime. Instead of staying home to enjoy the creative bursts of spring, I packed my winter coat, snow boots, a suitcase full of books and headed back to Minnesota.

When I had left in mid-December after the Advent Retreat at St. John's Abbey, a foot of new snow had just fallen. Most of it was still there when I arrived at St. Benedict's Monastery in St. Joseph, Minnesota, on March 8, Shrove Tuesday, the day before Ash Wednesday and the beginning of Lent. It seemed appropriate that my Lenten journey would begin in true winter instead of full-blown spring, as I longed for a stretch of time for silence and reflection to further explore the depths of my interior life with God. I was grateful to St. Benedict's Studium Scholars program for an extended period to focus on research and preparing an outline for this book.

The season of Lent in the Christian church is the most somber of our liturgical year. Sanctuaries and vestments are draped in deep purple, adding to the solemnity. Lent is all about purgation or purification through renewed repentance, confession, sacrifice, and preparation for the spiritual journey toward the cross each of us must take on our walk with Jesus. I wanted to spend this Lent within a spiritual community that understood its meaning and engaged in its own deep spiritual practices. Since I couldn't stay at St. Ben's for the whole fifty days of Lent—forty days plus Sundays through Easter—I elected to make a good beginning by arriving in time to experience Ash Wednesday with the community. So as revelers in New Orleans and elsewhere were celebrating Mardi Gras and letting off steam before the penitent season of Lent, I was settling in at the monastery, looking forward to a whole three weeks—God willing—of single-minded dedication to my task and my own purification process.

Even with this resolve, it wasn't easy to carve out three weeks away from home, as the primary caregiver for the household. To Tom, my son, my being away for three weeks seemed interminable. My husband, Alden, on the other hand, knowing he'd be inconvenienced, nevertheless graciously expressed his hope that I would make the most of this time to focus on my work and not worry about the home front. Reassuring Tom that I'd be available by cell phone and Skype, I prayed that all would be well in my absence and trusted it would be so.

My friend Sally, in Minneapolis, generously offered to pick me up at the airport and deposit me at St. Benedict's, nearly ninety miles away, and to return me back three weeks later. It would give us time to catch up, she said, and I was grateful for both the ride and her company

My Studium host, a Benedictine sister, was awaiting my arrival and graciously invited Sally to have lunch with us in the sisters' dining room. During my stay, the hospitality for which the Benedictines are known was beyond any I had ever experienced. I felt the welcoming warmth of the community from the beginning and received it gratefully. My accommodations included not only a spacious two-room apartment, a stocked kitchen, including the kind of peanut butter I preferred (they asked!), but also an office in case I wanted to spread out more than the apartment allowed. I found I didn't need the office, as there was more than enough space in the living quarters, conveniently located near the Studium staff and the Spirituality Center, and just a short walk from Sacred Heart Chapel, containing the oratory, chapel, dining rooms, and monastery offices. Despite the cold, I actually enjoyed walking several times a day back and forth from the residence area to the chapel. Not only was it good exercise but it also marked a transition between my personal work and my experience of worship and fellowship within the community.

It felt as though my every need was anticipated and quietly taken care of during my stay, so that I could concentrate on the writing and the intense process of self-purification. Since I was usually the one responsible for juggling work, family, church, and community needs, being cared for in such a gracious way was a new and precious experience. As I settled in, I was filled with gratitude and wonder at the gifts I was being given and resolved to blend in with the community life.

In chapter 53 of Benedict's Rule, "The Reception of Guests," the mandate is to welcome all guests as Christ, to honor them and meet them in loving courtesy. St. Benedict would be proud of the sisters of his namesake monastery, I thought. Hospitality is a learned spiritual discipline that eventually becomes natural as we grow in love of God and neighbor. It is also a mutual gift, as the stranger who is welcomed wants to reciprocate by offering the community friendship, sharing resources, and bringing new perspectives that broaden mutual understanding. People used to giving more than receiving often have difficulty accepting what is freely offered, so learning to receive graciously is a spiritual practice in itself. I found myself thinking of the grace of mutuality and reciprocity in relationships, like the self-giving so much a part of Christian Trinitarian understanding: God pours out God's love for us, Jesus pours out his life for humanity, and the Holy Spirit binds all into loving relationship, a true union of human and divine. "On earth as it is in heaven" is life under the reign of God, within the beloved community, and I was to catch more than one glimpse of what that life could be like during my three weeks at St. Ben's.

St. Benedict's Monastery is situated within the small town of St. Joseph, about five miles from Collegeville, where St. John's Abbey is located. Both monasteries are adjacent to the colleges that form a large part of their mission and service. The College of St. Benedict enrolls about 2,200 women, while St. John's University has about 1,800 male undergraduates in addition to its prep school and theological college. Students cross-enroll for classes, and buses run all day between the two campuses, which feel coeducational, although without the permissiveness that has prevailed in American higher education since the 1960s. Students are expected to live on campus and observe the community's rules, much as in my day when college administrations acted *in loco parentis*—in place of the parents—and enforced curfews and quiet times for study. That felt consistent with monastic life and reassuring for parents. Since during my first career in higher education I had served as a vicepresident of a church-related women's college, I felt right at home at St. Ben's from the outset.

On March 9, Ash Wednesday, I attended morning and midday prayers in the monastery's oratory, where the sisters and guests gather for private worship three to four times daily. I joined them and the college and local communities again at noon for the imposition of ashes and for the 5 p.m. Eucharist service in the beautiful Romanesque Sacred Heart Chapel. The music was especially moving, sung by the monastery's schola, or choir, and an ensemble of college students and staff. Music is such a significant part of worship, especially within this community, that it is exceptionally well performed. Listening to it heightened my own sense of joy to be present in this space with these people worshiping our God together and beginning our common journey through Lent. Near the end of this service, as we sang "May we be one in Christ" during the Eucharist, I silently prayed for Christ's divided church.

In Eastern Orthodoxy the season that begins with Lent and ends with Pentecost is called Triodion—three odes—and is devoted to strengthening faith through repentance, prayer, and self-purification. Our less liturgical Reformed tradition does observe this day of penitence, though practices differ. As a solo pastor of a Presbyterian church for several years, I had initiated a new practice for the Ash Wednesday evening service. Rather than using the ashes from last year's Palm Sunday fronds, as is often done, to mark the worshiper with the sign of the cross, I asked people to write on slips of paper their personal confessions and prayers for forgiveness and drop these into a bowl. As we prayed that God would create within us a new resolve to turn again and be healed, we watched as the papers burned to ashes, representing our compunction and sorrow for our transgressions and shortcomings. Then, as each congregant came forward, I dipped my thumb in the ashes and signed the cross on the forehead with these words: "We are dust and to dust we will return." Remembering that without God our lives count for nothing but ashes, we prepare ourselves to move through Lent with humility and reverence. We surrender ourselves to God's divine will, as Jesus did when he faced his destiny, emptying and sacrificing himself for the greater good of all.

It was this perspective of the penitential heart I wanted to carry into Lent.

That night I gave thanks for my safe arrival and all the blessings of the day. I especially asked for the grace to use this precious gift of space and time and support for my work to full advantage and placed my family firmly in God's care. The following morning I prayed for clarity on the focus of the book. Guidance came quickly: purity of heart and the holiness path within Eastern and Western Christian spirituality. Gratefully, I realized that's what I wanted most to research, experience, and write about.

The next day I was introduced to the community at dinner and asked to speak for a moment about my work. As I mentioned purity of heart, I felt this resonate with a number of the sisters. It turned out they had studied this subject together some years earlier. Notes from the leader of this study were produced. The sisters began to identify resources for me to look at, and books would appear at my door or were handed to me in the dining room. It seems that a member of the community who had passed away had written extensively on this subject in early monasticism, and a copy of her manuscript was given to me. A multi-author collection of essays on purity of heart in honor of this sister had been produced by another in the community. A copy of this long-out-of-print book miraculously appeared, along with the sister responsible for it, and we enjoyed a private dinner conversation together one evening. I realized that had I not come here I would not have known about or had access to these resources. God was placing exactly what I needed in my path.

I received a library card good for both the College of St. Benedict and St. John's University and began to take out books related to my subject. I had brought with me more than a dozen books I wanted to read during my stay, so I spent the first few days just soaking up all this abundance, along with the Liturgy of the Hours and meals with the sisters. I had requested a weekly spiritual direction session while there, and a senior member of the community, the one who had led the study of purity of heart, was chosen for me. Everything seemed to be falling into place.

My days began to take on the rhythm of the community. Always an early riser, I was generally up by 5:00, reading and praying for an hour or so, before heading out to morning prayer in the oratory at 7:00. Bowing to the community as I entered my reserved seat, I found the place in the prayer book and *ordo,* specifying the hymns and antiphons that would be used, and followed the liturgy, singing antiphonally with the choirs facing each other across the oratory. Following the service, because it was Lent, breakfast in the dining room was taken in silence. Then I returned to my room and spent another hour or more in *lectio divina* and contemplative prayer before beginning work. At 11:20, I stopped what I was doing and returned to the oratory for noon prayer at 11:30, followed by lunch and conversation with the sisters. Resuming work until around 4:45, I trekked again to the oratory for the 5:00 Eucharist, or worked until dinner at 5:30. Then I would return to the apartment for more reading, phone calls, or computer work. Sometimes I attended evening prayer at 7:00. At other times I continued my reading or, if too tired to concentrate, watched a little television or a movie, available from the college or monastic library. Bedtime followed between 9:00 and 10:00.

The schedule changed on weekends and during feast days or other special occasions, but I was kept informed. Name days were marked with a special song at dinner, to celebrate sisters named after whatever saint was being honored that day. On St. Patrick's Day, sisters named Patricia, Patsy, or Pat were feted, and nearly everyone wore something green. One Sister Pat, clearly of Irish heritage, had a special green shamrock sweater to mark her name day.

I thought how times had changed since Vatican II's reforms of the late 60s. Sisters today are freed from wearing habits and can express a bit of personality and individuality, always in moderation, of course. Some of the older sisters and those from other countries still preferred their habits, and that is accepted, too. One Benedictine sister from another monastery has written of her preference for the habit as a constant reminder of her identity in Christ. I could relate to that. When I led worship or officiated at a wedding or memorial service, I wore my black robe and stole as a symbol of the office of ordained minister. For years I even wore a clerical collar, customary at the first church at which I served. Habits and vestments have symbolic meaning relating to one's role in serving Christ within the various faith communions. Yet they may separate us from those we serve. We don't need them to express God's love.

St. Benedict's Feast Day on March 21 (one of two, the other on July 11) became an all-out occasion, with the dining room bedecked with special flower arrangements, linen tablecloths, and the "Sunday best" table settings. The sisters broke out the wine and beer that night, too.

The food was always nourishing and plentiful, served buffet style, which I appreciated since I was still on my extended fast. The protocol for seating was to fill in a table that had been started. This allowed me to meet most of the sisters during my stay, and I observed that they always included guests in the conversation. I was frequently asked how my work was coming, and I was interested in finding out more about their lives. Some had teaching or administrative positions at the college or at St. John's University, while others worked at one job or another within the monastery or wider community. They all took turns cleaning up after meals, sharing tasks as in a family.

While there are younger members within the community, the majority are over sixty-five, what our culture considers normal retirement age. But here no one seemed to retire until she was in need of personal assistance, at which time she transferred over to the monastery's assisted living facility, St. Scholastica's Convent, in nearby St. Cloud. Just recently, one ninety-nine-year-old sister moved to St. Scholastica's, but up to that point had managed just fine in independent living. Maybe it's the clean living or the supportive community, but these strong, capable women reminded me of the elders the psalmist speaks of in the verses that head this chapter, who flourish in the courts of the Lord, still bearing fruit, still green and full of sap when old. May we all be so blessed as these exceptional women who have devoted their lives to God and loving service!

For now at least, this older generation of sisters is not being replaced by younger women. Cultural roles have changed, and young women have many more options today. Most of the older sisters of St. Ben's came into the community following high school graduation or shortly afterwards, finding their opportunities for education and careers within the order rather than without. This is the largest Benedictine women's monastery in the U.S., with just under 300 sisters. Other smaller Benedictine houses have consolidated into this one, as they could not be self-sustaining.

Unless there are cultural or ecclesial changes that make monastic life more appealing to younger Catholics, in another generation many more monasteries will have disappeared. I've observed that the women of St. Ben's work hard at maintaining a public and community presence, not only because they enjoy outreach and service but also because they need to expand their base of support to survive. The college is a potential source of future sisters, and the students who attend St. Ben's certainly have had many opportunities to get to know the community. Young women today, however, generally don't regard celibacy and limited leadership roles for women in the church—the stained glass ceiling—as desirable.

Will the pendulum swing back? Will the church, out of necessity, change with the times? Only God knows. Meanwhile, places like St. Ben's are to be treasured for their values and lifestyles. The monastery's core values, taken from Benedict's Rule, are stated on their website: Awareness of God, Community, Prayer and Work, Listening, Hospitality, Stewardship, and Peace. A twice-weekly blog posted on Facebook keeps interested followers informed of the community's goings-on, and it amazes me how much they share of themselves with the world.

As I got to know this beloved community, it became clear to me that this was where I belonged as a Benedictine oblate. The transfer of my candidacy from St. John's Abbey was gracefully handled, and my Studium stay turned into the beginning of what I intend as a lifetime affiliation with this community. As St. John's also has much to offer, having access to both monasteries and campuses seemed to me the best of both worlds, especially for someone who had spent much of her adult life on college campuses and most of the rest of it in the church.

I attended a Lenten Retreat at St. John's during this time. The monk who led the retreat was an artist who shared with us his unique vision and his own spiritual journey, along with the history of the phenomenal Marcel Breuer-designed chapel, which also serves as the monks' oratory. It is an architectural treasure, and visitors come from all over the world just to see it and experience worship there. The Lady Chapel, a side chapel near the rear of the sanctuary, even has a fifteenth-century black Madonna, whose counterparts I had seen in France.

The retreat allowed me to reconnect with several of the oblates I had met in December as well as a few more. A luncheon that closed out the weekend at St. John's produced a surprise. Seated at my table of eight were two other Presbyterian ministers. None of the three of us knew each other. It was startling to find other "Presbyterian Benedictines" at this meeting, and that experience planted the seed for a small research project on why so many of us who minister in the Reformed tradition have been drawn to Benedictine spirituality.

On another occasion I was invited to accompany a few of the sisters to St. John's for a talk on peacemaking by a prominent Mennonite peace activist, part of Bridgefolk, a Mennonite-Catholic organization. He spoke of a twenty-first-century approach to making peace, which brought together interfaith and secular teams who involved themselves in grassroots political processes rather than trying to bring about change through existing intractable systems. His talk reminded me of similar approaches I'd been involved with over the years. A Middle East travel seminar that included a surreptitious trip into Gaza led by staff of the Middle East Council of Churches exposed our group of seminarians and church leaders directly to the Israeli-Palestinian conflict in all its ugliness, violence, and intractability. A visit to Bosnia with an interfaith group during that country's terrible war resulted in our creating a ministry to support the rebuilding of schools and lives under the direction of the Franciscans, who provided the only infrastructure that devastated country knew during the mid-90s. Participation at a peacemaking conference in Northern Ireland a year later, at the time when former Senator George Mitchell was an envoy to the peace process, exposed the entrenched thinking and emotion-filled loyalties of the parties preventing rather than working for peace. I remembered meeting a couple of Mennonites who lived on the "Peace Line" in Belfast, trying to hold sacred space for Catholics and Protestants to build relationships and learn to trust one another.

That night at the Abbey I gave thanks for the peacemakers, truly the children of God. I prayed that all people of faith and good will would join together to help usher in the reign of peace on earth that signals the fulfillment of God's desire for our restoration to wholeness and unity. Peace begins within. Forgiving and reconciling conflict within our own hearts is essential to our purification process.

Not long after my arrival at St. Ben's, a major earthquake and tsunami in Japan brought great destruction and more fear to an already fear-filled world. One of the sisters was supposed to travel to Japan just a few days after the quake to teach at a sister monastery there. It quickly became clear that wasn't going to happen. The world seemed very dangerous and the monastery a haven of stability, just as monasteries have been throughout much of their history.

I enjoyed being around the students and wondered, not for the first time, how my path would have been different if I had been able to combine my academic and religious careers as was done so well here. I had made my career decisions after marriage, so monastic life would not have been an option, but I could see its appeal as well as its potential limitations.

The spring equinox came and went, and I still hadn't seen any signs of spring in Stearns County, Minnesota. On March 23 a heavy new snow made walking to the oratory hazardous, but the sisters had that covered as well. Campus security arrived to take us to the door and deposit us back at the residences later. It was so nice to be taken care of!

Watching the snow fall reminded me of a poem I wrote at fifteen. I probably gave it an imaginative title, like "Spring." The poem spoke to me of my own journey then and now and the moments of illumination we receive when we pause to reflect. God speaks through the book of nature as well as through Scripture, and we are too little aware of earth's wisdom.

The poem went like this:

> A certain kindness settles softly with the snow
> That blots the year's impurity and mine,
> Then soaks in spongy earth to slake the thirst
> Of Spring and store bright promises for me.

The combination of snow as purity and spring as new life held a special meaning for me this year.

My time at the monastery passed all too quickly. Three days before I was to leave I still had not completed the outline for the book. That would have to wait until I got home. I was so absorbed in research and monastic life that I couldn't think about what lay ahead, only what was right in front of me. Living in the present moment is a spiritual discipline much admired by monastics through the ages, and I was experiencing this practice with a new appreciation for how freeing it is. Always one to plan ahead, I found this *kairos* experience of time to be another gift of my stay at the monastery. I saw the attraction of being fully present and reflected that at its best this state of presence is a release from fear and the need to control based on trust in God. A line from a favorite hymn, "Great Is Thy Faithfulness," came to mind: "All I have needed thy hand hath provided. Great is thy faithfulness, Lord, unto me." Living within the beloved community under the reign of God, trusting that all is just as it is meant to be, would truly be heaven on earth.

One of my desires for these three weeks of Lent was to deepen my prayer practice with two daily periods of contemplative or centering prayer that grew out of *lectio divina*. More will be said about these prayer forms later, but I was finding in this timeless state that characterized the rhythm and nature of monastic life that prayer was continual, and it was easy to pray without ceasing. Life itself became a prayer.

As was their custom, the night before my departure the sisters sang a blessing farewell to me, extending their arms as in a benediction—a Benedictine benediction, I realized, and I was deeply touched by this last gift of their hospitality.

And then it was March 31, the day of my departure. Sally had come to pick me up, and the Studium sisters helped me tote my gear to her car. After hugs all around, Sally and I headed toward the airport and home. I felt deep gratitude for all that I had received and experienced while at the monastery and for the grace that allowed me to be away from home the full three weeks.

When I returned, the peace of the monastery quickly faded into the reality of family life and catching up with all that had gone on in my absence. The blooming azaleas and mild weather eased the transition back into my domestic responsibilities. My son was full of anger over a mandated daily drive to his clinic and wanted to challenge the system. My husband had handled some household repairs on his own and was ready for me to take over. The dog was frantic for my attention. For nearly a full week, I needed to direct my energies to the home front. Given the contrast between life at the monastery and life at home, I experienced a bit of separation anxiety and longing for the simpler life I had just experienced. Oblates are expected to live according to the Rule of Benedict to the extent possible, consistent with their work, family, and community responsibilities. With a clear model before me, I resolved to modify my schedule, again release as much as I could of life's distractions, and settle into a comfortable rhythm of prayer, work, and everything else.

The day after my return home, it was my turn to lead a discussion in the class on Eastern spirituality at Duke Divinity School. St. Nicodemus of the Holy Mountain, an extraordinary eighteenth-century Mt. Athos monk, was my subject. Nicodemus had been largely responsible for the assembling of the written record of Orthodox monasticism now preserved as the *Philokalia*, those four volumes representing this tradition's faith, doctrines, and practices from the fourth through fifteenth centuries. Nicodemus himself was an extreme ascetic even during the Age of Enlightenment. I found him not only eccentric but one of the best informed men of his age, though it would be centuries before his work in gathering and preserving ancient manuscripts was appreciated. Tattered, toothless, and emaciated because of his ascetic practices, he died at sixty but left an immense legacy. Benedictine practice, in comparison, would not have allowed one of its monks to experience such extreme self-denial. A commitment to moderation in all things runs throughout the Rule. I realized that this was rooted in Benedict's understanding of what it takes to live within a stable community. The desert elders were a different breed, and St. Nicodemus lived more like one of them than like the cenobitic monks of his time.

One issue regarding where Alden and I would worship clarified for me while I was away, and I gave up singing in the choir of one congregation to return to my own faith communion in Chapel Hill. In a class on spirituality, I met several people who would become the basis of a community for me within this congregation. I began to attend a midweek alternative service called "Deep and Wide" that included music, a reading followed by a period of contemplative prayer, then gathering around the Communion table to share in the remembrance of Christ through intinction, the dipping of the bread in the common cup. This service felt nourishing and sustaining, and I continued to attend for the remainder of the season.

Holy Week, the most intense and demanding part of the Christian journey, approached, as late in the calendar year as it can be. The date of Easter's movable feast is determined by ancient calendars and cosmic cycles: the first Sunday after the first full moon following the spring equinox (in the northern hemisphere). Eastern Orthodox tradition uses two different ancient calendars, the Julian and the Gregorian, to fix the date of its Easter, usually a week or two after the Western Easter. This year, however, both dates fell on April 24. The date Lent begins is backed up from Easter, forty days plus Sundays. If March seemed to me a long and full month, April seemed even longer, with Easter coming so late.

I resolved this year to go deeper into the passion and crucifixion of Christ than ever before to experience, as had his first disciples, both the depths of despair and the joy of his resurrection. To prepare for Holy Week, my spiritual companions Meg and Mary and I gathered at Mary's home for an overnight retreat. Mary had completed the exquisite small chapel in her backyard converted from a storage shed, a few yards away from the labyrinth I had walked a few weeks earlier. I was eager to spend time with the two of them in this lovely, peaceful place.

As was now our practice we began the day with *lectio divina*, this time on John 14:15–31, a key passage from Jesus' Farewell Discourse the night of his delivery into the hands of his enemies. In it Jesus assures his disciples that he will not abandon them and will send the Advocate, the Spirit of Truth, to abide with them. The beauty of the loving interrelationship among the persons of the Trinity with the human is revealed in this passage, along with the words that never fail to move me: "Peace I leave with you; my peace I give to you. I do not give to you as the world gives. Do not let your hearts be troubled, and do not let them be afraid" (v. 27). The passage concludes with Jesus' declaration of obedience to God's will. "I do as the Father has commanded me, so that the world may know that I love the Father" (v. 31a). The entire passage, but especially these two verses, resonated deeply with me, as they represented the ultimate in self-emptying, *kenosis*, humbling oneself to the point of death in trusting acceptance of the divine purpose. While in our lifetimes we may never fully know or understand this purpose, releasing our fear and attachment to any outcome but God's brings its own deep peace.

That afternoon, as I walked the labyrinth with my two friends, I noticed how the journey inward to the center seemed slower, the pace more uncertain, more deliberate, than the outward return. The path seemed long, full of distractions, twists, and turns. When one finally arrives in the center, drawn into the heart of God, time stands still; yet it is never long enough before the return journey must be made. The way out seems quicker and surer, as the gifts of the first two phases of purification and illumination are integrated and brought back into one's own life and offered for the life of the world.

Following this retreat, my work on the book's outline flowed, and I experienced several vivid dreams, so often reflections of the inner work we are doing. I continued to study the mysteries of the labyrinth, contemplative prayer, and Protestant spirituality. One book on the Ignatian exercises with the spiritual practice of the daily examen seemed especially appropriate as Holy Week approached. Larry Warner's *Journey with Jesus: Discovering the Spiritual Exercises of Saint Ignatius* had a helpful section on walking through Holy Week with Jesus. Warner, a Protestant spiritual director and teacher, grasped how transformative working with the exercises can be. As he says, "The spiritual transformation that God brings about during your journey through the exercises [generally over thirty days or as long as nine months] is the result of time spent with God, not because you have worked your way through the entire Exercises."[1] I found this a useful reminder that however much effort we put into our processes, it is still God's Spirit within us drawing us on, luring us into closer relationship with the subject of our desire. Also, as we are drawn more deeply into Christ's own journey, we realize how much we desire his constant presence within us as our guide and beside us as our companion.

Warner quotes Martin Luther on the transformative power of meditating on Christ: "If one does meditate rightly on the suffering of Christ for a day, an hour, or even a quarter of an hour, this we may confidently say is better than a whole year of fasting, days of Psalm singing, yes, than even one hundred Masses, because this reflection changes the whole man and makes him new, as he was in baptism."[2] It is impossible, as Warner rightly notes, to reflect on the passion of Christ without experiencing his suffering. Protestant churches rarely keep the Suffering Servant before us, since our crosses are empty of the gruesome image of the dying Christ. Our theology and sense of decorum prefer the symbol of Jesus' triumph over death rather than the death itself. The older traditions, Catholic and Orthodox, say something significant about the redemptive quality of suffering. I decided to wear at home during Holy Week the Benedictine crucifix I had been given when I became an oblate candidate, to remind me of Christ's passion.

The Ignatian exercises combine a number of spiritual practices common during Lent, such as fasting. My own fast from sugar and carbs had continued since Epiphany, and I had lost about twenty-five pounds thus far. More importantly, I felt free of food cravings, which carbs and sugar feed, and food ceased to be one of my "eight afflictive thoughts." I also enjoyed being able to get into clothes I hadn't worn for several years.

During the days that preceded Palm Sunday, my son's health and emotional well-being declined. His condition mirrored one of my own challenges during this Holy season, to open my heart ever more deeply to the suffering of others. Remembering Christ's experience and its significance for humankind links us to others' pain and fear but also to faith and hope that through Christ even death will be overcome. Through

1. Warner, *Journey with Jesus*, 208.
2. Ibid., 214.

compassion, it becomes impossible to ignore others' needs while we drift off into dreamy contemplation. The suffering world commands our attention, and we are called to respond.

This reflection reminded me of the revelations of Julian of Norwich, the fourteenth-century English anchorite, who earnestly prayed that God would reveal to her Christ's passion and give her a mortal illness that would allow her to experience the depths of his suffering. Her prayers were answered. On the point of death, a priest came to give her the last rites. He held up to her the crucifix, and as she gazed upon it she had an intense vision of Christ's agonized face. Though she recovered, this haunting vision remained with her all her life, and she was to recall vividly the suffering that Christ undertook to fulfill God's will, writing about it soon afterward and again twenty years later when the illumination she received in that moment clarified for her. We will have more to say about this extraordinary mystic later. When reading about her experience and reflection, my own revelation was that our compassion is not fully engaged unless we can look directly upon the world's suffering and feel it viscerally.

As studies of responses to natural disasters have shown, human capacity to experience compassion for others' pain and loss drops off rapidly, especially if the media lose interest. Sustained compassion is a spiritual discipline to open the heart and keep it open, despite the vicarious pain we suffer. As parents know, their children's suffering is especially hard to bear. Whenever I recall it, I still feel in my gut the shock when my three-year-old son slammed the door on his finger and tore it nearly off, or the time when at five he fell off his bike and broke his jaw. Continuing to watch an adult child suffer is equally difficult. But when we come to love what God loves, we cannot live with the pain that causes us unless we recognize it in Christ's face, as Julian did, and know that God's love is with us and for us through it all. That gives us the strength to keep our hearts open and our generosity flowing in the service of those who need our compassion and help.

On Palm Sunday morning I attended a class on the spiritual journey. It seemed especially appropriate as Holy Week began. In the class was a woman who was to become a friend, a sister of one of the apostolic religious orders and a spiritual director. The worship service with its requisite palm fronds representing the cheering crowds as Jesus entered Jerusalem felt ironic and jarring, in light of how they would turn on him. I remembered other Palm Sundays when we lived in Santa Fe, New Mexico. Members of our congregation would parade through the streets with our palm leaves, singing hymns and gathering in the town plaza with members of the nearby Catholic church. Our coming together represented a foretaste of reconciliation and peace within the body of Christ.

On the day following Palm Sunday I began the actual writing of the book. It felt good to finally begin after the months of preparation, and the timing seemed auspicious. Intending to walk through the week with Jesus, I wondered how he had spent the days after his entry into Jerusalem on the back of a donkey, hardly an entry fit for a king. I imagined that it was devoted to readying himself and those closest to him for the end of his earthly life, preparing his disciples, as is evidenced in John's Gospel in the Farewell Discourses, and praying without ceasing. That's probably what I would have done under the circumstances, if I knew I was going to die. Most responsible, loving people would do this, and I'm sure we all know those who have spent their last days focusing on others' needs and encouraging them to go on living after their loss. Jesus was going to take the full brunt of his crucifixion—no drugs, no hospice, just full on pain, though mercifully shorter in duration than others similarly condemned. Walking with him during the week gives us an opportunity to reflect on how we might choose to spend our last days as well as to imagine ourselves as one of the characters in the drama of the passion, something acted out, preached upon, and sung about for centuries in the church.

I attended as many services as I could that week: the alternative "Deep and Wide" on Tuesday; my final class on eastern spirituality at Duke, followed by the Divinity School's Convocation at which a former seminary professor of mine preached on Wednesday; a Maundy Thursday evening service; and on Good Friday a noon-to-three labyrinth walk at a local congregation and an evening service of Tennabrae. Maundy Thursday, the night of the Last Supper, is often observed in churches with ritual foot-washing, following Jesus' example in John's Gospel. I have found that foot-washing, whether in the giving or receiving, contributes to a sense of humility and serves as a reminder that the last shall be first under the reign of God. Foot-washing is also about ritual purification, as Jesus and the disciples were Jews preparing for Passover, a holy feast day long before Easter came along. I elected to fast from dinner on Maundy Thursday to dinner on Good Friday, a simple acknowledgement of self-denial and self-emptying that is part of a Lenten journey.

The Tennabrae (Latin for darkness or shadows) service is one I find particularly moving. After each passage from Holy Week scriptures is read, the lights in the worship space are dimmed and a candle is extinguished. At the end the sanctuary is dark, symbolic of the light that goes out of the world through human sin. The congregation departs in silence to reflect on Christ's passion. This year I remembered the passage in Matthew's Gospel just after Jesus' arrest: "Then all the disciples deserted him and fled" (Matt 26: 56b). How alone he must have felt! The twelve male disciples during these days were for the most part a sorry lot, betraying, denying, and deserting Jesus, falling asleep during his hour of need when he asked them to watch and wait with him while he prayed in Gethsemane. We can't escape the parallels with our own desertion and denial of Jesus.

Only the women closest to Jesus were faithful throughout his time of trial: Mary, his mother, Mary Magdalene, his beloved companion, and a handful of others who had ministered to his needs. Their stories are now beginning to be told and heard, and there is much to say. The two Marys are among the spiritual masters I honor most, and I thought of them often during this week. How they must have suffered along with him! A replica of the famous Pietà, Mary holding Jesus' broken body after it was removed from the cross, sits on the bookcase in my study, expressing the darkest moment of her life.

The Good Friday labyrinth walk was especially meaningful for me this year. A canvas eleven-circuit labyrinth is offered each year to a local congregation willing to sponsor a community service and walk on Good Friday. I arrived shortly after noon, during the traditional three-hour period of Jesus' passion. A service was underway, and people were already taking their sacred journey through Jesus' final hours on the labyrinth, just as in medieval times. The labyrinth was well situated in the very center of the octagonal sanctuary, visible to all. When a number of people walk at the same time, it is customary to wait until one makes at least the first circuit before beginning, as everyone walks at her or his own pace. Overtaking someone is an option, as some linger at one point or another, and when you meet a person on the path who is returning when you are walking in (remember, there's only one way in and out), it is expected that each of you will move aside to make room for the other.

I stood at the entrance for a moment in silent prayer, asking that whatever I needed to understand about this experience and this sacred journey would be revealed to me during my walk and later in reflection. Then I began to move forward, head down, concentrating on keeping my feet on the path and being open to receive whatever might come. For many, walking this way is a form of meditation or pure prayer.

Stepping toward the center this time seemed to me to represent the journey to spiritual and emotional maturity through one's lifetime, while walking out represented taking all the insights and wisdom of experience and applying them—not reacting in the same ways as in our youth, but surrendering to God, trusting, being grateful in all things, being ready to go home to God, overcoming the fear of loss and death. Walking in felt slower, more wobbly, and I was aware of all of the serpentine turns of the inner and outer circuits. Coming out we expect these obstacles in our path, and our life experience and spiritual maturity allow us to locate detours around them or just to push on through. The journey usually seems longer going in because of all the stops and starts, confusion and uncertainty about where we are on the path. On the return we're more surefooted, used to situations that interrupt our journey or take us in another direction. We can't be linear thinkers while walking the labyrinth or journeying through life. As we start to see the patterns and get the lessons from our life experiences, we recognize that we are not alone on the path. God's Spirit accompanies, encourages, sustains, and draws us ever closer in infinite love.

As I entered the center of the labyrinth on Good Friday, I stood on each of the six petals of the rosette. In medieval times these six interlinked circles at the heart of the labyrinth represented the flower of life, an ancient sacred geometric symbol expressing that all life originates from a common source, our unity in God. The flower is also a metaphor for the mystical rose, representing the sacred heart, love, and the divine feminine. Allegorical meanings were attached to each petal. Some saw them as representing each kingdom or kin-dom: mineral, plant, animal, human, water and air, and finally the church. I stood on each in turn, praying and giving thanks for that kin-dom's place in God's creation. Then I stepped into the center, standing within what represented the very heart of God. I felt a surge of energy, goose bumps all over.

Once in the center, people sometimes sit or lie or find other ways to stay there as long as possible. But when a large group is walking at the same time, we need to step aside for others, also a part of learning to honor and support each other's journeys, not only our own. We encourage them but don't try to control their pace or push them through their stuck places. We may be on the same journey but each experience of it is unique, as is each soul. Walking the labyrinth parallels the soul's journey toward God, each circuit standing for another stage of life.

This journey on the labyrinth on Good Friday, surrounded by music, candles, and the spiritual energy of those walking the circuits, felt perfect to me, all in divine order. When I exited and gave thanks for all I had received, I also remembered that one tangible, embodied effect of walking is to balance the left and right hemispheres of the brain.

Before leaving the church, I moved around the interior of the sanctuary, where an exhibit was displayed of paintings in which Mary Magdalene appeared. This extraordinary collection of more than twenty prints through the ages reinforced for me her seminal role as the apostle of apostles. Her role remains hidden in plain sight within the Canonical Gospels but is also clearly revealed in the *Gospel of Philip*, part of the Nag Hammadi texts discovered in Egypt in 1945, and the *Gospel of Mary*, discovered in 1896. (The early church had made her, until the Vatican recently overturned its own dictum, a fallen woman, and much of the art portrays her as a penitent sinner rather than arguably the most spiritually advanced among Jesus' disciples.) The other prominent woman in Jesus' life, Mary, his mother, is considered a perpetual virgin by the Roman Catholic and Orthodox traditions. Mary is deserving of great veneration whether or not she was literally a virgin throughout her lifetime because at a deep spiritual level the church understood her role as the *Theotokos,* the God-bearer, representing the ultimate in receptivity to God's will. With her trusting acceptance, humility, and willingness to be an instrument of divine purpose, Mother Mary deserves our reverence and gratitude for her unique role. That kind of symbolic virginity links to purity of heart and is part of what we discover within ourselves on our journey to God. Mary Magdalene also deserves our veneration for her role as a great apostle of Christ, I mused, as I reflected on these works of art.

Earlier, on Good Friday morning, I had spent an extended time in meditation, imagining Jesus' passion, when an insight came to me. I was thinking about Jesus' final act of *kenosis*, the emptying of himself even unto death on the cross so that he truly experienced the death of the ego, what we humans experience as the self. I thought about how humiliating his experience would have been to any of us: wrongly accused, stripped nearly naked, tortured, paraded in front of jeering mobs, without a word of protest. I imagined him hanging on the cross, his physical body exposed to the elements and to the taunting crowd. In excruciating pain, he offered up his life willingly and without reserve. With a shock, I imagined even his physical body self-emptying in death, his bladder and bowels releasing as happens with the dead, dribbling down his legs along with the blood and other bodily fluids from his pierced side.

In death we have no defenses. Our bodies are shells of flesh empty even of our soul. The broken body that Mary holds draped across her lap in the Pietà, the body of her beloved friend that Mary Magdalene saw removed from the cross by Joseph of Arimithea and his men, must have been a horrific site to behold. When the Marys and other women close to Jesus showed up at his tomb in the Gospel accounts to anoint his body, still in shock from witnessing his death, they prepared to lovingly lay out, cleanse, and wrap the body for burial. That's what families did for thousands of years and still do in many parts of the world. Only we squeamish types whose faith is not fully embodied shy away from such tasks.

It is difficult when we've seen the body of a loved one in death to get that picture out of our heads, especially when the death is a traumatic one, as this was. The most recent death I witnessed of someone I loved was my mother's. She didn't look like herself in death, at least to me, her spark of life now completely gone. It had begun to leave some years earlier, as her mind failed and she suffered from dementia. For an intelligent, active woman through most of her ninety-three years, I thought at the time of her death how degrading it is for the mind to go, and then to have no control over the body, either. Maybe that's a gift, I had reflected later, that the mind doesn't stick around to see the body fail. I sang to her in those last hours before her death, everything I could think of that she might connect with: old hymns, popular songs, even a couple of tunes I'd composed in high school, just so that she'd have something familiar to journey with her to the other side. She was a person of great faith all of her life, and I'm sure that she was accompanied and welcomed by a heavenly host when at last her moment came.

For Jesus, that moment of death ultimately became a transition to a new life, as it is and will be for all of us. Even now, as we do our own releasing and self-emptying, we experience those moments of awareness when the ego with its incessant needs breathes its last, and we are free to be, if only for a moment, fully present to and with God.

As I prayed that Good Friday morning following this vivid, startling meditation, I asked God to spare me the loss of memory and self-control that I observed in my mother. Yet, if that is the way it happens, I accept it in advance. Acceptance is my only choice in the matter. I also prayed for loving people to surround and care for me in my final days. So may it be for all of God's creatures.

As Good Friday passed into Saturday, I realized that the Protestant tradition lacks rituals for this day when Jesus is passing from death to new life. In fact, I've heard it said many times that Christians who don't attend worship or walk through Holy Week with Jesus move too easily from Palm Sunday to Easter, going from one celebration to another, experiencing the heights but not the depths of this holiest of weeks.

Catholics and the Orthodox have ritualized through their liturgies virtually every aspect of the Passion of Christ. On my way to the church where the labyrinth was available on Good Friday, I observed a small crowd walking the familiar fourteen Stations of the Cross, the *Via Dolorosa* or the Way of Sorrow, on the grounds of the local Catholic church. I would have stopped to join them, but it happened to be pouring at the time. I remembered walking the *Via Dolorosa* in the old city of Jerusalem eighteen years earlier, my feet on the same path that Jesus may have taken on his way to Golgotha. In most Catholic and many Episcopal and Lutheran churches, the stations ring the walls of the worship space, inviting meditation on Jesus' final journey in this life, but especially on Good Friday.

Like the labyrinth, the stations are a kind of pilgrimage to Jerusalem. They date from the late medieval period and are attributed to the Franciscan Order, which created stations at sacred sites for hundreds of years. The traditional fourteen include a few "almost Bible" stations, like the one where a woman named Veronica was said to have wiped Jesus' brow with her veil. According to legend, his face imprinted itself on the cloth. The veil became a holy relic, known as the Vernicle of Rome, supposedly housed at St. Peter's Cathedral since the eighth century. Yet I have been in at least one other European cathedral that claimed to have a piece of that veil. Perhaps Veronica represents the kindness of the unnamed women who served Jesus throughout history. At any rate, as recently as 2007, Pope Benedict XVI approved an alternative to the traditional stations, the "Scriptural Way of the Cross," which moves from Jesus praying in the Garden of Gethsemane on Maundy Thursday through all the scriptural references for the events of Good Friday. Many beautiful works of art have been created as stations of the cross, and recollection, prayer, meditation, and repentance are very much in order as the faithful stand in front of each of these, praying and walking with Jesus through his passion.

Most of the Catholic world offers the experience of Triduum during Holy Week, the three days from Maundy Thursday evening through Easter evening. The observance includes a Saturday night vigil, as worshipers watch and pray with Jesus, accompanying him through the darkness of his betrayal, crucifixion, and burial until he rises again in the light of Easter's dawn. Just as many Protestant churches at the end of the Maundy Thursday service strip the sanctuary of liturgical cloths and banners or drape the cross with a purple cloth to represent the darkness of the world without Jesus' light, so the Easter eve vigil is generally conducted in near darkness and silence, a most profound experience for all who attend. Although seldom spoken about, this is the period known as the Harrowing of Hell, when Jesus traditionally was believed to have descended into hell, that place where the damned experience eternal separation from God, and returned having conquered death. Those destined for eternal life but still in that in-between place known as purgatory were released from bondage to sin and death through Jesus' own saving death and resurrection. The restoration and reconciliation of the dead to new life in Christ is a basic tenet of the Christian faith, and the Triduum vigil during this period commemorates this.

Eastern Orthodoxy is also rich in Holy Week tradition and liturgy. The Divine Liturgy itself reveals the Orthodox understanding of Christ's passion, or Pascha. The day before Palm Sunday honors Christ's raising of Lazarus from the dead, a prefiguration of his own resurrection and that of the faithful. On Wednesday of Holy Week, the Eastern church celebrates the Mysterion of the Holy Unction, one of the seven sacraments. This is a form of repentance and confession, of self-purification in preparation for Easter. On Holy Thursday, twelve Gospel readings act as reminders of the events of the passion and are often dramatized by the removal of a statue of Christ from the cross, wrapping his body in a shroud, and placing him in a sepulcher. After the Saturday night vigil, the darkness in the sanctuary begins at midnight to move toward light, starting with an Easter candle. The Orthodox do claim that their centuries-old unbroken traditions represent the earliest forms of Christian worship, so at least reading about them or, better, attending parts of the Divine Liturgy would be enlightening (pun intended!).

This year the journey through Lent felt like an extended self-examen that called to mind whatever I still needed to release as well as what I did not want to take in that might prevent me from approaching God through Christ on Easter. Both these sides of self-emptying—releasing the desires and attachments that separate us from God and allowing ourselves to be empty of desire for everything except God alone—are essential for the process of purification of the heart.

Easter finally arrived on April 24. Over the years I attended many sunrise services, celebrating the return of the light through Jesus' resurrection, but this year my husband and I went instead to a congregational breakfast followed by an uplifting worship service. I've always loved the drama of this day, celebrated in the liturgy with especially glorious music and a sense of joy. The service begins with the oldest confession of our faith, "Christ is risen!" The congregation responds, "He is risen, indeed!" The Christian church's greatest festival brought me a special joy this year for having walked intentionally through the darkness of the week, reflecting on my own failings that keep me from fully experiencing the light and love of Christ. Easter is like a renewal of marriage or religious vows, when we celebrate with renewed commitment Christ's sacrifice and God's saving love for us.

My Easter high didn't last long. Two days later I found out about a friend's crisis, which shocked and saddened me. I committed to surrounding her and the situation with love and light, again trusting that God would take care of her. This instance of falling from the height, the moment of illumination experienced on Easter, back into everyday reality felt like a test of my trust in God. Since we can't remain on the mountain top—the symbolic place for the inbreaking of God's reign into the realm of the human—we need to be able to function spiritually on a high level even in the midst of life's messiness. I was reminded that the reign of God is both here and not yet here, and that God works with each of us as we are ready to help bring about God's kin-dom on earth.

A couple of weeks later I elected to make a quick weekend trip back to St. Benedict's Monastery for an Oblate Day, since I hadn't attended one there before. It felt good to be back at St. Ben's, and as I took my accustomed seat in the oratory to pray with the sisters, a sense of peace and joy came over me. During this brief stay I was able to spend a little time renewing acquaintances as well as meeting a few of the oblates and enjoying an informative talk on the Rule of Benedict given by a sister who teaches at the college. An overnight in Minneapolis with my friend Sally ended a good weekend, and I arrived home on Monday ready to return to my writing.

Tom still wasn't feeling well, and later in May I had to cancel going with my husband to our granddaughter's college graduation to stay home with him. Again, the movement from a high to a challenge seemed to be an emerging pattern, and I released my disappointment and looked on the bright side: a couple of extra days to write.

One day in early June the thermostat reached 96 degrees. It had become my practice to stop work around 3:30, feed and toss balls for the dog, then walk the cul-de-sac as my daily exercise. The dog had sense enough to retreat into the air conditioning while I walked, but I persisted and began to feel that I was regaining some of my lost muscle tone and endurance. Caring for my physical well-being was now an important spiritual discipline for me. My lengthy fast continued, and by now I had dropped close to forty pounds without any desire for those foods I had eliminated from my diet. I was grateful for the grace in this extended fast.

On June 5 St. Benedict's Monastery installed its new prioress. Elected after an extensive discernment process by her peers, Sister Michaela Hedican would serve a six-year term as spiritual and administrative head of the monastery. The community was excited about their new prioress and held a joyful celebration following ancient traditions but with a modern touch. From videos and photos I saw later, the event couldn't have been more beautiful and uplifting. One ritual is for each sister to come forward and place her hands between those of the prioress, as a symbol of acceptance of and submission to her authority as Christ's representative. Obedience to God in all things is strongly emphasized in Benedict's Rule, and this symbolic expression of that obedience was very moving. I rejoiced for the community.

The date before Pentecost, a friend and I went to nearby Greensboro to attend a workshop on contemplative prayer given by one of the three Trappist founders of contemporary centering prayer, Father William Meninger. He was a delight, and his simple approach to this form of pure prayer renewed my own enthusiasm for it. That evening I began to read one of his books, *A Loving Search for God*, his commentary on the fourteenth-century mystical classic, *The Cloud of Unknowing*, and to reread *The Cloud*. That inspired me to read more of the classics of mysticism in the medieval and Renaissance periods, which will illumine later chapters for us.

Eastertide, the fifty-day season of Easter, ended on June 12 with Pentecost, which some call the birthday of the Christian church. The Thursday before Pentecost is traditionally celebrated in the older, more liturgical traditions as Ascension Day. In chapter 14 of John's Gospel, Jesus promises to send the Advocate, the Spirit of Truth, to guide the disciples and the newly forming church after he leaves them. The time between Easter and Ascension in the liturgical calendar is the period of Christ's resurrection appearances, during which he further prepares the disciples to carry on without his physical presence. Called the Pentecostarian by Orthodox Christians, this period commemorates the glorification of Christ, paralleling Lent, the preparation for Easter.

Moving from the liturgical purple of Lent through Easter's pure white drapings and vestments to the flaming red of Pentecost is a journey in itself. Usually the post-resurrection appearances are the subjects of sermons and homilies during this time. My own favorite is found in John 21, where Jesus joins those disciples who have returned to their homes in Galilee and occupy themselves once again with fishing. They catch nothing until Jesus appears on the shore and encourages them to cast the net once more. Their nets full to breaking, they recognize their Lord in this lavish abundance of grace. It is time for the seeds he planted in them to bear fruit. If they love him they are to feed his sheep, those starved for his living water, his intimate presence and love.

At Pentecost, the disciples gathered in Jerusalem are baptized with the Holy Spirit and become apostles ready to carry Christ's message, that the kingdom of God is at hand, to the ends of the earth. From this time forward, all who love Jesus are fed the sacred meal, his body and blood, in the church's celebration of the Eucharist.

Pentecost, the highest-energy festival in the life of the church with its roaring wind and dancing flames, is liturgically symbolized by the red of the fire as Jesus' promise to send an Advocate is fulfilled. God's Spirit creates the true beloved community, and its description in Acts is inspiring and amazing. Yet there are those who out of fear and ignorance continue to make fearful decisions to act in their own selfish interests rather than those of the community, like Ananias and Sapphira, whose deadly punishment is swift and extreme (Acts 5:1–11). Everything that happens in these first few chapters of Acts seems high-energy and exaggerated. When Pentecost comes, fasten your seat belts!

The sermon in my home church that day was preached by a fiery young associate minister with just the right touch of enthusiasm. He reminded us of the birth of the charismatic, "full gospel" Pentecostal movement within Christianity over a hundred years old on the West Coast. Based upon the original Pentecost's baptism of the faithful by the Holy Spirit and the speaking in tongues that followed, the charismatic Christians embody the movement of the Spirit through God's people, opening hearts and filling them with the spiritual gifts to share with one another. The message and energy of the service were uplifting, and I felt revived. The freedom of the Spirit of God to go where it will and choose whom it will to carry on the work of Christ is awe inspiring. Nothing or no one can prevail against it. That felt exhilarating!

This year Pentecost also signaled for me the end of another quarter in the calendar and the liturgical year, bringing this intense and dramatic period in the life of the church and my ongoing purification process to a close. Inflamed with God's love and Christ's example, I resolved to keep the fire lit within me for inspiration. On the spiritual journey, just as Easter represents the completion of the purification stage, so Pentecost represents illumination. It was now time to integrate all that I had experienced and to move into the center of the labyrinth.

EIGHT

Resting in the Heart of God

The light shines in the darkness, and the darkness did not overcome it.

—John 1:5

By the tender mercy of our God, the dawn from on high will break upon us, to give light to those who sit in darkness and in the shadow of death, and to guide our feet into the way of peace.

—Luke 1:78–79 (*Benedictus* or "Canticle of Zechariah")

Trinity!! Higher than any being, any divinity, any goodness!
Guide of Christians in the wisdom of heaven!
Lead us up beyond unknowing and light,
up to the farthest, highest peak of mystic scripture,
where the mysteries of God's Word lie simple, absolute, and unchangeable
in the brilliant darkness of a hidden silence.
Amid the deepest shadow they pour overwhelming light
on what is most manifest.
Amid the wholly unsensed and unseen they completely fill our sightless minds
with treasures beyond all beauty.

—Pseudo-Dionysius the Areopagite,
The Mystical Theology, early sixth century

AS WE MOVE INTO the illumination stage of the spiritual journey, we must speak first of darkness and light, not as duality but as divine presence. The "brilliant darkness" of the unfathomable God of whom Pseudo-Dionysius speaks and the "uncreated light" seen by Eastern Orthodox spiritual masters describe the same phenomenon: out of complete darkness comes complete light, fully dark and fully light at the same time, as God's presence for a brilliant moment is revealed to the

135

inner spiritual being. Always at God's initiative, the presence makes itself known and then fades back into hiddenness. What remains is an indelible imprint on the human heart and soul of unspeakable majesty, power, and love. Awe—holy fear—and wonder are the natural responses of the human who has experienced a theophany, a direct experience of God.

When God's light breaks upon us, it signifies divine presence, a moment of grace, the inbreaking of the kingdom into the now, a foretaste of the eternal life with God that is yet to come. Those graced with an experience of illumination find themselves transformed. Spiritual transformation enables us to see the divine in everything and to radiate, like Moses' face as he descended from the holy mountain, the light of God's presence. While rare and fleeting, an illumination experience is never forgotten. Human effort cannot bring it about, but the traditions see it as a fruit of purification of the heart, the release of attachments that no longer serve us in our spiritual journeys and the acquiring of the virtues that do. In extreme cases, like Paul's Damascus Road experience in Acts 9, a moment of illumination may itself be the transforming act that results in a purified heart, for the heart is the place of transformation. Such a moment is a great gift, not to be sought but to be treasured.

In the center of our being, the heart is the still point, the site of our spiritual connection with the God within and the place where we discover revealed our interconnection and resonance with the whole creation. Reaching the singleness of an undivided heart devoted to God, the purified are ready to see God. They are illumined.

The great archetypal labyrinth of Chartres Cathedral embodies in its symbolism this spiritual movement to the center. To reach that place is to rest in the heart of God. The six-petaled rosette, in addition to representing the kin-doms of God's creation, stands for the six days of creation itself. The telluric energies of that sacred site, one of the most energetically charged places on earth, heighten the accessibility of the divine energies. They are palpable, especially while walking the labyrinth. The nearby presence of the famous black Madonna, who represents the divine feminine, attests to this. She is treated with great devotion. Sensing a strong energetic field around her, I have felt more than once in her presence that I was about to levitate. The sacred geometry of the church unites heaven, symbolized by the circle of the labyrinth, with earth, symbolized by the square through which one moves to approach the altar. The labyrinth was laid so that one approaches the center from west to east, signifying the movement from darkness to light. All the spiritual knowledge revealed to the designers and master builders of this mystical treasure was drawn upon to create a temple in stone, a chamber of resonance of sound with the highest divine light through which creation was spoken into being.

These days this great labyrinth at the heart of the cathedral is usually covered with chairs, which may only be removed with special permission, and pilgrims are not permitted to rest in the center but urged to keep moving. Only once was I there with a group allowed to walk this sacred path. Pilgrims of old sometimes walked it on their knees as penance for their sins, often during Lent, to prepare for the great rebirth of Easter. Now we remove our shoes before entering it, for the place we walk on is holy ground. I can think of few more awe-inspiring experiences than traveling the sacred labyrinth of Chartres. The day our group completed our walk the setting sun began to stream light through the great stained glass windows. We huddled together on the street as a sexton threw open the huge eastern doors so that we might view this breathtaking spectacle of God's illuminating the darkness with the holy light of presence. Words cannot describe the miracle of that moment, or of any moment when the brilliant darkness pierces our limited vision and reveals its radiance and mystery.

As we explore the nature and experience of illumination for Christians through the ages, we must look first to Jesus, the light of the world, God-with-us, for glimpses of this heavenly light. Before his birth the angel Gabriel announces to Mary that she will conceive a son by God's grace through the power of the Holy Spirit. Her modest and humble response, "Here am I, the servant of the Lord; let it be with me according to your word" (Luke 1:38), is a perfect illustration of the pure heart and illumined soul, emptied of all desire except to serve divine love, accepting in trust what she does not understand.

The actual theophany, the manifestation of divine presence that results in Jesus' conception, is not shared in the Gospels, but two others are. The first occurs at Jesus' baptism. The Holy Spirit descends in the form of a dove, while a voice from heaven speaks to Jesus, saying, "You are my Son, the Beloved; with you I am well pleased" (Luke 3:22). In Matthew's Gospel Jesus sees the Spirit's descent (3:16–17) and hears the voice, while in Mark (1:10–11), Jesus also sees the heavens open as the Spirit comes to rest upon him and hears similar words. In all three of these accounts, it appears that only Jesus experiences the theophany, although in Matthew's the heavenly voice may have been heard by others. While John's Gospel alludes to the baptism, it is not recounted. Other slight differences exist among the Synoptic versions of Jesus' baptism, but all make it clear that God's favor rests upon Jesus and that God claims him as Son. The presence of the Holy Spirit completes this Trinitarian theophany for the first time as Jesus prepares to begin his ministry.

The second theophany in the Gospels, the transfiguration of Jesus, connects the spiritual leaders of his Jewish ancestors, Moses, the lawgiver, and Elijah, the prophet, to Christ, who now appears within this illumination to an inner circle of disciples. The presence alongside Jesus of the two Old Testament figures, both of whom had been graced with their own theophanies, elevates and expands this God manifestation and prefigures the resurrection of Christ.

It is little wonder that the disciples' privileged yet startling experience leaves them dumbfounded. Iconic portrayals of the transfiguration by the Eastern Orthodox generally show Peter, James, and John so blinded by the light that streams from the illumined countenance of the Christ and surrounds the whole scene that they fall down in fear. Peter must have seen and recognized the figures of Moses and Elijah around the Christ, for he blurts out his desire to build dwellings for them so that they may all stay in this *kairos* moment as long as possible. In Matthew's Gospel (17:5), a voice from a cloud speaks, as at Jesus' baptism: "This is my Son, the Beloved; with him I am well pleased; listen to him."

Although these disciples have remained close to Jesus throughout his ministry, until that moment they only believed that he was who they thought he was. Now they knew, through direct experience. That is characteristic of illumination moments. Belief turns to direct knowing. That knowing may be beyond human comprehension, as it was for Mother Mary, but the heart knows that it has been irrevocably changed. From that moment forward, as Jesus completed his journey into Jerusalem to accept his sacrificial death, the disciples had this precious experience to draw upon to nourish them through the dark days ahead. As with the baptism theophany, all three Synoptic Gospels carry the transfiguration accounts, underscoring its significance for both Jesus, now seen as the Christ, the Messiah, and those who will carry the good news of God-with-us to a world in great need of hope.

Blinding light and ethereal voices often seem to accompany these sudden, inexplicable experiences of illumination. Paul's story as recounted in Acts 26 is one of the most dramatic. Traveling the Damascus Road in pursuit of Jesus' followers he saw "a light from heaven, brighter than the sun, shining around me and my companions" (26:13). Literally blinded, he falls to the ground, like the disciples at the transfiguration, and hears a voice speaking in Hebrew, who identifies himself as Jesus. In this post-resurrection theophany, Jesus assigns Saul, the quintessential Jewish Pharisee, the special mission of becoming the apostle to the Gentiles, so that "they may turn from darkness to light" (26:18), just as Paul himself has done. Now that's a transforming experience! The zealous Pharisee who persecutes Jesus' followers himself becomes a chief apostle, whose words forever shaped the message and mission of the Christian Church. But first Saul, now Paul, requires an extensive period of recovery in which his mind and senses must align with what pierces his heart and spirit to the core of his being.

The more dramatic the illumination, it seems, the more dramatic the transformation that takes place. The post-resurrection appearances of Jesus in the four Gospels similarly transform belief to knowing for those who had followed him throughout his ministry and had been his beloved companions. Even Mary Magdalene, possibly his closest companion, did not expect the risen Christ to appear to her in the garden near the empty tomb on Easter morning (John 20). The disciples on the road to Emmaus only recognized him as their hearts burned within them and through the breaking of the bread in his presence (Luke 24). The disciples, hiding out in a room in Jerusalem to escape persecution themselves, did not recognize their Lord in his altered appearance, and Thomas needed even more reassurance than the others that this apparition who glided through a locked door was indeed the risen Christ (John 20). So if those closest to him had a hard time recognizing him, how likely is it that we will, if ever we are blessed with our own moments of illumination?

Many throughout the ages have experienced divine presence directly, and each of their stories is unique, yet with similar characteristics. The spiritual transformation that follows such experiences may not immediately be discernible, even to the one involved. Generally, it continues over time, as the indelible experience is lived into. A few of the better known instances described by the illumined of the church may shed more light—literally—on these moments of transcendence.

Gregory the Great's classic biography of St. Benedict (really a hagiography, mingling fact with legend) recounts a particular illumination that occurred late in Benedict's life. Gregory, pope from 590–603, himself became a saint and is considered a reliable source, writing within fifty years of Benedict's death in 547. *The Life of St. Benedict* appears in the second volume of Gregory's *Dialogues*. According to this account, Benedict was praying one night at his monastery in Monte Cassino, Italy, when "he suddenly saw a light pour down that routed all the shadows. It shone with such splendor that it surpassed daylight, even though it was *shining in the darkness* [italics mine]. A wonderful thing followed in this vision, for, as Benedict reported later, the whole world was brought before his eyes as if collected in a single ray of sunlight. As the venerable father gazed intently in the dazzling splendor of this light, he saw the soul of Germanus, bishop of Capua, carried to heaven in a fireball by angels."[1] Benedict then called for a fellow monk, who also caught a brief glimpse of this light and was stunned by it. Later it was confirmed that Germanus had indeed passed from this life into the next at the moment Benedict had seen.

Gregory explains that

> to a person who sees the Creator, every creature looks narrow by comparison . . . For the capacity of the mind is expanded by the light of interior contemplation. It is so enlarged by God that it becomes greater than the world. Indeed, the soul becomes greater than itself through contemplation. For when the contemplative soul is ravished by the light of God it is dilated. When it looks down in its elevated state it understands the insignificance of things in a way it could not when it remained below . . . Thus to that light that lights things for the exterior eyes, there corresponds an interior light in the mind.[2]

Gregory's explanation is as interesting as Benedict's cosmic vision itself. It reminds me of Dr. Edgar Mitchell's transformative experience when this Apollo astronaut saw earth from outer space and had an epiphany, a brilliant moment of insight, that changed his life. That insight has borne great fruit, for when he returned to Earth, Mitchell began his

1. Kardong, trans., 131–33.
2. Ibid., 133.

own deep engagement with the intersection of science and spirituality, which resulted in the creation of the Institute of Noetic Sciences, among other endeavors.

The vision that is "so enlarged by God that it becomes greater than the world" has figured in others' illumination experiences as well. One thinks of the mystic Julian of Norwich's sixteen revelations when she was thirty in 1374, which she contemplated for the remainder of her life. In the fourth revelation, Julian speaks of the Lord (Jesus) showing her

> something small, no bigger than a hazelnut, lying in the palm of my hand, and I perceived that it was as round as any ball. I looked at it and thought: What can this be? And I was given this general answer: It is everything which is made . . . It lasts and always will, because God loves it; and thus everything has being through the love of God. In this little thing I saw three properties. The first is that God made it, the second that he loves it, and the third is that God preserves it.

Through this showing, Julian perceives in her typically Trinitarian understanding that "God is the Creator and the lover and the protector" of all that is.[3]

Julian presents us with not only an extended experience of illumination but reflections on the meaning of these revelations as she continued to contemplate them over twenty years. Her showings are thus a particularly rich source of the interaction between the human and divine. Her reflections on her showings reveal that, although she is schooled in the teachings of fourteenth-century Catholic beliefs and doctrines, she is somewhat mystified by the gap between her experience and theological understandings. The monastic division between theology or scholasticism and spirituality had begun to expand in the late Middle Ages. Julian, however, isolated in her cell next to the Church of St. Julian, from which she takes her name, in Norwich, England, teaches those who knock at her cell's window to receive spiritual counseling through her own direct experience. Her knowledge is of the heart and the spirit rather than the mind, and it feels authentic, despite its incongruence with the church's doctrines in her own time as well as ours. She identifies differences between her perceptions and church dogma and puzzles over them but does not attempt to resolve them. This signifies her purity of heart and deep acceptance of the mysteries revealed to her.

3. Julian of Norwich, *Showings,* 130–32.

The enlarged perspectives gained through these divine encounters are plain to see. Skipping forward a few centuries to more modern examples, we find two additional contemplatives with mystical tendencies in John Wesley and Thomas Merton. John Wesley's luminous experience has been recounted often. In 1738, three days after Pentecost, the church's celebration of its illumination by the Holy Spirit, John Wesley had his own transformational experience of God. He wrote in his journal:

> In the evening I went very unwillingly to a society in Aldersgate street, where one was reading Luther's Preface to the Epistle to the Romans. About a quarter before nine, while he was describing the change God works in the heart through faith in Christ, I felt my heart strangely warmed. I felt I did trust in Christ, Christ alone for my salvation, and an assurance was given me that he had taken away *my* sins, even *mine*, and saved *me* from the law of sin and death.[4]   *Mine happened Dec 13, 2003 at confession with Fr. Malachy at monastery od 14.5 longer Ght*

This heartfelt experience of transformation led Wesley further down the path of the purified heart and gave his ministry a fuller, more spiritual focus. One considerable fruit of this became the eventual formation of the Methodist Church. His brother, Charles, who had a similar experience, wrote about this in the popular hymn "O for a Heart to Praise My God." The fourth verse describes his purified heart: "A heart in everything renewed,/And full of love divine/Perfect and right, and pure, and good,/A copy, Lord, of thine."[5]

The writing of Thomas Merton, a Trappist monk well known for his spiritual journey from a misspent youth to a contemplative hermit, is widely studied. Merton also had a life-transforming moment of illumination somewhat similar to that of Wesley. Merton's monastery, Gethsemane, the Trappist mother house near Bardstown, Kentucky, is not far from Louisville, where this insight took place. I know the spot where it occurred well, as Louisville is the headquarters of the Presbyterian Church (USA), and I have visited there many times, staying in hotels near the corner of Fourth and Walnut, now marked with a plaque commemorating Merton's experience. Merton described it as follows:

4. Wright, *Sacred Heart,* 67.
5. Ibid., 67–68.

In Louisville, at the corner of Fourth and Walnut, in the center of the shopping district, I was suddenly overwhelmed with the realization that I loved all those people, that they were mine and I theirs, that we could not be alien to one another even though we were total strangers. It was like waking from a dream of separateness, of spurious self-isolation in a special world, the world of renunciation and supposed holiness . . . This sense of liberation from an illusory difference was such a relief and such a joy to me that I almost laughed out loud . . . I have the immense joy of being man, a member of a race in which God Himself became incarnate. As if the sorrows and stupidities of the human condition could overwhelm me, now I realize what we all are. And if only everybody could realize this! But it cannot be explained. There is no way of telling people that they are all walking around shining like the sun . . . Then it was as if I suddenly saw the secret beauty of their hearts, the depths of their hearts, where neither sin nor desire nor self-knowledge can reach, the core of their reality, the person that each one is in God's eyes. If only they could all see themselves as they really are. If only we could see each other that way all the time.[6]

(handwritten margin note: Metamorfosis from feeling as low as a worm, through the cocoon of conversion to the feeling of as free as a butterfly.)

God broke into Thomas Merton's life on an ordinary day in 1958 on a busy street corner and enabled him to experience through God's eyes God's great love for humanity. This beautiful illumination confirmed for Merton, and for us, that such luminous experiences are not limited to monastic cells or churches but may occur anywhere in the midst of our lives.

I have had a few more modest experiences than these, which felt like the inbreaking of the divine. I mention one here because it was so unexpected and profound for me. This happened in 1991, a time when I was very engaged in my business, community activities, and local church. One day I had to slow down, as I wasn't feeling well, and lay on the sofa to watch an old movie. In this film a minister leaves his congregation to become a wartime fighter pilot. As he walks down a rural road in Korea, a wise elder who sees into his heart reveals to him his true identity: "I see you are a man of God." Both in the film and in my life, that perception triggered a profound shift. All of a sudden I felt downloaded with a complete knowing, a certainty, that I was to drop what I was doing and serve God through the professional ministry. Only once in my life, a few months earlier, had that idea even remotely entered my

6. Merton, *Conjectures of a Guilty Bystander*, 156–57.

mind. As I observed an older woman who served our congregation as associate pastor, I wistfully thought that I might have become a minister but now, at 48, was too old. God apparently didn't think so.

Over the next few days, as I found out what I had to do to become an ordained minister, I asked for confirmation that this call to ministry was for real. The confirmation came in several ways. The most dramatic was that one morning upon awakening I felt pinned to the bed by an immense power. From the depths of my being I responded without thought, "Your obedient servant, Lord; your obedient servant, Lord," and after a few minutes the power left me.

After that I didn't look back. I felt I had no choice but to obey, no matter that this claim on my life cost me my business, involved a weekly 600-mile round-trip commute to seminary, and called for the gracious forbearance of my recently retired husband. It brought with it a profound sense of humility and awe. Later, when I completed seminary and the denomination's preparation for ministry process, I felt that awe and humility again, coupled with inexpressible joy, as I was ordained in my home church on June 5, 1994. During the ordination, the weight of that powerful force fell on me again as I knelt in front of the sanctuary, when all the ordained ministers, elders, and deacons in our large congregation came forward and laid hands on me—head, shoulders, arms, and back— a weight that signified the gravity of what I had undertaken through the grace of God and the help of many along the way.

While illuminating moments such as the ones described are not uncommon for serious seekers of God, they are normally few and far between. True illumination, as taught by those who have experienced it or known those who have, is deeper and more advanced on the spiritual journey than we have yet gone. To explore this level of illumination we are guided by several well-known contemplatives and mystics.

John of the Cross, a Spanish Carmelite monk (1542–1591), is best known for his *Dark Night of the Soul,* a narrative poem with commentary that describes the soul's journey toward union with God. St. John identifies the soul's three stages, corresponding to those of the spiritual journey we have been exploring: beginner, progressive, and proficient. Those at the progressive stage have moved through purification and are being drawn by God into the way of illumination through which God "feeds and refreshes the soul"[7] before taking it through the next dark night it must endure before being truly illumined.

7. Peers, trans., *Dark Night of the Soul,* no pagination.

John notes that proficients, those well on their way toward union with God, still have two kinds of imperfection. The first includes habits and affections that still remain unpurified and, as they are deeply rooted, are harder to eradicate. The second, actual imperfections, range from fanciful spiritual visions to spiritual sins of another order from those encountered on the first stage of the journey. Before a soul may reach union with God it must be tested and refined through this dark night phase. John defines its essence as "an inflowing of God into the soul, which purges it from its ignorances and imperfections, habitual, natural and spiritual, and which is called by contemplatives [including Teresa of Avila] infused contemplation, or mystical theology." He goes on to say that "God secretly teaches the soul and instructs it in perfection of love without its doing anything, or understanding of what manner is this infused contemplation. Inasmuch as it is the loving wisdom of God, God produces striking effects in the soul for, by purging and illumining it, He prepares it for the union of love with God."

As we saw in the Pseudo-Dionysius text that heads this chapter, this "infused contemplation" takes place in the "brilliant darkness" of God's illuminating light penetrating through clouded, blinded human understanding. When the soul has experienced all the trials of this purgation, it is then filled with the divine light.

At this stage, God reveals to the soul the spiritual sins that must be replaced by their corresponding virtues before it can move on. This revelation chastens the soul and causes it great grief. It also experiences the dark night as spiritual dryness, like the sin of *acedia* or apathy we encountered in the writings of the desert elders. What the soul had perceived as spiritual consolations or gifts of the Spirit are replaced by desolations, such as feelings of abandonment and grief, during the dark night. This difficult period of trial is only for those who can endure this further transformation because they truly desire to overcome their own remaining faults and learn to desire God for God's sake alone, not for their own selfish purposes.

In reading John's descriptions of the seven spiritual sins of this stage, I realized that I had committed them all at one point or another on my journey. Spiritual pride, greed, luxury, wrath, gluttony, envy, and sloth are not sensual, as on the physical level. Rather they are the result of trying too hard to be esteemed by self, others, and even God, or of believing oneself farther along the path than one actually is. We become so enamored of our spiritual life that we cut off those we think aren't spiritually at our level, or obsess about finding the time to complete our spiritual practices instead of being present to the people in our lives who need us, or get discouraged when we imagine that God isn't responsive to our prayers. I have experienced all of these, and reading John of the Cross brought clarity and tears of compunction when I reflected on my own shortcomings. This act brought its own solace, through God's mercy, for we are meant to come to this point on our path and allow God to further cleanse and refine our hearts and spirits. We must also humbly accept that we will not be completely free of these spiritual sins in our lifetimes.

These shortcomings are meant to be replaced during the dark night by the seven spiritual virtues: pride by humility, greed by simplicity, wrath by contentment, luxury by peace, gluttony by moderation, envy by joy, and sloth by strength. Unless we allow God to work within us at God's initiative, we will remain blind to our own lack of inner light.

Encountering the spiritual sins after a long period of purification may be compared to the last couple of circuits on the journey inward to the center of the labyrinth. If ever we thought the spiritual path was linear and only upward, as so many of the classics of Eastern and Western spirituality suggest, the dark night of the soul will confirm that it is more labyrinthine than ladder-like. Just when we think we're getting close to the center, our destination, the path turns back, and we find ourselves traveling on one of the longest circuits of all, certainly one of the most significant. To finally arrive at the center, representing the heart of God, is to admit that we could not have found our way there on our own. Once there, we want to stay forever, resting in that great heart of loving, pulsing energy which enfolds us like a mother or a tender lover.

John of the Cross's Carmelite associate, Teresa of Avila (1515–1582), wrote near the end of her life her spiritual masterpiece, *Interior Castle*. In it she speaks of the castle of the soul as a house of seven mansions in which God is king. The soul as it progresses moves through these mansions, although few make it to the last two. Through a lifetime of contemplative prayer and monastic leadership, St. Teresa experienced, as did John of the Cross, more than one dark night. She writes: "So that [God] may show His marvels clearly, He does not want our will to have any part to play; for the will has been already entirely surrendered to Him. Nor does He wish the door of our faculties and sense which are all asleep to be opened to Him. For He will come into the center of the soul without using a door, as He once did when He came unto His disciples."[8] The beginning of a "personal encounter with the living God" begins in the fourth mansion, which belongs to the illumination stage. What St. Teresa called the "Prayer of Quiet" in which one listens for and is present to God in loving relationship is a central spiritual practice for those approaching this stage. St. Teresa belonged to a cloistered community in the age of the Inquisition, and much of what she addresses in *Interior Castle* is written for her order with care taken to color inside the lines of Catholic doctrine.

Lest it seem that only monastics and clergy experience illumination, we note that another widely read Western classic of the spiritual journey has inspired millions of Christians since the early fifteenth century. *The Imitation of Christ,* written or edited by a Dutch Augustinian monk, Thomas à Kempis, also recounts the soul's journey, the challenges it meets, and the questions of faith these raise. The book's third section, "On Interior Consolation," is a dialogue between Christ and a disciple. The disciple expresses throughout the book his own desolations and consolations along the journey, and in this section Jesus encourages him to trust in and rely on him alone, turning from worldly desires through prayer and resignation:

> Many a time I have said unto thee, and now say again, Give thyself up, resign thyself, and thou shalt have great inward peace. Give all for all; demand nothing, ask nothing in return; stand simply and with no hesitation in Me, and thou shalt possess Me. Thou shalt have liberty of heart, and the darkness shall not overwhelm thee. For this strive thou, pray for it, long after it, that thou mayst be delivered from all possession of thyself, and nakedly follow Jesus who was made naked for thee; mayest die unto thyself and live eternally in Me.[9]

Rarely are contemporary Christians challenged to this degree, to commit the whole self to Christ. Yet if we do not accept this invitation with both its challenges and promise we remain beginners on our spiritual journeys. It is crucial to know we have a choice: either remain on the early steps of the path, repeating them endlessly or abandoning them because they don't seem to produce the results we desire, or keep mov-

8. Teresa of Avila, *Interior Castle,* 164.

9. Kempis, chapter 37, no pagination.

ing along the winding path with determination and trust even though we can't see what lies ahead. All who have passed ahead of us on this journey throughout the ages confirm that God accompanies and awaits us as we are drawn like magnets to true north.

For the Eastern Orthodox, the illumination stage of the spiritual journey is linked to light mysticism based upon the theophany in which Moses encounters the uncreated light of God on Mt. Sinai in Exodus 34. The interior of the oratory of St. Catherine's Monastery at Mt. Sinai, mentioned earlier, contains a mosaic of the transfiguration, in which Moses appears, as we have seen, with Jesus and Elijah. This divine light and presence Moses experienced has been actively sought by the reclusive hesychasts of the Eastern church through the ages, who, even when living in monastic communities, preferred solitude and silence. The Jesus Prayer or pure prayer spoken of earlier is central to their tradition, which at the illumination stage is ceaseless and as automatic as breathing, having dropped from the mind where it begins to the heart where it stays. The hesychast connects with the Christ within in the apophatic way, the way of the imageless *via negativa*, in which he or she awaits in silence the divine presence and light. Many have over their years of practice and devotion experienced what they refer to as the uncreated light of God's presence described in Scripture in the two theophanies, first on Mt. Sinai, when Moses' face shone in the reflected luminousity of that holy light, and on Mt. Tabor, where he appeared in Jesus' transfiguration.

Orthodox tradition teaches that during the illumination stage, as the passions are released and the senses guarded, the light becomes stronger within, and the gifts of the Holy Spirit are received. Seven gifts are named as fear of God (in the sense of reverence and awe), strength, counsel, understanding, knowledge, comprehension, and wisdom.[10] These give birth to the light mysticism described earlier, characteristic of Eastern hesychasm. As for the Western contemplatives and mystics, direct, constant contemplation of God and of the mysteries of the Trinity accompanied by unspoken ceaseless prayer are expected to lead on to eventual deification, *theosis*, or union with God, about which we'll speak in Part Three.

One of the two contemporary accounts of Orthodoxy written by sociologist Kyriacos C. Markides, *The Mountain of Silence* (2001), again shows us that illumination is not only for these dedicated monks on

---

10. Staniloae, *Orthodox Spirituality*, 196.

Mount Athos. The book's central figure is Father Maximos, himself a Mount Athos monk now living in Cyprus, who manages, through Markides'S flowing style, to state clearly what his tradition teaches and how it applies to contemporary life. If we look only at the hesychasts, we would despair of ever reaching the illumination stage, as few of us imagine that we can devote ourselves with such intensity and lifelong commitment to prayer and contemplation.

Father Maximos, however, encourages us to make the effort. "Christ himself revealed to us the method," he says in a conversation with Markides ("He told us that not only are we capable of exploring God but we can also live with Him, become one with Him. And the organ by which we can achieve that is neither our senses nor our logic but our hearts.")He reminds his companion that "according to the tradition of the holy elders, a person's existential foundation is the heart . . . the center of our psychonoetic powers, the center of our beingness, of our personhood. It is therefore through the heart that God reveals Himself to humanity . . . It is only the cleanliness and purity of the heart that can lead to the contemplation and vision of God."[11]

Father Maximos goes on to say that the "entire methodology of the authentic Christian mystical tradition as articulated by the saints is to reach that stage where we become conscious of the reality of God within ourselves."[12] This is fully consistent with what we have explored of the spiritual journey as transformation. He makes it clear that the spiritual methodology taught and practiced in this tradition is available to all. The essence of the relationship between God and human is love, its purpose to restore us to full humanity, the fullness we see in Christ. To participate in that relationship "is a matter of shifting your energy exclusively in the direction of God. Then through continuous prayer and spiritual practices something begins to happen within the consciousness of the praying person,"[13] a flood of love so strong that the person may find it overwhelming. When the heart is purified, Fr. Maximos goes on, "at a certain point there is a sudden inner transformation and illumination"[14] through which one sees as God sees. All, one then realizes, is grace, even pain and suffering.

11. Markides, *Mountain of Silence,* 43–44.
12. Ibid., 45.
13. Ibid., 47.
14. Ibid., 64.

The key to Orthodox practice is staying present to God through ceaseless prayer, normally the Jesus Prayer. When that becomes automatic, so deeply ingrained that it happens whether we are awake or asleep, it becomes pure prayer or the prayer of the heart, establishing our constant connection with God.

Those with limited spiritual aspirations still may make themselves available to God in the hopes of receiving these gifts of the enlightened through the experience of God. The practices we have focused on—sacred reading, prayer, and participation in worship and the sacraments—are central to all three great streams of Christian spirituality.

At this point we note what may seem to be a significant point of departure between the contemplative Christian traditions and the more mission-focused churches of today that bring Christ's love to the wider world. Recently I heard Father Richard Rohr, the Franciscan priest and teacher, downplay the importance of the contemporary centering prayer movement—described a little later—because he finds it too inner-focused. As the founder of the Center for Action and Contemplation, Father Richard emphasizes both the inner and outer dimensions of the spiritual journey. In the third stage we will be traveling in Part Three, the return trip on the labyrinth for his tradition and my own Reformed tradition would be to integrate what we have learned and carry it out into the world. Contemplatives and mystics, however, are committed to praying for the world and to changing themselves so that the light and love of God flows through them. There are fewer of them than are needed. Monasticism, particularly in the Western tradition, while it tends to the contemplative, is far more diverse and more engaged in scholasticism, mission, and social justice than is commonly understood. And those who are more contemplative still must engage in the world in ways consistent with their faith. Contemplation and action, the inner and outer journeys, are both necessary for a whole, healed Christianity, experienced and expressed in a multitude of ways.

One earlier Western tradition that included both contemplation and works of charity was that of the Victorines, the religious community attached to the Abbey of St. Victor in Paris, which began to flower in the great twelfth century and flourished for several hundred years. Spirituality professor Steven Chase has written about their work in his enlightening book, *Contemplation and Compassion: The Victorine Tradition*. Richard and Hugh of St. Victor were able to wed these two dimensions of spirituality in ways we can learn from today. Chase concludes:

> Contemplation of the divine mystery as it pervades and gives meaning to all aspects of our existence is a way of life. Contemplation affects the whole life of the individual and of the community, in all the complexities of human relationships. It is not primarily an avenue to perfection, except in the sense that it fosters a desire to realize God's presence in the world. In this sense contemplation fosters compassion. Contemplation as a way of life integrates the so-called 'contemplative and active' life, recognizing that all of creation is sacred and that the spiritual life—our call to holiness—pervades and gives meaning to all aspects of life. In Victorine teaching contemplation is deeply relational, positive, inclusive, and recognizes that human and spiritual development are complementary. A delicate balance exists between ordered spiritual practice, the divinely given freedom of the human spirit, and the relational quality of creation, humanity, and God.[15]

Earlier I shared Father Bruno Barnhardt's insight that the eastern religions, including Christian Eastern Orthodoxy, are more about inner stillness than the western Christian tradition, where movement and progress are so frequently emphasized. We are now at the point where even Western Christianity becomes still. Eastern and Western thought and practice meet in the practice of contemplation. We recall here the four stages of *lectio divina*, the sacred reading of Scripture, other writings, and experiences that draw us closer to God: *lectio* (reading), *meditatio* (deep reflection on what one receives from the reading), *oratio* (prayer, usually beginning with cataphatic prayer), and finally *contemplatio*. It is here where we may reach the still point of contemplation, when our minds are emptied of thoughts and our hearts are free of all desires except to be in the eternal presence in which we have our being. All of the spiritual journey may thus be contained in these four movements of *lectio divina*, which is why it is such an essential practice.

As mentioned before, contemplative prayer is apophatic, imageless, wordless prayer that properly belongs to this stage of the spiritual journey. Cataphatic prayer is characteristic of the earlier stage, prayer *vocal* in which we speak the names of God, praise God's attributes (gracious, just, merciful, and so on), offer thanks for blessings received, confess our shortcomings, make petitions for ourselves, and request interces-

15. Chase, *Contemplation and Compassion*, 149.

sions on behalf of others. One or more of these elements, whether individually composed from the heart or read from a book of common
prayer, probably comprise 99 percent of all prayer offered to God. We
speak and hope that God is listening. In contemplative prayer, we listen and hope that God speaks or is present to us. "For God alone my
soul waits in silence," the opening of Psalm 62 [61], is characteristic of
the contemplative stance. We make ourselves available and present to
God, open ourselves fully, and wait with hopeful expectation that we
will encounter the living God. We do so not in order to bombard God
with words and petitions but to give and receive love in that perichoretic dance that exists within the Trinity and extends to the creature
beloved of God. We wait in silence, releasing distractions, simply offering ourselves and our love.

Contemplative prayer is an expression of the self-emptied, kenotic
humility we spoke about as central to our purification process, and that
is why it generally calls for more experience than the prayer forms we
have been taught to pray and are accustomed to hearing in the church.

In his helpful commentary on Teresa of Avila's *Interior Castle*,
Father Dennis Billy notes nine levels of prayer that correspond to the
three stages of the spiritual journey, as follows:

1. *Vocal Prayer* is spontaneous or liturgical, prayed individually or in
   groups. This is the most common form of prayer people use and
   experience in worship.

2. *Meditation* or *Mental Prayer* is silent reflection on a passage of
   scripture or mystery of faith as in *lectio divina*.

3. *Affective Prayer* is a deeper form of meditation, more from
   the heart than the mind, which grows out of reflection and is
   spontaneous.

4. *Acquired Recollection* is "a simple, loving gaze upon a concrete
   representation of the divine" such as an icon. One's spirit is "awak-
   ened to the divine and is content with doing nothing else but sitting in the divine presence."[16]

These four forms are considered part of the purification stage of the
journey although may be practiced at all stages. The last is transitional
to the next stage, illumination.

16. Teresa of Avila, *Interior Castle*, 14.

5. *Infused Contemplation:* the person praying "receives an intimate experiential knowledge of God. This knowledge comes in the form of an intellectual light that illumines the mind and enables the person to have an intuitive, connatural knowledge of the divine. Infused contemplation is a pure gift from God."[17]

John of the Cross also spoke of this type of prayer when he described the journey through the dark night of the soul.

6. *The Prayer of Quiet* allows the illuminating light of the divine to penetrate the will. "The result is an experience of intense joy and inner consolation . . . the person blessed with this experience tends toward solitude and repose."[18]

The last three forms of prayer, the Prayer of Union, Spiritual Betrothal, and Spiritual Marriage, properly belong to Part Three, Union with God.[19] Five and six, however, Infused Contemplation and The Prayer of Quiet, are associated with illumination. St. Teresa clearly experienced all of these types of prayer herself, as she described not only in *Interior Castle* but also her other writings.

For seekers of God, these prayer experiences of illumination are enticing. Once experienced, one longs for more. However, that can translate, as John of the Cross teaches us, into spiritual greed or gluttony. We must be content to receive what God offers us when it comes and seek God solely for Godself, not for a spiritual experience. It is also important to be careful about sharing such experiences, to avoid spiritual pride in the speaker or envy in the listener. No sincere Christian wants to feel that God doesn't love him or her enough to be present in that way, and that is certainly not the case.

One reason why experiences of illumination aren't very common is that we need to make ourselves available for them and be ready to receive them when and if they come. As we saw earlier with the Wesley and Merton examples, that doesn't necessarily mean alone in our rooms in prayer. These experiences can happen anywhere. But praying often, in any form, communicates to God that we are open and listening. A time set aside each day to not only speak with God but to listen is important.

17. Ibid.
18. Ibid., 15.
19. Ibid., 13–16.

Many are uncomfortable with silence and want to fill it with speech, music, laughter—anything that maintains the reality they know and can control. Younger people today, trained by our fast-paced media, seem to be unable to exist without music, video, cell phoneS, and other distractions pushing their brains toward overload. What I've experienced with people who are unused to observing silence in a religious or spiritual setting is that they find ways to fill it. Recently I noticed that one of our congregation's pastors purposely left half a minute of silent reflection time at the end of her sermon. People looked around, confused, and leafed through their worship bulletins to figure out who had missed the cue to speak next. The intended sound of silence instead became a rustling of paper.

The first time I went on a silent retreat at a monastery, I felt uncomfortable with sitting in silence without doing something. When we are quiet, we hear our own endless mind chatter, labeled by some the "monkey mind," that stream of consciousness that has been waiting for us to pay attention to it. Retreat leaders tell us, and I've found it is true through personal experience, that it takes a good three days of silence to process all that chatter before we can allow what we have stuffed down deep inside to surface so that we can deal with it in prayer and spiritual direction. After that, we may be able to really listen for the spirit of God. That's why a weekend retreat isn't usually enough. Just when our overloaded minds and stuffed feelings are about to quiet down and let us experience a moment of inner peace and presence to God, it's time to go home.

Unless we include a practice of stillness for at least a few minutes each day, we are always playing catch up. Getting to silence is part of releasing and surrendering even our thoughts to God: "For God alone my soul waits in silence." This is not mindfulness derived from Eastern religious traditions. It's honoring God by presence. We're detaching from the world for a few precious moments to deepen our attachment to God. In the silence we may speak a favorite name for God, to let God know we are present and ready for a loving exchange of energy. This is our time with God, and we honor both God and ourselves when we offer our attention and desire for connection.

To explain today's contemplative prayer movement we have to return to the fourteenth century. Father William Meninger found within the medieval spiritual classic *The Cloud of Unknowing* four steps leading to contemplation, which he simplified as follows: 1) Start with a doorway to silence by praying a simple prayer, such as a line from Scripture or a slow recitation of the Lord's Prayer. 2) Choose a prayer word of one or two syllables, a name of God that for you symbolizes your desire to love God. It may be something like "God, Abba, Jesus, Love, or Spirit." Let that prayer word go deep within your heart to center you on God. 3) When distractions inevitably come, gently return to the prayer word. Even if you drift off in your thoughts or sleep, since your intention is to stay present to God the Holy Spirit will pray for you. 4) Continue your practice for twenty minutes or longer—or work up to that if you need to. Conclude your time of silent prayer with the Lord's Prayer slowly said or another simple prayer. Sit in contemplative prayer twice a day.[20]

The simplicity of this form of prayer is the key to its wide practice. It's a basic prayer of presence. However, as most who practice it for months or years discover, the description is deceptively simple. Layer after layer of the overlaid self will be stripped away by years of practice as we get to our essence, our essential self in relationship with God. There is much more to learn about contemplative prayer. Not only are there a plethora of recent books available, but a whole international movement has grown up around the version of this prayer form that Father Thomas Keating and others teach, named "centering prayer." The four steps given on the latest centering prayer brochure are similar to those given above. There are nuances and differing techniques that are taught to experienced practitioners, as the layers of this prayer form and of the self are revealed.

Father Thomas's organization, Contemplative Outreach (www.contemplativeoutreach.org), includes levels of training for all who are interested, including the training of facilitators of centering prayer, resources, and a listing of upcoming retreats and workshops. A flyer that comes with the brochure explains that Father Thomas was concerned years ago that young people were "turning to Eastern practices for contemplation and had little knowledge of the contemplative traditions within Christianity. So he set out to present those practices in a more accessible way, and is recognized as the founder of Centering Prayer." You may notice the connection of that statement to the major theme of this book, that what has been forgotten or hidden within the Christian tradi-

20. Father William Meninger, as presented in a workshop in Greensboro, North Carolina, on June 11, 2011, which I attended.

tion needs to be made more widely available to people who have lost or never developed their Christian roots. Following Vatican II, Catholic leaders were mandated to bring the faith to the people, to revive their own older traditions which still had value in new, more accessible and life-giving ways, not simply to retain only for the clergy the spiritual classics and practices that had informed Catholic religious life for nearly two millennia.

I remembering discovering centering prayer during seminary and afterwards through the Certificate in Spiritual Formation program I completed. At that time I knew just enough about it through doing a little practice on my own and reading books like Keating's *Open Mind, Open Heart*, Basil Pennington's *Centering Prayer*, and Morton Kelsey's *The Other Side of Silence* to try to teach it at a church retreat. I quickly realized that not only was I teaching ahead of my practice, as Sister Meg Funk would say, but also that the people who attended my workshop had no context for what I was talking about. Sitting in silence for twenty minutes after listening to my brief introduction to centering prayer probably turned most of them off of it for life! There is much more to this deep practice than first appears, and while I applaud the efforts of the Contemplative Outreach organization, I know that this practice comes out of a spiritual path that prepares those who would seek God in this way to have a strong chance to find God—or, better, to allow God to find them.

Hopefully, those who are introduced to centering prayer or the broader contemplative prayer that others write about will read to gain the understanding they need, participate in communal worship, find ongoing spiritual guidance, continue to practice the forms of prayer leading up to contemplative prayer while they are developing their spiritual gifts, and connect with a centering prayer group that can reinforce and support their practice. Otherwise, I doubt that many will stick with centering prayer through the periods of dryness and frustration in order to experience its gifts.

Three texts in my own library that I find illuminating on this prayer practice are Merton's *Contemplative Prayer*, Cynthia Bourgeault's *Centering Prayer and Inner Awakening*, and *Spirituality, Contemplation & Transformation: Writings on Centering Prayer*, a multi-author volume edited by Thomas Keating.

In the last book he wrote before his death in 1968, Merton comments:

> People who try to pray and meditate above their proper level, who are too eager to reach what they believe to be "a high degree of prayer," get away from the truth and from reality. In observing themselves and trying to convince themselves of their advance, they become imprisoned in themselves. Then when they realize that grace has left them they are caught in their own emptiness and futility and remain helpless . . . A long course in humility and compunction is the remedy![21]

The purpose of prayer, especially the kinds of prayer we have described throughout this book, is "to prepare the way so that God's action may develop this . . . capacity for inner illumination by faith and by the light of wisdom, in the loving contemplation of God," says Merton.[22] Much of this little gem of a book contains the short version of the path of the purified heart we've been pursuing, winding through early monasticism up to the present. It reinforces that getting to contemplative prayer is a journey, not a destination, and that it is not the first stop along the way. The higher kind of listening in silence Merton speaks about depends on

> a general emptiness that waits to realize the fullness of the message of God within its own apparent void . . . [T]he true contemplative is not the one who prepares his mind for a particular message . . . but who remains empty because he knows that he can never expect or anticipate the word that will transform his darkness into light . . . He waits on the Word of God in silence, and when he is "answered," it is not so much by a word that bursts into his silence. It is by his silence itself suddenly, inexplicably revealing itself to him as a word of great power, full of the voice of God.[23]

Later, he makes the point that the way of contemplation is not the way to God: "Christ alone is the way, and he is invisible."[24] In his conclusion, Merton states emphatically that "The prayer of the heart must penetrate every aspect and every activity of Christian existence . . . The only full

21. Merton, *Contemplative Prayer,* 13.

22. Ibid., 22.

23. Ibid., 68.

24. Ibid., 71.

and authentic purification is that which turns a man completely inside out, so that he no longer has a self to defend."[25] Finally, he says, "The most important need in the Christian world today is this inner truth nourished by this Spirit of contemplation: the praise and love of God, the longing for the coming of Christ, the thirst for the manifestation of God's glory, his truth, his justice, his Kingdom in the world."[26]

Cynthia Bourgeault, the Episcopal priest and author of several enlightening books exploring the wisdom tradition within Christianity, has worked and taught with Father Thomas Keating for over twenty years. Her book on centering prayer begins with the concern that contemplative prayer is little understood in the contemporary church, citing its largely untapped potential to transform Christian life. This book and the Keating collection of essays on centering prayer deserve fuller attention than is possible here. The energy that has built up and surrounds this contemplative outreach movement is an example of how God is doing a new thing. If the church wants to tap into this effort to awaken the human spirit to a state in which it will allow God's love to transform and heal us, it needs to provide the contexts and the worshiping communities that the movement cannot provide on its own.

The Eastern Orthodox particularly stress that the Divine Liturgy continues the process of purification. Through prayer, confession, repentance, and especially through the Eucharist, participation in the living body of Christ, the worshiping community is given the strength and grace to stay on the path of the purified heart and to keep moving toward God. So I will give the last word in this chapter to Father Edward Rommen, the Orthodox priest I studied with at Duke Divinity School. In his succinct summary of his own tradition, he states: "The one who is purified of the passions reaches the height of pure prayer, sees the divine light, and has spiritualized his own nature to such an extent that it has become the warmth and the light of the love of God."

25. Ibid., 88.
26. Ibid., 94.

PART THREE

Union with God

Walking into a New Life

NINE

Summer
Ordinary Time, Again

> Friendship can be the most dangerous of all types of love since
> other kinds may be had without intercommunication, but friend-
> ship is completely based on it . . . Love everyone with a strenuous
> love based on charity, but form friendships only with those who
> can share virtuous things with you . . . that spiritual friendship
> by which two, three, or more souls share with one another their
> devotion and spiritual affections and establish a single spirit
> among themselves . . . Honest friendship is at all times and in all
> ways honest, courteous and amiable. It never changes except into
> a purer and more perfect union of minds, a living image of the
> blessed friendship that exists in heaven.
>
> —Francis de Sales, *Introduction to the Devout Life*

PENTECOST CAME LATE THAT year, on June 12. Summer followed on
its heels. Its all-enveloping heat and humidity already lay over our
area like a steamy blanket. I was profoundly grateful for air-conditioning
and felt deep pity for the people, plants, and animals that couldn't escape
into a cool space like my comfortable home. Even our normally active
dog was reluctant to venture out in the midday heat.

My own concern about the sustainability of our planet and its
inhabitants in the face of increasing natural and human-caused earth
changes has involved me in efforts over the years to raise awareness
and change behavior both within the church and the wider community,
but results come slowly. While the mainstream denominations generally have earth ministry resources to offer individual congregations, it
is still relatively uncommon for church leadership to engage members
in taking up the challenge to live more simply and sustainably. Our serious overconsumption patterns in the developed world create severe
economic inequities, heightened by the current global recession. We are
living in volatile and precarious times.

161

As people of faith in the God who created a world of abundance so that all may have enough, it is long past time for us to face individually and communally how we must change and live more simply so that others can simply live. At the place where we live into the heart of God and recognize the connectedness of all life and God's love for the whole creation, we realize that union with God is not just about our individual bliss but about our collective survival. If we have truly been changed by our walk into the center of the labyrinth where we have met the living God, if we have freed ourselves from our addictions to what feeds our bodies and egos, our images and narrow beliefs, when our concerns are for all, not just for me and mine, then it remains to stand humbly before our God, beg forgiveness, and recommit our lives to loving all of creation. Jesus gave us the vision and the model to shift and expand our perspectives. True union with God comes through following Jesus, even to the cross, the gateway to new life, and making our personal self-sacrifice for the greater good of all.

While I have felt this way for years and wrote about environmental and financial stewardship in my 2002 book, *Graceful Living: Your Faith, Values, and Money in Changing Times*, I still feel challenged and humbled daily by my own failure to live out radically what I know is required. Our family's efforts to downsize our housing may have been unsuccessful in a depressed market, but there were many other ways in which we could cut back, manage with less, and share more of our abundance with others.

Consuming less and giving away more is liberating and gratifying. My lengthy fast resulted in a weight loss of over fifty pounds, and I was thrilled to pack up several large bags of clothes now too big for me and drop them off at the local thrift shop. No one needs that many clothes, anyway! After many months of walking the path of the purified heart, I felt more conscious of the need to reduce, reuse, recycle and gift more liberally, so I committed to stepping up my own and the family's efforts.

During these months I had to lay aside community involvement. Except for continuing service on the board of a neighborhood development organization in my hometown of Detroit, a city that has suffered more severely than most throughout the ongoing economic crisis, other commitments had been put on hold. As the process of completing the book and my year of purification was coming to a close, I found myself thinking about how I wanted to take a more active role in the church and communities of which I was part. Already a small writing project had surfaced, an article on why so many Presbyterian ministers have become Benedictine oblates, and I began a process of identifying these fellow oblates so that I could turn my attention to this project in the fall, when the book was complete. I also wanted to lead classes and workshops on Christian spirituality. I knew other ways of serving the wider church and community would emerge when I was ready.

Now that Pentecost had celebrated once more the initial moment of the church's illumination, by the middle of June the liturgical year returned to Ordinary Time, that long stretch through the summer and fall that affords the church a period of refreshment and recollection of its purpose and energies to prepare God's people for both their inward and outward journeys. As we've seen, Ordinary Time is anything but ordinary. Each day offers opportunities to transform our minds, hearts, and spirits.

My intention during this period was to complete a draft of this book manuscript by mid-August, when I was to return to the Studium Scholars program at St. Benedict's Monastery to make the final revisions before turning the book over to the publisher. While there, I would also make my final commitment as an oblate. By late June it was already clear that things were not going to go according to plan—at least my plan. A few more challenges lay in store. As if to thwart my desire to move into a more intimate relationship with God, the road got narrower and bumpier and would test all I thought I had mastered.

I was not plagued by doubts or crises of faith. Those I'd had earlier in life, even during my years of ministry. If anything, my certainty of God's presence grew stronger and more intense during this period. What threatened to destabilize me and distract me from my work were the serious health crises of two of the people closest to me: my son, Tom, and my close friend and spiritual companion, Meg. A third crisis, which affected other friends, was playing itself out in the background at the same time.

Tom's situation was the most immediate and chaotic. For months he had been having major problems. In December, his clinic, more than sixteen miles away, demanded that he show up daily because of the combination of prescribed medications he was taking. This dictum felt to him unjust and undeserved. He determined then that he would get off the medication he received at that clinic and began an aggressive reduction. Each week he dropped further down on the medication, and this rapid withdrawal began to take its toll. He barely slept or ate, and the least bit of stress would trigger an anxiety attack. I cooked for him twice a day and by late June was driving him to his clinic every morning at 6:30 because he was too sick and weak to drive himself. Meanwhile, he was consulting with his doctors at the University of North Carolina health care system about making a transition to their clinic to improve the quality of his care and eliminate the need for the other clinic. The date for the transition was set for early July. As the date approached, Tom was just barely hanging on. Like any typical parent, I suffered along with him, distressed by his condition but hopeful the transition would improve his quality of life.

Ironically, on July Fourth, Independence Day, Tom paid his last visit to the first clinic. Three days later he entered the one at UNC. The transition to the new medication was supposed to take place quickly, and he was expected to be better in a matter of hours. Instead, the medication caused reactions that would last for months.

In the midst of his pain and panic, I endeavored to keep my calm, peaceful center, but on many days the stress overtook me, too, and I couldn't work or focus on anything but making sure Tom was all right. If he was having a relatively good day, so was I. But for several weeks those were few and far between. Finally, toward the end of July, after many doctor and hospital visits, things calmed down a bit but remained difficult.

Meanwhile, I continued to write as I could and prayed for the crisis to pass. I summoned all my capacity to submit to these circumstances and trust that all would be well. It was a challenge to sit in silence as a contemplative when all of this was going on, but that was where I found the inner stillness I needed. It came as a reminder that stability, one of the strongest of Benedictine values, is vital for those seeking the contemplative life. Stillness is essential, as is waiting with patience for the God who comes at the time and in the manner of God's own choosing.

On the same day that Tom finished with the first clinic, Independence Day, Meg, Mary, and I had our biweekly spiritual sharing phone call. It was then that Meg revealed that her recurring cancer, which she had been trying to heal on her own, now required medical attention. As a health educator and holistic practitioner, Meg knew how to take care of herself. To seek conventional medical treatment meant that the situation was life-threatening. A conversation with a doctor friend left her considering only one option she found acceptable: palliative radiation to try to reduce her tumors enough to relieve her severe nerve pain. <u>Palliative treatment is only for comfort</u>. <u>It is not a cure</u>. She was planning to see a radiation oncologist later that week to discuss her treatment.

I talked with her the evening after her meeting with the oncologist. It turned out that her cancer was very aggressive, and the doctor held out little hope. In addition to this devastating news, the radiation was going to be five days a week for six weeks and was sure to make her even sicker than she was already. I know she considered not doing it at all. At nearly sixty, single and without dependents, she was free to make the decision to let God take her sooner rather than later, and I assured her that I supported her decision either way. In the end, she chose to try to prolong her life by enduring the radiation and continuing to practice her own forms of healing. <u>As a holistic healer, it was especially difficult for Meg</u> to commit to a harsh treatment that would <u>kill massive amounts of cells and tissue and leave the areas around them scarred and dysfunctional.</u> I committed to sending her prayer and healing energy twice a day every day.

My heart was aching for my dear friend, such a gift to the world, yet not once did it occur to me to challenge God or ask the old theodicy question, "Why her, O Lord?" God doesn't wish for us to have illnesses and disease but allows us to make our own choices about how we will respond to them. <u>The only response I could make was to offer her loving energy and ask for Jesus, the great healer, to give her each day whatever she needed most, whatever was for her highest good.</u> (I had learned over the years not to ask for any particular outcome for prayer and healing but only that whatever happened would be in alignment with God's desire for her highest good, "Thy will be done," in effect.) <u>Neither Meg nor I fear death</u>, for we know something of what awaits us, but no one wants a loved one to experience prolonged suffering. Only a few months earlier we had lost a dear mutual friend in her fifties to a sudden heart attack. That friend had passed on to the next life before she hit the floor. While the shock was devastating to her children and grandchildren, at least our friend hadn't suffered.

Thinking about that triggered a childhood memory. I was nine years old. My sister, almost seventeen, had just been killed in a car accident. My mother told my other sister and me that Nancy hadn't suffered before her death. No, I realized then and later, it's the ones left behind who suffer. Yet for Christians, when we sit at the foot of the cross and meditate on Christ's suffering, undertaken as his destiny and his choice, we know that God's great, unconditional love for us abides through our pain and grief. Our worst mistake at times like these is to turn away from or blame God as the cause.

Even before we unite with God more fully in a neverending exchange of loving energy and presence, we receive through Jesus, God-with-us, the consolation that will see us through our desolation, and I clung to that assurance during this long, hot summer of "ordinary time." One day, as I sat in prayer with my head bowed, feeling a bit despondent, my chin lifted and a warm, loving presence enveloped me for about ten minutes. When it left, I felt re-energized. This was surely a gift of grace, to let me know not to despair, that God is as close as our breath.

Crises always bring renewed perspective and blessings. Among those for me at this time were gratitude for Tom's progress in healing and for Meg's friendship. I was grateful that I could accompany them through these difficult times and that nothing can separate us from the love of God or from each other, as reflections of that divine love.

Other blessings came too. The Sunday after Pentecost I was able to join a contemplative prayer group that met on Sunday mornings at the Methodist church across the street from where I worshiped. The summer schedule meant that I could make the 9:00 gathering and still attend my own church. The group was a Godsend for me, literally, as it was the only one in the community that kept meeting through the summer. It was a blessing to sit companionably in silence with several others for twenty minutes before engaging in conversation about an assigned spiritual reading. While I continued my contemplative prayer practice at home, it was challenging in the mornings because of the chaos around me as well as the writing schedule. By evening it was usually far easier to relax into a deep inner stillness and rest in the heart of God.

I remembered that Meg had shared with me a meditation on stillness that had been given to her by a wise elder. I pulled out a copy and found that it settled and comforted me. It reads:

There is so much power in stillness.

In the stillness, the ego is silent and love flows.

In the stillness, the human limitations cease to surface, and the Divine emerges and flows.

In the stillness, we find the best in ourselves.

In the stillness, there is patience and sweetness and insight . . . there is everything you need.

In the stillness are infinite possibilities waiting to be invited into action.

In the stillness, one meets infinity in all its vast glory.

In the stillness lies the access road to your path, clearly delineated.

In the stillness lies the friendship and love of friends and family . . . stripped of their human agendas and foibles.

In the stillness is the fullness of "I AM" . . . of who you are in your limitless power and potential.

In the stillness lies your heart's dearest and deepest desire.

In the stillness lies the fullness of your being.

In the stillness, you can connect with all the love we have for you.

In the stillness is life . . . teeming with opportunities and options.

In the stillness is the void in which you find your self . . . your divine self . . . your fully actuated self.

"Be still and know that I am God." Hold to this.

Now go in peace. All is well.

In communing with God we learn who we are and in abandoning the fearful, ego-driven self to the stillness, we find the God who seeks our whole selves.

Each day brought its challenges as well as its blessings. When I couldn't write I would read. I re-encountered several of the great Christian contemplatives and mystics: Julian, Teresa of Avila, John of the Cross, the author of *The Cloud of Unknowing*, and Hildegard of Bingen, the extraordinary twelfth-century Benedictine visionary, among them. I also enjoyed the brief excerpts from spiritual classics included in Richard Foster's *Devotional Classics*, which we were reading in the contemplative prayer group. I explored an interest in medieval and Reformation era history, delving into *Cluny: In Search of God's Lost Empire*, about that greatest of the medieval Benedictine monasteries eventually destroyed after the French Revolution, and *The Last Divine Office*, about the Durham Cathedral, which I had visited a few seasons ago. One of the finest of the Middle Ages, it was desecrated during the reign of Henry VIII, when the king cut ties with the Roman Catholic Church.

Even during the most intense weeks in July I managed to continue my extended *lectio divina* on chapters 4 to 7 of the Rule of Benedict in preparation for a class to be taught in the fall by Sister Meg Funk. I chose those chapters of the Rule because they had much to teach me on two virtues central to monastic spirituality: obedience and humility. It is difficult for people living in contemporary America, even within the church, to grasp the importance of these interlinked virtues. We are too used to living under our own authority rather than accepting God's. For the Benedictines, obedience to God through keeping the commandments, obeying the abbot or prioress who stands in Christ's place, and following the Rule are imperative. In Christian traditions, humility is considered the highest virtue, encompassing all the others, for it is through self-emptying humility that we not only are able to accept what we discern as God's will but to do so freely and gratefully.

The longest chapter in Benedict's Rule is chapter 7, on humility. In it, Benedict references Jacob's Ladder, an ancient metaphor for spiritual ascent. He presents his own twelve-step program for humility based on the premise that ascent comes through descent, that through humbling our hearts God will raise us through the rungs of the ladder to heaven. By placing God at the center of our lives and overcoming all that would separate us from God (the "eight afflictive thoughts" or "Seven Deadly Sins" we encountered earlier on our journey), by understanding who we are and growing in relationship with the Triune God, by learning from the wise guides we have met on our path, we will eventually reach the top rung of the ladder of humility where, Benedict notes, we arrive at the perfect love that casts out fear (1 John 4:18). "Through this love," the saint goes on, "all that we once performed with dread, we will now begin to observe without effort, as though naturally . . . out of love for Christ, good habit, and delight in virtue."[1] Kenotic love, through which we release our own ego needs and desires, modeled for us so perfectly by Jesus, lights the way to our destination: union with God. Few of us reach the top rung of the ladder, but, just as with our journey on the labyrinth, we keep on going with faith and trust that God will meet us where we are.

Obedience, too, has its own rewards and appeal. During this trying period there were days when all I wanted was for someone wiser than I to lead me like a loving shepherd to the green pastures so that I might

1. Chittister, *Rule of Benedict*, 99.

lie down in safety and peace and drink from the still waters that restore the soul. This is what God, through Jesus, offers us, and I was more than ready to surrender my autonomy to follow him.

I felt again the need for a spiritual director who would listen, share insights and help hold me accountable for staying intimately connected with and attuned to God. The person I had asked to do this now had a crisis to deal with herself and wasn't available at that time. I spoke on occasion with my former spiritual director, now a friend, but respected her need to step back from that role. Meanwhile, a local woman, herself a spiritual director, approached me to be her director. We agreed to meet a few times to discern together whether that would be good for us both. I told her that in any case I couldn't begin before September, given my commitments. I knew that I needed to be in direction myself in order to offer that soul connection to another and trusted that God would choose a director for me. Spiritual direction is part of the discipline of the daily examen and used to be connected more to confession than it is now, especially for monastics. I find it helpful to have someone in my life who will help me care for my soul, but those who are able and willing are rare when we reach a certain point on our paths.

Towards the end of June, before the traumas of July, I took a couple of days off to attend the first Wild Goose Festival on the emerging church, held outdoors in a rural area not far from my home. The festival drew speakers and participants from around the country to share the new things God is doing through the church. Since it was so close to home and featured several people I knew or wanted to hear, like Richard Rohr and Phyllis Tickle, I ventured out, even though it meant taking time away from the writing. I hoped the event would stimulate fresh insights and provide spiritual nourishment.

It was good to see Richard again. He is one of the wisest spiritual teachers of our time and continually shares his own new insights. This time he talked about his latest book, *Falling Upward: A Spirituality for the Two Halves of Life*. He noted that what is healthy ego development in the first half of life becomes unhealthy if continued in the second half. Too many people in the culture and the church remain stuck in the first half and don't learn from life's transitions and passages in order to find meaning in all they encounter. Christians who lose faith when things don't work out as they expected haven't matured along their spiritual path. I see that as the huge task and challenge for the church today: to help people become mature Christians.

This festival was attended by many younger people and evangelical Christians who consider themselves part of the emerging church movement. What is emerging isn't clear. There has been considerable experimentation in the last twenty years with programmatic changes, such as alternative worship, that relies more on entertainment and innovation to attract new members than spiritual formation and reverence for God. Some leading evangelicals are discovering that and beginning to place more emphasis on preparing mature Christians. Brian McLaren, one of these, spoke at the festival about his own faith development as revealed through the succession of books he has written. I read one of these recently, *Finding Our Way Again: The Return of the Ancient Practices*, and smiled when I found that it dealt with a theme similar to mine and introduced the reader to basic spiritual practices. It occurred to me, not for the first time, that the path to the future of the Christian tradition may well lie in recovering the best of the past, the wisdom of deeply formed Christians.

We all still have much to learn on our spiritual walks, and the more open we are to each other's wisdom, the stronger and better for all of us. If the church is ever to be one in Christ, it must embrace the whole, despite theological or cultural differences.

Phyllis Tickle's 2008 book, *The Great Emergence: How Christianity Is Changing and Why*, places the emerging church within a much broader context. In her presentation she noted that traditional authority within the church's structure and leadership are no longer accepted by many Christians. What the church is undergoing now, she says, is equivalent to the great transformation that Jesus brought to the world. According to Phyllis, who borrowed this concept from Joachim of Flora (a twelfth-century Cistercian mystic who followed the Rule of Benedict), the Old Testament period conceived of God as the Father. When Jesus came, the New Testament church moved into the age of God the Son. Although Joachim envisioned the third age of the Holy Spirit as coming in the thirteenth century, it is only happening now, in our own time. The age of the Holy Spirit, symbolized by the Celtic wild goose, is to eventually usher in an era of peace and universal love.

The third stage of the spiritual journey as transformation, union with God, will then be all-inclusive, I reflected as I listened to Phyllis speak. Through God's grace the creation will be restored to its intended wholeness. That is the age our hearts and souls long for, the divine union in all its fullness. While the emerging church movement seems to recognize that we've put God in a box, letting God the Holy Spirit loose in the church and the world is still a scary proposition to many.

The summer and my ponderings wore on. A month after the Wild Goose Festival, on July 22, Mary Magdalene's Feast Day, Richard Rohr and Cynthia Bourgeault began a seminar called "God as Us! Sacred Feminine/Sacred Masculine." I downloaded the webcast and listened with interest to ten hours of presentations by these master teachers.

Cynthia, whose recent book *The Meaning of Mary Magdalene* has much to add to the conversation about this Apostle of Apostles, began with the provocative statement that she was appalled by the lack of conversation about *The Da Vinci Code* in the church. I was with her on that one, as I'd taught an adult Sunday class on that topic not long after the book came out in 2003. What interested Cynthia was not the bloodline argument made in the novel, that Jesus and Mary Magdalene were married and had children, but that hidden in plain sight was evidence that Mary was the chief among the apostles and possibly the beloved disciple who stood at the foot of the cross with Mother Mary. What she argues in her book and in this seminar is that recent good scholarship that includes the lost gospels discovered in the last hundred years or so has shot holes in the master story of our faith, that all the disciples were men and that Jesus put them alone in charge of carrying forward the good news of God's love. All four canonical Gospels confirm that Mary Magdalene was commissioned by Jesus as an apostle, the one sent to tell others.

To reclaim Mary Magdalene from her centuries-old diminishment, says Bourgeault, is to reclaim Christianity, particularly in the West, as the Eastern Orthodox revere her along with Mother Mary. In addition, Cynthia spoke of Jesus' model of open, compassionate, self-giving as the true heart of Christianity. Rather than renunciation, the pushing away from the passions and what is considered sinful that was such an essential part of the early Christians' path, especially the desert fathers, she argues that Jesus practiced and taught letting go, releasing with open hands whatever would divide and separate the heart from God. This is the form of *kenosis* that leads to the gifts of the Spirit of which we've spoken: compassion, generosity flowing from a sense of abundance, humility, and undemanding love, among them. This, I would add, is what is understood at the level of the purified heart illumined by and attuned to God.

Both Bourgeault and Rohr strongly affirm a Trinitarian God who offers Godself completely, a God of wholeness, genderless but inclusive of positive gender qualities, a relational God who connects us to that wholeness. This is what they see mirrored in the loving friendship between Jesus and Mary Magdalene. Whether they were married or not isn't essential. Bourgeault asserts that they are the one perfect example presented in our faith tradition of a healthy male-female relationship in which the whole is greater than its parts, the unitive love that creates a third entity, the Abler Soul, as it is called in the wisdom tradition. Their loving relationship as friends and equals shows us what divine love and human love are like at their best. This love does not divide the heart but rather co-creates a greater love. The description of this kind of love as divine friendship by the Counter-Reformation era saint Francis de Sales, opens this chapter. This restoration of wholeness is what we seek in our search for God, for we rarely find it in our human relationships.

The concept of such divine friendship reflected in human life reminded me of a well-known passage in Gregory of Nyssa's *Life of Moses*. Gregory, the fourth-century Greek Cappadocian, brother of Basil the Great, was influential in the development of Eastern Christian spirituality. He wrote about stages in our relationship with God that parallel in some ways the three stages of the spiritual journey. At the first stage people fear God, like slaves who expect their master's wrath and punishment for real or imagined failings. Second-stage believers perceive God as the source of great rewards for living a virtuous life, like an employer handing out Christmas bonuses to her employees. By the third stage, we neither fear judgment nor expect rewards. What we desire is being with God, in God's presence. That is the stage we hope to reach, the destination we seek, not as slaves or employees but as Jesus' friends. There is mutuality in that relationship, as in the continual outpouring and flow of divine love within the Trinity.

These reflections nourished and strengthened me, as Ordinary Time wore on through the summer. By early August my son showed improvement. Although he wasn't out of the woods yet, I gave thanks for the positive changes occurring in him physically and emotionally.

Meg's situation was still critical, but three weeks into the painful and grueling radiation treatments, her attitude, quality of self-care, and spiritual practices were carrying her through. I continued to offer twice-daily prayer and healing energy for these two dear ones in my life, along with other friends in crisis.

With Tom improving, I was able to give more time to my writing and began to see the light at the end of the tunnel. I was confident that with God's help a complete draft of the manuscript would be ready by mid-August, as planned, so that during my two weeks at St. Ben's Studium program I could concentrate on revisions and be prepared to make a presentation on the project to the Studium board.

One Sunday I led our centering prayer class on selections from Dietrich Bonhoeffer's work. I took time to read *Life Together* and to reread parts of *The Cost of Discipleship*, and found his intensity and directness challenging in the same ways that the great church leaders of old challenged nominal Christians to follow Jesus as if our very lives depended on it. Bonhoeffer's did, as we know. Beginning Christians and seekers may shy away from the prophetic word of Bonhoeffer and others in this tradition. Prophets shake us out of our complacency. Those of us long on the path must hear again, as if for the first time, the words that call us away from a place of comfort back to risking everything for new life in Christ.

With Bonhoeffer's words ringing in my ears, I completed the final chapter of this book during a week punctuated with family visits and Tom's doctors' appointments. If we can't hold fast in the midst of stress and disruptions to our routines, we're not up to this path, I thought, grateful for God's grace in seeing me through the difficulties of the past year.

Confident that the manuscript was sufficiently complete so that I might meet my self-imposed deadline and entrusting my family to God, I returned to Minnesota. Once again, my friend Sally drove me from the airport to St. Joseph and the sisters responsible for Studium were there to greet me. I had barely settled into my comfortable apartment and office when it was time to meet with the oblate director about making my final commitment as an oblate of the monastery that evening. Noon prayer and lunch followed, and before I knew it I was back into the rhythm and gracious hospitality of the community.

At evening prayer another woman and I stood before the sisters as the prioress led us through the brief but meaningful ritual. "What do you seek?" she asked us. "I seek to serve God as an oblate of St.

Benedict," we responded. Then each of us in turn read our statement of commitment and signed the document on a table representing an altar. The prioress added her signature, and the oblate director handed each of us a certificate and an oblate pin to mark the occasion. The original documents would be added to the monastery archives. Then, as we stood with bowed heads and open hands, we received the community's sung blessing. I was deeply moved by the ritual and the whole occasion. I felt the same kind of divine presence and love I had felt at my ordination to the ministry many years ago. Sharing this moment within this beloved community was a great gift, and I resolved to maintain a lifelong affiliation with these special women of St. Benedict's Monastery.

Getting to this sacred place and moment had not been easy, nor should it have been. Not only had I devoted myself to studying and following the Rule of Benedict to the fullest extent possible in my life, to responding to more than a dozen sets of questions prepared by the oblate directors of both St. John's and St. Ben's, and to spending time within the communities to acquaint myself with their culture, practices, and people. I also had to find the connections between this 1500-year-old tradition and my own faith communion. This I had been able to do through the year by uncovering and attempting to follow the path of the purified heart that opened itself to me like a flower as I sought it through the records left in Scripture and by the wise guides of our common tradition. The challenges in my own life I was able to accept as lessons and gifts of God's grace. There would be more of these to come, I knew, but I felt ready to accept them and to trust that all shall be well.

The remainder of my two weeks at St. Ben's flew by. Other special moments began to accumulate: Donor Appreciation Day, when the sisters offered their special brand of hospitality to their supporters and put on a show that concluded with a hilarious "Sister Act" spoof; coffee time each morning with the Studium staff and scholars; a picnic with the sisters in our residence and dinners in their homes; long walks on weekends around the grounds and the small town of St. Joseph in the most beautiful summer weather I'd experienced in years; a restorative exchange of spiritual healing with one of the sisters; the return of the college students to campus; lunch with the prioress; and a final sung blessing again on the day of my departure. I was also grateful that the spiritual director I had sought and prayed for emerged, and I was able to begin the process of listening with her for what God was working within me.

The writing and editing process seemed to flow in this environment. I was given the opportunity to present my work to the community at a Studium Board meeting attended by a number of the sisters and guests. I felt that it went well, confirmed afterwards by generous comments.

Meanwhile, the home front in North Carolina experienced the shockwaves from an unusual earthquake in the region and a hurricane that skirted our area—both in the same week. It seems that the chaos that had characterized our family life over the summer was being mirrored in the wider world, from these severe earth changes to the congressional spectacle in Washington over raising the debt ceiling, to revolution in Libya and flash mobs in Great Britain. All of this unsettling change felt like a prelude to transformation, not only for those on the spiritual path but for all life in God's creation. Whatever lay in our individual and common futures, over the past year I had learned to release fear and surrender expectation to God. I hoped to be able to receive all that would come our way in these uncertain times with open hands and heart.

During Sunday Mass in the monastery's Sacred Heart Chapel, we sang a beautiful hymn whose words were written by one of the sisters, "Sing a New Church." The final verse touched me deeply: "Draw together at one table all the human family; shape a circle ever wider and a people ever free. Let us bring the gifts that differ and, in splendid, varied ways, sing a new Church into being, one in faith and love and praise."[2] I realized then that although we may not as yet share fellowship around one table, Christians throughout the world celebrate the Lord's Table within our own traditions at one and the same time. In that way, we are united in one ever-expanding circle, singing God's praises as we express our love and trust that one day we will truly be one.

One last effort to walk the monastery's labyrinth remained before me. During my visit in March it had been hidden by snow. In May a cold rain had thwarted my intended walk. When I first arrived this time, I couldn't find the path through it. The basic, seven-circuit grass labyrinth was overgrown and the path poorly defined. It occurred to me that this obscured pathway through the Christian journey was where I had started last summer and that this book and my own process throughout

2. Text by Delores Dufner, OSB. GIA Publications, 1994.

the year had been an effort to uncover and clarify that path and to assure all who sought it that they would find it by following Christ. The day before leaving, I returned on a sunny afternoon to try again to find the path and this time was able to walk the freshly cut circuits.

As I entered the labyrinth, I gave thanks for my own journey through the year and for all I had learned and received through God's grace and love. I was grateful, too, for my companions along the way, both living and beyond this life, who illumined the path for me. I thought of them as I rounded each circuit with confidence that I would arrive safely at the center. I remembered the spiritual practices that had supported my journey to the heart of God. While resting on the bench thoughtfully placed in the labyrinth's center, I noticed the beauty of God's creation all around me: the mature trees providing shade from the sun, habitat for animals, and clean air for us to breathe; the plants and flowers with their rainbow of colors and sustenance for the bees who provided honey for the community; and the humming insects and chirping birds who created a natural harmony of song. The cornstalks and community garden in the nearby fields signaled a land teeming with life. I fell under the spell of the nourishing warmth and the breeze that rustled gently around me and didn't want to leave the peace of the place.

For a few moments I slipped through time into the liminal space where heaven and earth meet. My hands began to open and close in a rhythm of their own. It felt as though the Spirit of God was breathing through me, that we were one. The world went on around me, but I was rapt with a deep contentment and sense of the unity of all life. I felt complete and the experience of the year felt complete as well. After a while, as my awareness returned from this contemplative state, I knew it was time to take the gifts of the journey with me and return the way I had come, from my home in God to my home in North Carolina. The deep peace remained as I walked back out of the labyrinth, turned, gave thanks, and headed down the gravel path leading through Ordinary Time toward whatever was yet to come.

The transition from the monastery to home flowed more smoothly this time, even though the first week back was again filled with family visits and household responsibilities. My husband and son had managed just fine during my absence. It was good to be back in my own space, following the rhythms of my life and those of the family and community. A conversation with Meg and Mary was disconcerting, as Meg's condition had worsened since we last talked and Mary's husband had been hospitalized, but I was able to release my anxiety for them and instead to hold God's love and light around them for their highest good. In a similar way I surrendered control over Tom's life and his journey to God, trusting in the infinite grace and goodness that would accompany him on his path.

My year of purification and its labyrinthine journey now complete, I looked forward once again to the renewed energy the fall would bring: classes I would attend and lead, the progress of the book toward publication, time to deepen friendships and explore new work, and a return to the monastery in October to participate in the installation of a permanent labyrinth. Every moment felt precious, full of the promise of abundant life, full of the radiance of God, and with a heart filled with gratitude, I embraced it all.

TEN

Companions on the Journey

Truth sees God, and wisdom contemplates God, and of these two comes the third, and that is a marvelous delight in God, which is love. Where truth and wisdom are, truly there is love, truly coming from them both and all are of God's making. For God is endless supreme truth, endless supreme love uncreated; and a man's soul is a creature in God which has the same properties created. Therefore God rejoices in the creature and the creature in God, endlessly marveling, in which marveling he sees his God, his Lord, his maker, so exalted, so great and so good in comparison with him who is made that the creature scarcely seems anything to itself. But the brightness and clearness of truth and wisdom make him see and know that he is made for love, in which love God endlessly protects him.

—Julian of Norwich, *Showings*

But solid food is for the mature, for those whose faculties have been trained by practice to distinguish good from evil. Therefore, let us go on toward perfection, leaving behind the basic teaching about Christ, and not laying again the foundation: repentance from dead works and faith toward God, instruction about baptism, laying on of hands, resurrection of the dead, and eternal judgment. And we will do this, if God permits.

—Hebrews 5:14—6:3

THESE TWO PASSAGES, THE first from the fourteenth-century contemplative Julian of Norwich, the second from the anonymous author of Hebrews who exhorted the early church to move beyond beginning Christianity, bracket the movement of the spiritual journey from illumination to union with God. The eternal truths, wisdom, and love revealed in the *perichoretic* flow among the persons of the Trinity illumine the means through which a healed humanity and a spiritually mature church may co-create with God heaven on earth. Perceiving God's truth, contemplating its wisdom, and loving God with an open heart comprise the movement of this final stage of the spiritual journey. Fashioned by the Potter's hand, purified by the divine refining fire and molded into the likeness of Christ by the journey itself, the deep Christian becomes a vessel to serve the beloved community gathered around the Lord's Table. The disciple, the student, is now the apostle, the wise elder.

Where are the wise elders of today to be found, the spiritually mature companions who will walk alongside us on our journeys through faith and life, help us discern how God is working through us, offer correction when it is needed and new perspectives when ours are too limited? Until we are formed in Christ's image ourselves, without these guides we may get stuck on the path or lose our way.

We turn to the post-Pentecost early church for insights. In Jesus' farewell to his disciples in John's Gospel, he gave them a new commandment: "Just as I have loved you, you also should love one another. By this everyone will know that you are my disciples, if you have love for one another" (John 14:34b–35) and "No one has greater love than this, to lay down one's life for one's friend. You are my friends if you do what I command you. I do not call you servants any longer . . . but I have called you friends, because I have made known to you everything that I heard from my Father" (John 15:12–15).

As the disciples were touched by the Holy Spirit with the transforming tongues of flame in Acts, they became not only Jesus' wise elders but also his beloved friends. They were to be known by the *perichoretic* love that flowed among the Father, Son, and Spirit through them, pouring out the self for the whole in the cosmic dance of unity. Loving what God loves and what Christ taught through God's word and the example of his life leads to union with God.

The friends of Jesus became the primary spiritual companions and community for one another, and they may become that for us, as well. We may need to search them out or they may appear before us at just the right time, divinely sent.

Although the stories and legends of what happened to these early wise ones have largely disappeared from history, the discovery of the *Gospel of Thomas* and the *Gospel of Phillip* among the Nag Hammadi texts and the earlier discovery of the *Gospel of Mary* (Magdalene) take us further into the story of the earliest formation of Christian community.

These texts are still being examined critically and interpreted by biblical scholars in ways that stretch our knowledge and understanding of this nucleus of Jesus' friends. Whether or not the texts were known when the canonical Gospels and letters were selected in the fourth century, there is still much to be revealed about the interplay of personalities and angles of perception among the spiritual companions of Jesus.

From Luke's Acts of the Apostles we learn that the post-Pentecost disciples, transformed by the power and love of the Holy Spirit into apostles, the ones sent by Jesus to carry and live out the message of God's unending, abundant love, lived in a heightened state of awareness. Everything seemed new, full of possibility. However, even as they gathered together to figure out how to express their newfound faith and build community with one another, problems emerged. It was challenging enough to live in a hostile political and religious environment that threatened their very lives. But even from the very beginning, as the apostles began to form communities centered on Christ's teachings and the sacraments of baptism and Holy Communion, disagreements surfaced over worship practices and community behavior. Power struggles took place, causing a split over who were the "true" disciples. Peter went off to establish churches in Antioch and Rome. Jesus' kinsman James became the head of the church in Jerusalem. Paul was given a mission to the Gentiles. According to one set of legends, Mother Mary went to Ephesus, where she eventually died. According to another set, Mary Magdalene ended up in France, where she lived and taught for many years. Much cultural evidence of this remains embedded in the Languedoc region of southern France and the abbey town of Vezelay, one site that claims her relics. It is still a major starting point on the pilgrimage road to the cathedral of Santiago de Compestela, which claims James' remains, and Saint-Maximin-la-Sainte-Baume in Provence, where Mary Magdalene's remains still may rest. Whatever the truth about these accounts, it is clear that she is highly revered in France as a close companion of Jesus and teacher of many.

Hundreds of accounts about Jesus and his followers were being written, redacted, and circulated in the first and second centuries. Even those accepted into the New Testament canon reveal conflict from the very beginning within the body of Christ. Dissent grew and divisions formed, despite all the worthy attempts of the new church leadership to instruct, placate, and exhort the faithful to become mature in their faith, to move beyond the infantile quarrels and inappropriate behaviors that continue to plague the church today. The body of Christ, it seems, has been divided throughout its two-thousand-year history. Must it always be so? Where is the beloved community to be found in our own time?

Over the years I have sought to resolve my own concerns about the divided church in two ways: first, by searching out and highlighting the commonalities among our many faith communions, especially the three main streams, as has been my intention in this book; and, second, by studying closely and attempting to follow the path Jesus laid out for us, even when it gets narrower, steeper, and more confusing. Differing historical accounts, theologies, dogmas, doctrines, worship styles, church politics, and the like give us, it seems to me, opportunities to practice mutual forbearance. Our perceived differences can be transcended through the grace of God by our common humanity and desire to heal ourselves, one another, and the world. That healing, centered in forgiveness and reconciliation, remains our most basic task, as much as it was for the early church leaders. Meanwhile, we keep our feet on the path as we know it and do the best we can.

Sometimes walking the path of the purified heart feels lonely and impossibly difficult. At these times we especially need spiritual companions who have been through the same trials and can offer us encouragement to keep going. We need deeply formed, loving Christian community.

As the path leads to a radical self-giving love poured out for the life of the world, we discover that we no longer want or need to live in disharmony with one another or to distance ourselves from God. We have detached from those thoughts and activities that turn us away from the path and reattached ourselves to the source of life itself.

The God that Jesus showed us through his birth, baptism, ministry, death, resurrection, and continual presence is as close as our breath. "We are God breathed," a friend and spiritual teacher, Ron Roth, used to say. We are the expression, literally, of life-giving, life-sustaining energy. We breathe in God; we breathe out God. There is no way to separate ourselves from God except in our own minds. Our hearts know the truth, our bodies feel it. We just need to get all parts of ourselves singing out of the same hymnal, on the same page, in full harmony—and so does the church. The great spiritual teachers and guides we have encountered on this journey all understood that at some level, when they were their deepest and truest, they were most connected with God. The ones who moved beyond their own passions and worldly attachments, beyond spiritual greed, envy, and selfish desires, lit up our path with divine illuminations. These inspired them to keep connected, to share the truth of God's mercy and grace to all who would hear, and they, in turn, continue to inspire us. Now it is our turn to inspire the next generation of Christians.

"Listen, child of God, to the guidance of your teacher," begins the Rule of Benedict. "Attend to the message you hear and make sure that it pierces to your heart, so that you may accept with willing freedom and fulfill by the way you live the directions that come from your loving [God]."[1] Benedict's words seem prophetic in light of the journey we have taken together. I know that they and the Rule have pierced my heart and transformed my life.

The path we have been following together does not depend on one stream of Christianity for its truth, wisdom, and love, but on all of them together, even though filtered through the human mind and heart and colored by history, culture, gender, and tradition. God continues to speak, as we have learned from the practice of *lectio divina*, itself a microcosm of the spiritual journey. Through reading and meditating on Scripture we listen with the ears of our hearts. Through prayer and contemplation we allow ourselves to be drawn into divine union.

In the same way worship and liturgy, especially the sacrament of Eucharist or Holy Communion, feed and nourish us with the bread of life and the cup of salvation, and form us as the beloved community, the body of Christ on earth. While styles of worship may differ from one part of the church to another, we all still celebrate the mystery of Christ's living presence that lies at the heart of our faith. In sharing the sacrament around the common table of the Lord's Supper we locate both the church's greatest division and its greatest potential for healing.

As a woman ordained to the office of Minister of the Word and Sacrament, I am authorized by my faith communion to baptize, marry, and celebrate Communion as well as to preach God's word and serve in church leadership. It saddens me that this is not an option for all women who feel similarly called and desire to serve God in this way. Gender and sexual preference issues still divide the church, as in society. Who

---

1. Patrick Barry, OSB, trans. Prologue to the Rule of Benedict in *The Benedictine Handbook*, 10.

may serve and who may not is a highly charged topic, although there are hopeful signs of change. God is free to call whomever God chooses and throughout history has consistently chosen from among those the dominant culture would label the least likely—Moses, Jonah, and Mother Mary among them. What they had in common was that they listened to and obeyed God's word.

Recently I attended a local governing body meeting of my faith communion at which seven new candidates for ministry were presented for approval of the body in order to proceed to ordination and accept the calls to ministry offered them. I wasn't alone in feeling that this was a gifted, passionately committed group of young and older, second-career women and men who would breathe new life into the church. They had heard God's call and claim on their lives and had sacrificed in order to stand before us that day, ready to take on the leadership of the church for the next generation.

In addition to who may serve in church leadership, another issue dividing the church at its core is who is welcome at the Lord's Table. Since Jesus' radical, open-handed, open-hearted grace expressed God's love, he welcomed all who sought him, all who wanted to be healed, all who were ready to be transformed, no matter their station in life. Zaccheus, Nicodemus, the Samaritan woman at the well, and the man born blind come to mind. Why is it that the church erects barriers beyond baptism and confessing faith in Christ?

Wherever and however this most holy of Christian sacraments is administered, whatever its celebrants and recipients believe the bread is or represents, whether the cup is filled with wine or grape juice, whether it is shared from a common cup or a common spoon or from little plastic individual cups, whether the congregants come forward and stand or kneel or remain in their seats, whether or not the celebrant has a pure heart, what is given and received in the name of Christ is transformed, as are we, through the power of the mysterious presence of Christ in our midst. The bread and the fruit of the vine become life-giving when shared among those who want to know and follow Christ.

While I support the spiritual formation many faith communions require before the baptized and confirmed may participate in the Eucharist, human-made divisions across communions rob the church of wholeness and reconciliation to God and one another. It is here, at the heart of our most sacred sacrament, that we must eventually come together if the church is truly to become the one body of Christ in and for the world. The motto of the Presbyterian Church is "Reformed, always being reformed." Perhaps our common motto could be "Transforming, always being transformed." That acknowledges our desire for union with God and one another. Both the Protestant commitment to reform coupled with the Catholic, especially Benedictine, commitment to stability are needed. If we were to reform from within our own hearts and our primary communities of faith, we might discover common ground with our brothers and sisters in Christ rather than defecting in place or voting with our feet and leaving the church.

Eucharistic sharing, as it is known in ecumenical circles, continues to be a challenge even to those who desire to find common ground across faith communions. While the World Council of Churches in 1982 set a goal of one Eucharistic fellowship for all Christians and Vatican II in 1963 opened the door to conversation that promotes Christian unity, seven rounds of dialogue between U.S. Catholic bishops and representatives of the Reformed churches illustrate the distance we still remain from one another. The most recent six-year dialogue resulted in a document called "This Living Bread." One of its participants wrote to me that "there is still a long way to go" before Eucharistic sharing can be openly practiced across the traditions. The ecclesial climate appears to have become more restrictive in recent years over issues of theology, doctrine, and polity.

A basic humility seems missing in church legalism about who may or may not serve or partake in Holy Communion. The Scripture passage from Matthew 15:1–20, which Meg, Mary, and I chose for *lectio divina* at our fall retreat, illustrates that this problem was present in Jesus' day as well. The Pharisees observe that his disciples broke a commandment by not washing their hands before eating. Jesus responds, "Why do you break the commandment of God for the sake of your tradition?" (v. 3). Later, he teaches his disciples that "what comes out of the mouth proceeds from the heart, and this is what defiles . . . To eat with unwashed hands does not defile" (v. 20).

It is God's work in us that ultimately will bring about the transformation that leads to union, but we must put forth effort to "work out our own salvation with fear and trembling," as Paul teaches in Philippians 2:12. Effort is not "works-righteousness," suggesting that we "earn" grace, for that is God's free gift alone, but rather our cooperation with God as we seek to draw closer and experience more of divine love. Our individual efforts require support within our communities of faith. Spiritual formation and ongoing nourishment are basic needs for all Christians, however these are provided. People will stay if they find the beloved community in which they are fed and encouraged on their journeys.

The great Lutheran theologian and martyr in Hitler's Germany, Dietrich Bonhoeffer, gave his life in response to a call to create a seminary to prepare and preserve church leadership for the time it could once again emerge in his homeland. The book that describes his vision for the seminary is simply called *Life Together*. The urgency of the times and the conditions under which this underground group of disciples assembled called for plain, direct speaking, and Bonhoeffer did not mince words: "Christianity means community through Jesus Christ and in Jesus Christ. No Christian community is more or less than this. Whether it be a brief, single encounter or the daily fellowship of years, Christian community is only this. We belong to one another only through and in Jesus Christ."[2]

"What does this mean?" Bonhoeffer goes on. "It means, first, that a Christian needs others because of Jesus Christ. It means, second, that a Christian comes to others only through Jesus Christ. It means, third, that in Jesus Christ we have been chosen from eternity, accepted in time, and united for eternity."[3] Without Christ, he notes, we are separated from God and from one another. Christ is the mediator who can reunite us to live as one, in peace and harmony under the reign of God.

When he speaks of Christian community, Bonhoeffer teaches that "The more genuine and the deeper our community becomes, the more will everything else between us recede, the more clearly and purely will Jesus Christ and his work become the one and only thing that is vital between us . . . [T]hrough Christ we do have one another, wholly, and for all eternity."[4]

For Bonhoeffer, that community begins in the home, within the family unit. As did the early Reformers, he encourages daily worship both morning and evening, including hymns, prayers, and substantial readings from the Psalms and both testaments. Like the monastic

2. Bonhoeffer, *Life Together*, 21.

3. Ibid.

4. Ibid., 26.

orders, he advocates the practice of *lectio continua*, the continuous reading from day to day of whole chapters and books of scripture, rather than taking passages out of context and losing the sense of the grand sweep of the human relationship with God.

When Bonhoeffer comes to the fellowship of the table, he observes that "giving thanks and asking God's blessing, the Christian family receives its daily bread from the hand of the Lord,"[5] and whether within the family or the church, partaking in the sacrament opens the disciples' eyes so that they know God, as on the road to Emmaus in Jesus' post-resurrection appearance in Luke.[6]

Bonhoeffer also recommends alone time for prayer and meditation, noting that strength is to be gained both from silent communion with God and fellowship with the family and community. He calls, too, for frequent confession as preparation for participation in the sacrament of the Lord's Supper. His concluding paragraph of *Life Together* illustrates the significance of this sacrament for the whole body of Christ:

> The day of the Lord's Supper is an occasion of joy for the Christian community. Reconciled in their hearts with God and the brethren, the congregation receives the gift of the body and blood of Jesus Christ, and, receiving that, it receives forgiveness, new life, and salvation. It is given new fellowship with God and men. The fellowship of the Lord's Supper is the superlative fulfillment of Christian fellowship. As the members of the congregation are united in body and blood at the table of the Lord so will they be together in eternity. Here the community has reached its goal. Here joy in Christ and his community is complete. The life of Christians together under the Word has reached its perfection in the sacrament.[7]

It is community created with and for Christ that Bonhoeffer describes. That community must distinguish between human and spiritual dimensions in its life together. It is Christian community when "it understands itself as being a part of the one, holy, catholic, Christian Church, where it shares actively and passively in the sufferings and struggles and promise of the whole Church."[8]

5. Ibid., 65.

6. Ibid., 66.

7. Ibid., 122.

8. Ibid., 37.

That is the kind of community we must become for one another: the beloved community for which we all long. We catch glimpses of it every now and then, often in worship when the sacraments are celebrated, in moments when we rise above our petty divisions and feel the Holy Spirit surging through our midst, uniting and transforming us, and when we work side by side with brothers and sisters, whether Christian or not, who need our help but more importantly need our love and we theirs. Occasionally we find that community, but more often than not we experience its absence. That is why so many have left churches and faith communions and have created their own or just given up on the church, turning instead to spiritualities that seem to offer a path to union with God. And yet, as I hope this book has shown, this path has been present in Christianity all along. It has just been obscured, obfuscated, and overgrown by the church as institution rather than the church as the body of Christ.

How can the path of the purified heart be restored within the Christian tradition? Since the path begins and ends with Jesus, he must always be the center of the church and of the lives of Christians. Christian community is intended to illuminate and strengthen our relationships with Jesus and the Triune God. Everything the local congregation is and does should make that its central aim. As I used to suggest to members of congregations I served, our task is not primarily to grow the church by attracting new members; it is to grow ourselves spiritually so that people will see our light and want to be part of such a faith communion. The Eastern Orthodox believe that unity with God is attainable in this life, not just after death. So do those within our traditions who have experienced directly the uncreated light of God and have become illumined and transfigured themselves. We have encountered some of these spiritual guides on our journey together through these pages. Most, but not all, were monastics. In monasteries spiritual formation, both individual and collective, is essential and continual. *Conversatio morum,* ongoing conversion on the path to wholeness in God, is expected.

Church members can be shown how to help one another develop into the spiritual companions, the friends of Jesus, they desire to become and to walk alongside. We send people on mission trips to experience diversity and help the less fortunate, and that is an essential part of Christian life, but even more essential is that we model loving community within our congregations. Spiritual formation and development beyond the level of confirmation or new member classes are much needed as the solid food for the spiritually mature the author of Hebrews speaks about. Otherwise, the greater mysteries of our faith, discovered only by following over a lifetime the path Jesus laid before us, remain beyond the grasp of the average Christian.

Before literacy was virtually universal, people learned about Scripture from the priests during worship. Even if they could read, until recently in some traditions the laity were discouraged from studying the Bible on their own because interpreting scripture was considered the task of an educated clergy. The people in the pews learned about worship and the sacraments through regular attendance, not through individual study or taking classes. Even a brilliant monastic woman like Hildegard of Bingen was not allowed to learn Latin so that she could read Scripture on her own. She learned its rudiments from praying the Divine Office.

Ultimately the path of the purified heart reveals the God we seek and strengthens us in becoming true friends of Jesus. The path is ours to find and follow, whether supported within our congregations or not. The kind of daily practice that the monastics follow or that Bonhoeffer and Calvin before him advocated undergirds our efforts on this demanding path.

Each of us may begin by gathering a small group of family or friends for daily *lectio divina*—Scripture reading, reflection, and prayer. We may practice on our own as well. A minister I knew longed for a deep spiritual community with whom he could meet for morning or evening prayer. He began by inviting one friend to join him each day. As others heard about the group they wanted to be part of it. It just takes one or two interested people who share our desire to get a group going. Family members in households are ready made communities, but often scatter in different directions so that even sharing a common meal around the table must be made a priority and built into the schedule. That's what we need to do with our daily time with God. It will quickly become an indispensible part of the day. A weekly gathering for worship is also essential. As stressed throughout this book, these practices are basic. Staying with them over time will support every dimension of our lives.

One of the reasons so many of us have gravitated toward monastic communities as oblates and affiliates is that they offer both the worship opportunities and community support we need for spiritual growth. They also usually offer wise spiritual directors who may serve as our guides, just as the abbas and ammas did for the desert communities or the monastics did for one another throughout history. Monastic communities are not full of perfect people, any more than are the churches. However, those who choose that path and stick with it through a lifetime have a kind of authenticity and depth of experience with matters of faith not readily found in the wider church population. We can learn from them and offer them our own gifts and experiences in a loving exchange of mutual benefit.

Each of us must take responsibility for our own spiritual work and relationship with God. The core spiritual disciplines mentioned—worship, sacred reading, and prayer in its many forms—may be practiced anywhere. One friend has met for years with a group on Friday evenings at someone's home to study Scripture and share experiences of God. Another friend who has advanced degrees in theology wants to start a spiritual book group in her home for a few like-minded friends. Seminaries and divinity schools may offer certificates in spiritual formation, as do some independent programs. Retreats, workshops, and pilgrimages may be found through a web search. Labyrinths are everywhere.

Even online spiritual community is available. I mentioned earlier the Benedictine Sisters of Erie, Pennsylvania's online "Monastery of the Heart," inspired by Sr. Joan Chittister's book of that name. Other such communities are forming. People's hunger for spiritual growth and community is evidenced by the abundance of available options.

Serious seekers on the path of the purified heart may also want to explore living in a spiritual community. The new monastic movement is spreading, as groups of people who want to live in intentional vowed communities find each other. Celibacy generally is optional in such communities. The core belief supporting celibacy, as I understand it, is that one must have an undivided heart to participate in the highest levels of spousal mysticism, in which monastic men and women feel united in a spousal kind of love with God. I believe that kind of union is possible in any self-giving, reciprocal love relationship. The intimate, open-hearted love experienced within marriage or between friends joined at the heart also reflects the divine exchange of love among the persons of the Trinity. To love is not to divide but to overcome division, to make one out of two. That is unitive love, and that's where our journey to God

<u>brings us</u>. Celibacy, marriage, and spiritual friendship are all relation-ships through which humans experience divine love.

When we have been fed and nourished by God and our commu-nities of faith, we are prepared to walk back along the labyrinth's path and share what we have found with others. Within churches, mission and evangelism are the usual expressions of this sharing. The missional activities of the church take many forms and are enriching for the par-ticipants but are not substitutes for traditional spiritual formation and practices. Jesus didn't send out the disciples to heal and spread the gos-pel until he had trained them for their service. At times they did well; at other times they failed their assignments and required more training. Being with Jesus, understanding what he said, observing what he did, following his lead, discerning God's will and obeying it comprised their training manual. When he departed from his closest followers, they were no longer his servants but his friends, ready to support one another and to pour out their lives for the healing of the world. No less is asked of us.

In his best-known book, *The Cost of Discipleship,* Bonhoeffer makes this startling statement: "When Christ calls a man he bids him come and die."[9] This won't necessarily mean physical death, as it did for this heroic pastor-theologian, but it certainly will mean dying to the old life and rising to the new. That is understood and expected on the path we have been traveling. It leads to transformation into the likeness of Christ. Restored to our full humanity and united through him with the God we have sought, our journey is complete. The pearl of great price may cost us everything we thought we wanted but offers in its place a life with and in God now and forever.

We have come to the end of our journey together on the labyrinth, whose winding path we have followed into the heart of God. Returning, we take up our own crosses, now much lighter because supported by our companions in Christian community. Looking back to see the distance we have traveled, we smile, give thanks, and move on with faith and trust in the God we have met on this path of the purified heart.

9. Bonhoeffer, *Cost of Discipleship,* 89.

Bibliography

60 Minutes. "A Visit to Mt. Athos." CBS News, April 24, 2011.

Artress, Lauren. *Walking the Sacred Path: Rediscovering the Labyrinth as a Spiritual Tool.* Albany: State University of New York Press, 1995.

Avila, Teresa of. *Interior Castle: The Classic Text with a Spiritual Commentary by Dennis Billy, C.Ss.R.* Notre Dame, IN: Ave Maria, 2007.

————. *A Life of Prayer: Faith and Passion for God Alone.* Edited by James M. Houston. Vancouver: Regent College Publishing, 1998.

Barnhart, Bruno, and Joseph Wong, editors. *Purity of Heart and Contemplation: A Monastic Dialogue between Christian and Asian Traditions.* New York: Continuum, 2001.

Barry, Patrick, et al. *Wisdom from the Monastery: The Rule of St. Benedict for Everyday Life.* Collegeville, MN: Liturgical, 2005.

The Benedictine Handbook. Collegeville, MN: Liturgical, 2003.

Bingen, Hildegard of. *Hildegard of Bingen: Selected Writings.* Translated by Mark Atherton. New York: Penguin, 2001.

Bondi, Roberta. *To Love as God Loves: Conversations with the Early Church.* Philadelphia: Fortress, 1987.

Bonhoeffer, Dietrich. *The Cost of Discipleship.* New York: Touchstone, 1995.

————. *Life Together.* New York: HarperOne, 1978.

Borg, Marcus. *The Heart of Christianity.* San Francisco: HarperSanFrancisco, 2003.

Bourgeault, Cynthia. *Centering Prayer and Inner Awakening.* Lanham, MD: Cowley, 2004.

————. *Chanting the Psalms: A Practical Guide with Instructional CD.* Boston: New Seeds, 2006.

————. *The Meaning of Mary Magdalene: Discovering the Woman at the Heart of Christianity.* Boston: Shambhala, 2010.

————. *The Wisdom Jesus: Transforming Heart and Mind; A New Perspective on Christ and His Message.* Boston: Shambhala, 2008.

————. *The Wisdom Way of Knowing: Reclaiming an Ancient Tradition to Awaken the Heart.* San Francisco: Jossey-Bass, 2003.

Brown, Robert K., and Philip W. Comfort, translators. *The New Greek-English Interlinear New Testament.* Wheaton, IL: Tyndale, 1990.

Casey, Michael. *Sacred Reading: The Ancient Art of Lectio Divina.* Liguori, MO: Triumph, 1996.

————. *The Undivided Heart: The Western Monastic Approach to Contemplation.* Petersham, MA: St. Bede's, 1994.

Cassian, John. *The Conferences of John Cassian.* Christian Classics Ethereal Library. Kindle edition.

Charpentier, Louis. *The Mysteries of Chartres Cathedral.* New York: Avon, 1974.

Chamberas, Peter A., translator. *Nicodemos of the Holy Mountain: A Handbook of Spiritual Counsel.* Mahway, NJ: Paulist, 1989.

Chase, Steven. *Angelic Spirituality: Medieval Perspectives on the Ways of Angels.* Mahway, NJ: Paulist, 2002.

———. *Contemplation and Compassion: The Victorine Tradition.* Maryknoll, NY: Orbis, 2003.

———. *A Field Guide to Nature as Spiritual Practice.* Grand Rapids: Eerdmans, 2011.

———. *Nature as Spiritual Practice.* Grand Rapids: Eerdmans, 2011.

Liturgical *Calendar* Chittister, Joan, OSB. *The Monastery of the Heart: An Invitation to a Meaningful Life.* New York: BlueBridge, 2011.

———. *The Rule of Benedict: A Spirituality for the 21st Century.* New York: Crossroad, 2010.

———. *Wisdom Distilled from the Daily: Living the Rule of St. Benedict Today.* San Francisco: HarperSanFrancisco, 1991.

The Church of England. *The Book of Common Prayer.* London: Random Century House, 1992.

The Cloud of Unknowing and Other Works. Translated by A.C. Spearing. New York: Penguin, 2001.

Collins, Gregory, OSB. *The Glenstal Book of Icons: Praying with the Glenstal Icons.* Collegeville, MN: Liturgical, 2002.

Cross, John of the. *Dark Night of the Soul.* Translated by E. Allison Peers. Wilder Publications, 2008. Kindle edition.

Curry, Helen. *The Way of the Labyrinth.* New York: Penguin Compass, 2000.

Davis, Bruce. *Monastery Without Walls: Daily Life in the Silence.* Berkeley, CA: Celestial Arts, 1990.

De Caussade, Jean-Pierre. *Abandonment to Divine Providence: The Classic Text with a Spiritual Commentary by Dennis Billy, C.Ss.R.* Notre Dame, IN: Ave Maria, 2010.

Dean, Eric. *St. Benedict for the Laity.* Collegeville, MN: Liturgical, 1989.

De Sales, Francis. *Introduction to the Devout Life.* Edited by Charles Dollen. Staten Island, NY: Society of St. Paul, 1992.

De Waal, Esther. *Living with Contradiction: An Introduction to Benedictine Spirituality.* Harrisburg, PA: Morehouse, 1997.

———. *Seeking God: The Way of St. Benedict.* London: Fount Paperbacks, 1984.

———. *The Way of Simplicity: The Cistercian Tradition.* London: Darton, Longman and Todd, 1998.

Driskill, Joseph D. *Protestant Spiritual Exercises: Theology, History, and Practice.* Harrisburg, PA: Morehouse, 1999.

Ehrman, Bart D. *Lost Christianities: Christian Scriptures and the Battles over Authentication.* Chantilly, VA: The Teaching Company, 2002. DVDs.

Farley, Lawrence. *Let Us Attend: A Journey through the Orthodox Divine Liturgy.* Chesterton, IN: Conciliar, 2007.

Field, Anne M., OSB, editor. *The Monastic Hours: Directory for the Celebration of the Work of God and Directive Norms for the Celebration of the Monastic Liturgy of the Hours.* 2nd edition. Collegeville, MN: Liturgical, 2000.

Forest, Jim. *The Ladder of the Beatitudes.* Maryknoll, NY: Orbis, 1999.

Foster, Richard J., and James Bryan Smith, editors. *Devotional Classics.* New York: HarperOne, 1993.

Foster, Richard J. *Streams of Living Waters.* New York: HarperOne, 2001.

French, R. M., translator. *The Way of a Pilgrim and The Pilgrim Continues His Way.* New York: Quality, 1998.

Funk, Mary Margaret, OSB. *Humility Matters: For Practicing the Spiritual Life*. New York: Continuum, 2005.

———. *Into the Depths: A Journey of Loss and Vocation*. New York: Lantern, 2011.

———. *Lectio Matters: Before the Burning Bush*. New York: Continuum, 2010

———. *Thoughts Matter for Practicing the Spiritual Life*. New York: Continuum, 2007.

The Glenstal Book of Prayer: A Benedictine Prayer Book. Collegeville, MN: Liturgical, 2001.

The Grail. *The Psalms: An Inclusive Language Version Based on the Grail Translation from the Hebrew*. Chicago: GIA, 2000.

Gruber, Mark, OSB. *Journey Back to Eden: My Life and Times among the Desert Fathers*. Maryknoll, NY: Orbis, 2002.

Guthrie, Shirley C. *Christian Doctrine*. Rev. ed. Louisville, KY: Westminster/John Knox, 1994.

Hart, Patrick, OCSO. *A Monastic Vision for the 21st Century: Where Do We Go from Here?* Kalamazoo, MI: Cistercian, 2006.

Harvey, Andrew, editor. *Teachings of the Christian Mystics*. Boston: Shambhala, 1998.

Holdaway, Gervase, OSB, editor. *The Oblate Life*. Collegeville, MN: Liturgical, 2008.

How, William Walsham, and Ralph Vaughn Williams. "For All the Saints." *The Presbyterian Hymnal*. Louisville: Westminster/John Knox, 1990.

Jamison, Christopher, OSB. *Finding Sanctuary: Monastic Steps for Everyday Life*. Collegeville, MN: Liturgical, 2006.

Julian of Norwich. *Showings*. Translated by Edmund Colledge and James Walsh. New York: Paulist, 1978.

Kardong, Terrence G., OSB, translator. *The Life of St. Benedict by Gregory the Great: Translation and Commentary*. Collegeville, MN: Liturgical, 2009.

Keating, Thomas, OCSO. *Open Mind, Open Heart: The Contemplative Dimension of the Gospel*. Salisbury, Great Britain: Element, 1991.

———, et al. *Spirituality, Contemplation and Transformation*. New York: Lantern, 2008.

Kelsey, Morton T. *The Other Side of Silence: A Guide to Christian Meditation*. Mahway, NJ: Paulist, 1976.

Kempis, Thomas à. *The Imitation of Christ*. Uhrichsville, OH: Barbour, 1984.

Kisly, Lorraine, editor. *The Inner Journey: Views from the Christian Tradition*. Sandpoint, ID: Morning Light, 2006.

Kulzer, Linda, OSB, and Roberta Bondi, editors. *Benedict in the World: Portraits of Monastic Oblates*. Collegeville, MN: Liturgical, 2002.

Lane, Belden C. *Ravished by Beauty: The Surprising Legacy of Reformed Spirituality*. New York: Oxford University, 2011.

———. *The Solace of Fierce Landscapes: Exploring Desert and Mountain Spiritualities*. New York: Oxford University, 1998.

Leclercq, Jean, OSB. *The Love of Learning and the Desire for God: A Study of Monastic Culture*. New York: Fordham University, 2009.

Lubtchansky, Jean-Claude, director. *Living Prayer in Christianity*. Geneva: Axis Mundi Foundation, 2011.

Luckman, Harriet A., and Linda Kulzer, OSB, editors. *Purity of Heart in Early Ascetic and Monastic Literature*. Collegeville, MN: Liturgical, 1999.

Maddocks, Fiona. *Hildegard of Bingen: The Woman of Her Age*. New York: Doubleday, 1991.

Markides, Kyriacos C. *Gifts of the Desert: The Forgotten Path of Christian Spirituality.* New York: Doubleday, 2005.

———. *The Mountain of Silence: A Search for Orthodox Spirituality.* New York: Doubleday, 2001.

Martimort, A. G., editor. *Principles of the Liturgy,* vol. 1: *The Church at Prayer.* Collegeville, MN: Liturgical, 1987.

McColman, Carl. *The Big Book of Christian Mysticism: The Essential Guide to Contemplative Spirituality.* Charlottesville, VA: Hampton Roads, 2010.

McGinnis, Mark W. *Wisdom of the Benedictine Elders.* New York: BlueBridge, 2005.

McKee, Elsie Anne, editor and translator. *John Calvin: Writings on Pastoral Piety.* Mahway, NJ: Paulist, 2001.

McLaren, Brian. *Finding Our Way Again: The Return of Ancient Practices.* Nashville: Thomas Nelson, 2008.

Meeks, Wayne A., editor. *The HarperCollins Study Bible: New Revised Standard Version.* New York: HarperCollins, 1993.

Meninger, William A., OCSO. *The Loving Search for God.* New York: Continuum, 2011.

Merton, Thomas, OCSO. *Conjectures of a Guilty Bystander.* New York: Doubleday, 1968.

———. *Contemplative Prayer.* New York: Image Books, 1996.

———. *An Introduction to Christian Mysticism: Initiation into the Monastic Tradition 3.* Kalamazoo, MI: Cistercian, 2008.

Meyendorff, John. *St. Gregory Palamas and Orthodox Spirituality.* Crestwood, NY: St. Vladimir's Seminary Press, 1974.

Moorhouse, Geoffrey. *The Last Divine Office: Henry VIII and the Dissolution of the Monasteries.* New York: BlueBridge, 2008.

———. *Sun Dancing: A Medieval Vision.* London: Phoenix, 2001.

Mullins, Edwin. *Cluny: In Search of God's Lost Empire.* New York: BlueBridge, 2006.

Needleman, Jacob. *Lost Christianity: A Journey of Rediscovery.* New York: Tarcher/ Penguin, 2003.

Norris, Kathleen. *Acedia and Me: A Marriage, Monks, and a Writer's Life.* New York: Riverhead, 2008.

———. *The Cloister Walk.* New York: Riverhead, 1996.

The Northumbria Community. *Celtic Daily Prayer.* London: Collins, 2000.

Nouwen, Henri J. M. *The Return of the Prodigal Son: A Story of Homecoming.* New York: Image, 1994.

———. *The Way of the Heart: Desert Spirituality and Contemporary Ministry.* San Francisco: HarperSanFrancisco, 1991.

Okholm, Dennis. *Monk Habits for Everyday People: Benedict Spirituality for Protestants.* Grand Rapids: Brazos, 2007.

Pagels, Elaine. *Beyond Belief: The Secret Gospel of Thomas.* New York: Random House, 2003.

Palmer, G. E. H, Philip Sherrard, and Kallistos Ware, editors. *The Philokalia: The Complete Text.* 4 vols. London: Faber Paperbacks, 1983–1998.

Presbyterian Church (USA). *Book of Common Worship.* Louisville, KY: Westminster/ John Knox, 1993.

Raasch, Juana, OSB. "The Monastic Concept of Purity of Heart and its Sources." Unpublished manuscript. St. Joseph, MN: St. Benedict's Monastery. Originally published in *Studia Monastica,* vols. 8–12, 1966–1970.

Rice, Howard L. *Reformed Spirituality: An Introduction for Believers.* Louisville, KY: Westminster/John Knox, 1991.

Robinson, David. *Ancient Paths: Discover Christian Formation the Benedictine Way.* Brewster, MA: Paraclete, 2010.

Rohr, Richard, OFM. *The Naked Now: Learning to See as the Mystics See.* New York: Crossroad, 2009.

Rohr, Richard, OFM, with John Bookser Feister. *Jesus' Plan for a New World: The Sermon on the Mount.* Cincinnati: St. Anthony Messenger, 1996.

Sangster, W. E. *The Pure in Heart: A Study in Christian Spirituality.* New York: Abingdon, 1954.

Schlabach, Gerald W. *Unlearning Protestantism: Sustaining Christian Community in an Unstable Age.* Grand Rapids: Brazos, 2010.

Senn, Frank C. *Protestant Spiritual Traditions.* New York: Paulist, 1986.

Sienna, Catherine of. *The Dialogue of St. Catherine of Sienna.* Translated by Algar Thorold. Gladstone, OR: Gladstone, 2011.

Smolley, Richard. *Inner Christianity: A Guide to the Esoteric Tradition.* Boston: Shambhala, 2002.

Staniloae, Dumitru. *Orthodox Spirituality: A Practical Guide for the Faithful and a Definitive Manual for the Scholar.* South Canaan, PA: St. Tikhon's, 2003.

Steidl-Rast, David, OSB, and Sharon Lebell. *Music of Silence: A Sacred Journey through the Hours of The Day.* Berkeley, CA: Ulysses, 2002.

Stewart, Columba, OSB. *Cassian the Monk.* New York: Oxford University Press, 1998.

Taylor, Richard. *How to Read a Church: A Guide to Images, Symbols and Meanings in Churches and Cathedrals.* London: Rider, 2003.

Teasdale, Wayne. *The Mystic Heart: Discovering a Universal Spirituality in the World's Religions.* Novato, CA: New World Library, 2001.

Teilhard de Chardin, Pierre. *The Divine Milieu: An Essay on the Interior Life.* New York: Harper & Row, 1960.

Temple, Richard. *Icons and the Mystical Origins of Christianity.* Longmead, Great Britain: Element, 1990.

Thompson, Marjorie J. *Soul Feast: An Invitation to the Christian Spiritual Life.* Louisville, KY: Westminster/John Knox, 1995.

Tickle, Phyllis. *The Great Emergence: How Christianity Is Changing and Why.* Grand Rapids: Baker, 2008.

Timidasis, Metropolitan Emilianos. *Toward Authentic Christian Spirituality: Orthodox Pastoral Reflections.* Brookline, MA: Holy Cross Orthodox, 1998.

Tvedten, Benet, OSB. *The View from a Monastery.* New York: Riverhead, 1999.

Underhill, Evelyn. *The Spiritual Life.* Harrisburg, PA: Morehouse, 1984.

Warner, Larry. *Journey with Jesus: Discovering the Spiritual Exercises of Saint Ignatius.* Downers Grove, IL: InterVarsity, 2010.

Watts, Alan W. *Myth and Ritual in Christianity.* Boston: Beacon, 1968.

Webb-Mitchell, Brett. *School of the Pilgrim: An Alternative Path to Christian Growth.* Louisville, KY: Westminster/John Knox, 2007.

Wright, Wendy M. *Sacred Heart: Gateway to God.* Maryknoll, NY: Orbis, 2003.

About the Author

LAURA DUNHAM is an ordained minister in the Presbyterian Church (USA) and a Benedictine oblate. She holds a BA in social sciences, an MA and a PhD in English. Following a career in higher education, during which she taught and administered at several colleges and universities, and a second career as a Certified Financial Planner, she felt God's call to ministry. She attended Columbia Theological Seminary for her Master of Divinity degree and subsequently completed the Certificate in Spiritual Formation through the seminary.

Since her ordination, Laura served as a pastor of churches and a governing body and board leader. Her 2002 book, *Graceful Living: Your Faith, Values, and Money in Changing Times*, was commissioned by the Ecumenical Stewardship Center for use by congregations and individuals.

Since retiring from active ministry, Laura has engaged in teaching, leading workshops, and writing about spiritual formation and transformation. Now residing in Chapel Hill, NC, she invites inquiries about her work and visits to her blog and website, www.healingandwisdom.com.